HEALTHCARE
DESIGN

Wiley Series in Healthcare and Senior Living Design

SARA O. MARBERRY
HEALTHCARE DESIGN

ALFRED H. BAUCOM
HOSPITALITY DESIGN FOR THE GRAYING
GENERATION: MEETING THE NEEDS OF
A GROWING MARKET

HEALTHCARE DESIGN

Edited by
SARA O. MARBERRY

JOHN WILEY & SONS, INC.
New York / Chichester / Brisbane / Toronto / Singapore

Library of Congress Cataloging in Publication Data
Healthcare design / edited by Sara O. Marberry.
      p.   cm. — (Wiley series in healthcare and senior living
  design)
    Includes bibliographical references and index.
    ISBN 0-471-13349-3 (cloth : alk. paper)
    1. Health facilities—Design and construction. 2. Health
facilities—United States—Design and construction—Equipment and
supplies—Directories.   I. Marberry, Sara O., 1959– .
  II. Series.
  RA967.H45   1996
  725'.5—dc20   96-12446

Printed in the United States of America

10 9 8 7 6 5 4 3 2 1

CONTENTS

DESIGN   PART I

FOREWORD

The healthcare industry in the United States has gone through several incarnations. Prior to the 1940s, physicians administered to the sick and dying primarily in their homes. At that time, the hospital was reserved for terminally ill individuals who lacked the financial resources required to bring a doctor to the home or who lacked a permanent place of residence. The development of therapeutic modalities (specifically, antibiotics) needing intravenous administration and new surgical techniques requiring a hospital setting resulted in a shift of critically ill patients from the ambulatory or home setting to a hospital environment. This was followed by a proliferation of new and expensive diagnostic and therapeutic techniques, which led to the development of hospital-based subspecialty care.

Throughout the 1960s and 1970s, there was a technological explosion in medicine. This further accelerated the shift from a low-cost ambulatory healthcare delivery system to a high-cost hospital-based delivery system wherein healthcare providers and hospitals were rewarded based on quantity of delivered services, resulting in a period of medical inflation that dwarfed the overall inflation rate. The costs incurred as a result of this shift, largely borne by American industry, were identified by American manufacturers as a major impediment to the competitive pricing of American goods and services in what was evolving into an increasing global economy. Accordingly, more and more pressure was placed on payors to identify cost-saving methods of healthcare delivery and to pass these costs savings on to the major purchasers of healthcare services, mainly, American industry.

The government has experienced a similar phenomenon wherein the cost of healthcare delivery to the poor and elderly—principally through Medicare and Medicaid—has consumed an over increasing share of federal and state budgets. Thus, state and federal governments, following the lead of American industry, have sought to identify cost-saving methods of healthcare delivery and to utilize these savings to reduce taxes and balance budgets.

These forces have dramatically changed the landscape of healthcare financing, forcing a reengineering of healthcare delivery, such that an ever increasing portion of healthcare delivery is shifting from the high-cost hospital environment back to a lower-cost ambulatory setting, thus coming full circle. The initial shift of healthcare delivery from the ambulatory setting to the hospital environment was driven by changing technology. The more recent shift of healthcare delivery from the hospital setting to the ambulatory arena is a financially driven phenomenon wherein payors are seeking lower-cost alternatives. Thus, private payors have embraced the concept of *managed care* with the development of health maintenance organizations (HMOs), which generate cost savings through more efficient use of diagnostic and therapeutic goods and services with these savings being reflected in lower premiums.

Similarly, governmental payors are increasingly embracing managed care as a cost-savings measure. The original concept of controlling costs through managed healthcare delivery, which limits access to the hospital environment with its associated high-cost diagnostic and therapeutic modalities, has been of limited success. Accordingly, the concept of *capitated* healthcare has been developed, wherein the providers of care are given a fixed fee per patient per year and assume the financial risk associated with providing comprehensive healthcare services to a defined population. Thus, rather than being rewarded for providing more goods and services, the providers receiving a capitated fee enjoy a financial reward for limiting consumption.

This evolution in healthcare financing and delivery has wide regional variation. Managed care with or without capitation is more common in the West and Southwest and in many midwestern cities of the United States. The Northeast, in particular, has traditionally been an area of low penetration for managed care delivery systems. Factors contributing to this low penetration of managed care in the Northeast include: the lack of large, organized medical groups necessary to support managed care; a reluctance of patients to give up longstanding relationships with personal physicians; an economy dominated by small employers reluctant or unable to force managed care on their employees; resistance from organized labor.

The changes in healthcare financing have shifted the focus of healthcare delivery from a hospital-based setting to an outpatient setting. In order to survive into the next century, hospitals need to understand the changing marketplace and redefine themselves as integrators and managing members of healthcare systems that can assume risk. Developing an integrated delivery system will require hospital leadership to focus on several critical areas, including development of a system to deliver primary care, the restructuring of subspecialty services, the creation of a hospital network, the provision of subacute and long-term care, and the development of integrated insurance products. The key to network positioning and patient enrollment is the development of primary care capability with the expansion of healthcare providers in the specialties of internal medicine, pediatrics, obstetrics and gynecology, and family medicine. These physicians serve as the primary providers of healthcare and as *gatekeepers* in their capacity of managing the delivery of diagnostic and therapeutic goods and services.

With the increasing pressure of managed care and the resultant decline in hospital-based care, specialists and specialty programs will decrease in number, requiring the reeducation of many subspecialists in primary care delivery. In addition, despite the decreased need for inpatient capacity, there is a need for hospitals to organize themselves into integrated delivery systems. This includes strategically located, financially viable hospitals that work together to develop administrative economies, a full range of nonduplicative services, and geographic access that is attractive to the purchasers of healthcare services.

The need to develop the capacity to deliver home care, subacute care, and long-term care is a financial imperative as healthcare networks assume responsibility for comprehensive healthcare delivery. In addition, providers have recognized the need to develop independent health insurance products wherein the profits derived from the healthcare premium can be utilized to subsidize the traditional hospital-based activities of teaching, research, and the provision of healthcare to the uninsured.

It is clear that hospitals—the traditional focus of healthcare delivery—are in the midst of a financially driven healthcare revolution in which they are often viewed as financial liabilities rather than profitable centers of healthcare delivery. The increasing trend of providing healthcare in a low-cost nonhospital-based setting has created excess hospital capacity within the industry and has led to the closure of many inpatient facilities.

In order to survive, hospitals must recognize their limited role in the new paradigm for healthcare delivery. Specifically, in the future, hospitals will care for a smaller number of patients who are more seriously ill and hospitalized for a shorter period of time. The model for the hospital of the twenty-first century includes operating rooms, recovery rooms, and intensive care units linked to hotel accommodations. Rather than the focus of healthcare delivery, the hospital of the twenty-first century will be but one part of a large healthcare delivery system caring for an ever declining patient population. Those who fail to recognize their hospitals' changing role in healthcare delivery will suffer the same fate experienced by the railroad industry in the 1950s—it failed to recognize that it was but one part of a transportation system and not simply an isolated entity.

William T. Speck, M.D.

Dr. Speck is president and CEO of The Presbyterian Hospital at Columbia-Presbyterian Medical Center in New York City.

PREFACE

Although I'd like to claim it, the idea for this book was not mine. For that, I have to give credit to my editor at John Wiley & Sons, Amanda Miller, and Marty Gurian, a technical specialist at DesignTex fabrics. Marty, who teaches an excellent course on healthcare textiles for the New York University (NYU) School of Continuing Education's Healthcare Environments program, was called by Amanda in late 1994 to see if he wanted to write a book based on his course. Marty suggested to Amanda instead that John Wiley & Sons publish a contributor book based on all the courses offered at NYU. The daunting task of putting the book together, he reasoned, could be handled by a writer who knew the healthcare design industry. He suggested me. Since I already had a relationship with Amanda and John Wiley & Sons, it seemed like a natural fit.

Consequently, this book is loosely based on the healthcare design certificate program offered by NYU (and formerly by Cañada College in Redwood City, California). It is a textbook 101 course on healthcare design. No doubt, each of the topic areas covered in this book could probably be expanded into a single book, as Amanda originally envisioned with Marty's textile course. But this book gives a good overview of the important concepts, methods, and ideas that are shaping healthcare design today.

Some, but not all, of the contributors are instructors at the institutions mentioned above. I applaud their efforts and am grateful for their desire to share their knowledge for little more than just recognition.

And, despite the changes that are being brought on by managed care, I believe there are many opportunities in healthcare design in the United States. Hospitals are reinventing themselves, and their facility needs are undergoing a tremendous revolution. I hope that this book will help you be a part of this revolution.

Sara O. Marberry

ACKNOWLEDGMENTS

So much work by so many individuals goes into producing a book like this, and I would like to acknowledge the contributions of the 22 professionals who wrote the text and supplied the illustrations. Their willingness to share their knowledge is a true contribution to the healthcare design field.

In addition, I would like to thank the following people for their help and ideas:

Amanda Miller, my editor at John Wiley & Sons, whose patience, guidance, and support is much appreciated

Mary Alice Yates, Amanda's very capable assistant who handles all the details beautifully

Marty Gurian, DesignTex's technical specialist, who gets credit for having the original idea for this book

Wayne Ruga, president and CEO, The Center for Health Design, who helped me select most of the topics and contributors and whose advice and friendship I count on almost daily

Joan Rangelli and **New York University** School of Continuing Education, upon whose Healthcare Interior Design Certificate Program this book is based

Jules Horton, who went out of his way to write a paper for this book at the last minute

I
DESIGN

SITE VISITS

Craig Zimring, Ph.D.
Bruce Nepp, AIA
Rhonda Hillman

Change in society in general and healthcare in particular is rapid and increasingly unpredictable, bringing an unprecedented level of risk for healthcare organizations facing new projects. This chapter discusses a specific tool that healthcare organizations and design professionals can use to help manage uncertainty: the facility visit. In almost every healthcare project, someone—client, designer, or client-design team—visits other facilities to help to prepare for the project. A probing, well-structured, and well-run visit can highlight the range of possible design and operational alternatives, pinpoint potential problems, and build a design team that works together effectively over the course of a design project. It can help individual team members to be creative in breaking their existing paradigms for their current project and can provide a pool of experience that can inform other projects. All of these can help reduce risk for healthcare organizations.

However, current facility visits are often ineffective. They are frequently conducted quite casually, despite the rigor of much other healthcare planning and design. Visits are often costly—$40,000 or more—yet they often fall short of their potential. Sites are often chosen without careful consideration; little attention is given to clarifying the purpose or methods of visits; there is often little wrap-up; frequently, no final report is prepared. Not only is the money devoted to the visit frequently not used in the most effective way, but also important opportunities to learn and to build a design team are too often squandered.

These lost opportunities are both an instrumental problem—clients are not getting the full value of their investment—and symptomatic of a crisis in healthcare design that might be called *allasophiaphobia*—the fear of learning in public. In our research, many designers have expressed the belief that their clients had hired them because they already knew the answers to their problems, and several clients expressed this view as well. This leads to anxiety about appearing uncertain, even when facing new situations. This view of professional practice, where the professional is seen as knowing the answer in advance, stifles innovation. It is particularly troublesome in a rapidly changing area such as healthcare, which must respond to many new technical, economic, and social conditions.

This chapter focuses on what a facility field visit can accomplish and suggests ways to achieve these goals. Although a facility visit may occur in a variety of circumstances (including the redesign of the *process* of healthcare without any redesign of the physical setting), this chapter focuses on situations in which architectural or interior design is being contemplated or is in process.

The following sections describe our research, findings, and revised process. The chapter concludes with a discussion of a crisis we perceive in healthcare design and how processes such as the facility visit might begin to address it. Some of the text of this chapter is adapted from *A Guide to Conducting Healthcare Facility Visits* (Zimring 1994). Readers interested in more detail about procedures as well as worked-out case studies and sample forms should refer to that book.

SCOPE OF THE RESEARCH

This project is the result of a contract with The Center for Health Design, a nonprofit design advocacy organization in Martinez, California, which decided that, since most design teams conduct facility visits as part of their current design process, the practice should be upgraded to be more instructive. Hence, the goals of this project were to learn about the existing practice of conducting healthcare facility visits, to learn about the potential for extending their rigor and effectiveness, and to develop and test a new approach. We interviewed over 45 professionals in the fields of healthcare and design from every region of the United States, including interior designers, architects, and clients who had participated in design projects, as well as healthcare professionals who conduct visits in their own facilities. We sampled professionals from large and small design firms and from large and small medical organizations. To get a picture of both "average" and "excellent" practice, we randomly selected members from professional organizations, such as the American Institute of Architects (AIA) Academy on Architecture for Health and the American Society of Hospital Engineers, and augmented these with firms and individuals who were award winners or were recommended to us by top practitioners. We developed a multipage questionnaire that probed the participants' experiences with visits, including their reasons for participating, their methods, and how they used the information produced. We faxed each participant the questionnaire and then followed up with an interview on the phone or in person. Everyone in our sample had participated in some sort of visit to healthcare facilities within the past year.

After conducting the interviews, we developed, field-tested, and revised a new facility visit method, which is presented in this chapter.

GOALS OF FACILITY VISITS

There are many reasons for doing a facility visit and many different kinds of visits. However, we discovered that visits fall into roughly three categories: specific visits, departmental visits, and general visits. Specific visits focus on particular issues, such as the design of patient room headwalls, nurse stations, or gift shops; departmental visits focus on learning about the operations and design of whole departments, such as outpatient imaging or neonatal intensive care; general visits are concerned with issues relevant to a whole institution, such as how to restructure operations to become patient focused. Usually, departmental and general visits occur during programming or schematic design; specific visits often occur during design development, when decisions are being made about materials, finishes, and equipment.

More broadly, there are several general reasons for conducting visits: learning about state-of-the-art facilities; thinking about projects in new ways; creating an effective design team; and responding to trends in healthcare.

Learning About State-of-the-Art Facilities

Visit participants want to learn what excellent organizations in their field—both competitors and other organizations—are doing. Participants are often particularly interested in learning how changes in technology, increased focus on outpatient facilities, or increased criticality of inpatients might affect their own operations and design. For example, in Story 1, a U.K. team was interested in grafting U.S. experience onto a U.K. healthcare culture. In another example, hospital personnel at Georgia's St. Joseph's Hospital visited five emergency rooms over the course of several weeks before implementing an "express" service of their own. According to planner Greg Barker of Jay Farbstein & Associates, they "use site visits as a method of exposing the clients to a broader range of operating philosophies and methods." This gives the clients and design professionals a common frame of reference on which to base critical operational and design decisions.

STORY 1.	WILLIAM HEADLEY
	North Durham Acute Hospitals, U.K.

Traditionally, hospital design in the U.K. has been established centrally, with considerable emphasis placed on standard departmental areas and on a standardized planning format known as "Nucleus." The 20-year-old Nucleus system is based on a standard cruciform template of approximately 1,000 square meters housing a multitude of departments, which can be interlinked to provide the nucleus of a District General Hospital.

Durham wished to develop a hospital that in its vision would meet the challenges of the twenty-first century and produce a custom-designed hospital solution built to suit the needs of the patient, not just individual departments.

Therefore, the brief had to be developed from a blank sheet of paper and not from standard chapter lines. It was also the Trust's objective to have the brief developed by staff from the bottom up. The purpose of the study tour was to give frontline staff the opportunity to experience new ideas firsthand and to talk to their medical counterparts about some of the philosophies of patient-focused care and to input their findings into the briefing process. We acknowledged the differences in the U.S. and U.K. healthcare systems, but we were interested in ensuring that the best U.S. practices—including the patient-focused approach, facilities design, and the use of state-of-the-art equipment—was studied and subsequently tailored to suit the new North Durham hospital.

Thinking About a Project in a New Way

Participants who are currently engaged in a design or planning project are concerned with using visits to advance their own project. They use a visit to analyze innovative ideas and to help open the design team to new ideas. At the same time, they are interested in building consensus on a preferred option. In Story 2, a hospital serves as a frequent visit host because it shows how special bay designs can be used in neonatal intensive care, and participants can consider how these designs apply to their current project. Other visit organizers see a visit as an opportunity to focus the team on key decisions that need to be made or to help the team focus in a systematic way on a range of strategic options and critical constraints. The visit exposes each team member to a variety of ways of accomplishing a similar program of requirements and thus starts the debate on how to achieve the best results for the facility being designed.

We get visitors at our facility about once a month. Right now the neonatal intensive care unit (NICU) is the most frequently visited location. The main reason is that Ohmeda uses our unit as a showcase for a special design of NICU bays. People want to see it because most think that Hill-Rom is the only vendor of this type of equipment.

Early on, we were also one of the only state-of-the-art labor delivery recovery (LDR) facilities around. So if people wanted to visit an LDR unit, they had little choice but to come here. Now, however, people come to see us because we are a freestanding, yet still-attached, facility. Over time the visits have evolved away from the design of the facility and more into programming, services, and operational issues.

We give three types of visits:

1. Overview visits for laypeople who just want to come see the area
2. Functional visits for other hospital people or architects who want to see the LDR design, mother/baby floor, NICU design, and so on
3. Operational flow visits to learn how the LDR concept impacts operations

In general, we start the visitors wherever the patient would start in the facility.

To arrange a successful visit of our facility, we need to know the interests of the visitors; then we can focus the schedule on that. Also knowing who they are bringing is helpful. You need to have their counterparts available. The types of information needed to conduct facility visits are:

1. What specific operational information to ask for in advance—size, number of rooms, number of physicians, staffing, C-section rate, whether they are a trauma center
2. How to prepare for the visit
3. Who to bring

We've found that periodically the visitors are disappointed because they didn't bring enough people. Better to have too many than not enough.

Creating an Effective Design Team

Participants use visits as an opportunity for team building. Many visits are conducted early in a design project by a team that will work together for several years. The visit provides participants with a useful opportunity to get to know each other and to build an effective team. As Stories 3–6 illustrate, clients often look to a visit to see how well designers can understand their needs; designers use it as a way to learn about their clients and to mutually explore new ideas. A visit can also provide an opportunity for medical programmers to work with designers and clients. This is particularly important if programming and design are done by different firms.

Many visit participants focus on interpersonal issues—spending several days with someone helps build a personal relationship that one can rely on during a multiyear project. A visit also provides the opportunity to achieve other aspects of team building: clarifying values, goals, roles, and expertise of individual participants; and identifying conflicts early so they can be resolved. One result for some teams is that it establishes a common vocabulary of operational and facility terms translated to the local healthcare facility.

STORY 3.	**BING ZILLMER** *Director Engineering Services, Lutheran Hospital, La Crosse, Wisconsin*

Conducting a facility field visit is an opportunity to have that one-on-one contact and find out if the architect "walks the talk or talks the walk." The biggest benefit is in finding out how the visit team of the architectural firm has been assembled, to see their level of participation, and how they have interacted with and listened to the clients and the hosts. What we look for in a consultant is not a "yes man." We look for someone who knows more about existing facilities than we do. Our key concerns are how the team worked together, how they listened.

STORY 4.	**DENNIS C. LAGATTA** *Vice President, Ellerbe Becket, Washington, D.C.*

The main reason for conducting a visit is to settle an issue with the client. The clients usually have only two frames of reference: the current facility and the one where they were trained. These two frames of reference are hard to overcome without a visit. We conduct visits to help settle an issue between various groups within the institution. The visit process tends to be a good political way to illustrate a problem or a solution to a problem. A good example is when you have a dispute between critical care physicians and surgeons. Both parties may be unwilling to compromise. Usually a visit will be a good way to defuse this conflict.

| JAMES W. EVANS | **STORY 5.** |
| *Facilities Director, Heartland Health System, St. Louis, Missouri* | |

What kinds of team-building activities were conducted before the actual visit took place? The functional space program stage is where you start building a team. Functional space programming is a narrative of what you want to do. If the programming includes a laboratory or some other specialty area, you would also want to have the consultant (if you are using one) involved in this process. You want to go on visits between blocks and schematics. By working together and staying together through big and small projects, you develop a lot of rapport and credibility.

| LES SAUNDERS | **STORY 6.** |
| *Nix Mann And Associates, Architects, Atlanta, Georgia* | |

In the case of marketing visits, we try to present our unique abilities to our clients and to get to know each other better. Our visits are generally tailored to what the client group is trying to accomplish. Our functional experts will go on the visit so they can get to know the client and try to enhance "bonding."

Responding to Trends in Healthcare

Facility visits allow healthcare organizations and design professionals to address several important trends in healthcare.

TREND 1: As competition for patients increases, healthcare organizations are becoming more customer oriented. A visit allows a team to understand the experience of stakeholders whom they do not currently serve and to examine the design and operations of facilities that are more customer oriented.

TREND 2: Social, economic, and regulatory changes are resulting in some stakeholder groups gaining importance, such as outpatients involved in more complex procedures, higher acuity inpatients, older people, or non-English speakers. A visit may allow a team to learn about the experiences and needs of some groups who may be unfamiliar to some healthcare organizations or design professionals.

TREND 3: A greater emphasis on efficiency, learning from customers and staff, and Total Quality Management are placing more importance on benchmarking and data collection. A visit can provide quantitative and qualitative data that support future decision making.

TREND 4: **Tighter budgets, shorter design and construction schedules, and more complex projects are requiring design teams to form more quickly and work more effectively.** A visit can be an effective tool for building a design team early in a design project.

FALLING SHORT OF THEIR POTENTIAL

In a design project, the client healthcare organization generally pays for a visit, either directly or as a part of design fees. Do healthcare organizations usually get good value for their investment? Do visits generally achieve their ambitious goals of learning about competition and change, moving the design project along, and building teams? We found very different answers. Despite the usual rigor of healthcare planning and programming, many current visits are very casual. Whereas some planners of visits do careful searches of available facilities to fit specific criteria, most choose sites to visit in other ways—sites that participants happen to know already because they have read about them in magazines, or sites where there is a contact that someone on the team knows. Although using these criteria to choose sites may be appropriate, it raises a question as to whether most teams are visiting the best sites for their purposes.

Overall, many visit teams simply do not spend much time structuring the visit. Most teams do not even meet in advance to decide the major focus of the visit. We did not find many groups who use checklists or sets of questions or criteria when they go into the field. Whereas some teams compile the participants' notes, and one team actually created a videotape in a large project, most teams do not create any kind of written or visual record of their visit. Many teams hold no meeting at the end to discuss the implications of the visit, although many participants felt that these emerged in subsequent programming or design meetings.

Despite the apparent casualness of these visits, designers and clients alike—almost without exception—felt they were a valuable resource. Simply visiting a well-run facility can be vivid and exciting. It is fascinating to see how excellent competitors operate, to talk to them and learn of their experience. (It is also an excellent opportunity for administrators and designers to get away from their daily routine and talk to professional counterparts.)

But there are large opportunity costs in the way most current visits are run, and they represent considerable lost value for the healthcare organization, designer, and design project. Visits commonly fall short of what they could achieve for a similar investment of time and money elsewhere.

Common Pitfalls

Opportunity costs of current visits come from several common pitfalls, discussed in the following sections.

LOW EXPECTATIONS—LIMITED BENEFITS

Often, participants see field visits as a way to get to know other team members and simply to see other sites, but have no clear idea about what additional information can be helpful to the project at hand. They don't think through how the visit can help the goals of their project or organization.

TOO BUSY TO PLAN

The planner of a visit faces multiple problems. Often the visit is seen as a minor part of the job of most participants and doesn't get much attention in advance. Schedules and participants may change at the last minute. In many cases, no one is assigned to develop the overall plan of the visit or to ask if the major components—choice of sites, choice of issues to investigate, methods for visits, ways of creating and disseminating a report—match the overall goals of the organization and project. This is especially ironic because participants are often advocates of careful planning in other areas.

TOO FOCUSED ON MARKETING

Many visits are explicitly established to choose designers or consultants. However, others, while billed as data-gathering visits, are in fact aimed at marketing. A design firm may literally be marketing services, or the firm or a member of the client team may be trying to get a client to accept a solution that has already been developed—marketing the idea. This may lead to an attempt to create a "perfect" situation in the facility being visited, one without rush, bustle, or everyday users and the information they can provide. From designer-client teams, we heard many designers complain that they couldn't control their clients, that they couldn't keep them focused on pre-arranged ideas or keep them limited to prearranged routes. (This is often the result of not enough advance work aimed at understanding the interests the participants have and not enough time spent building common goals.)

CLOSING THE RANGE OF DESIGN OPTIONS TOO EARLY

Many visits occur early in the design process or when an organization is considering significant change, a perfect time to consider new possibilities or address issues and solutions not previously considered. This timing, and the chance to see and discuss new options in a visit, presents an opportunity for a design team to open its range of choices and consider novel or creative alternatives. However, many visit participants feel strong pressures to "already know the answer" when they start the visit. Many designers and consultants feel that their clients do not want them to genuinely explore a range of options, that they were hired because they know the solution. Similarly, some medical professionals establish positions early to avoid seeming foolish or uninformed. As a result, the team may choose sites that bring only confirmation, not surprise, and people will be interviewed who bring a viewpoint that is already well established. This is not simply a matter of the individual personalities of people who set up visits, but rather a problem of the design of teams and the context within which they operate. It is often important for a design firm to show a client the approach it is advocating and for them to jointly explore its suitability for the client's project. However, if the client expects a designer to know the answer before the process starts, rather than developing it jointly with the client, the designer is forced to use the visit to exhort rather than to investigate.

TOO LITTLE STRUCTURE FOR THE VISIT

Whereas no one likes to be burdened with unnecessary paperwork before or during a visit, it is easy to miss key issues if there is not an effort to establish issues in advance, with a reminder during the visit. Seeing a new place with lots of activity and complexity makes it easy to miss some key features. Many team members come back from visits with a clear idea of some irrelevant, unique feature, such as the sculpture in the hallway, rather than the aspect of the site that was being investigated.

INTERVIEWING THE WRONG PEOPLE

Often, out of organizational procedure or courtesy, a site being visited will assign an administrator or person from public relations to be the primary contact. It is almost always preferable to interview people familiar with the daily operations of the department or site.

MISSING CRITICAL STAKEHOLDERS

Almost every healthcare facility is attempting to become more responsive to customers, both patients and "internal" customers such as staff. Patients now often have a choice of healthcare providers. Staff members are costly to replace. Despite these trends, many visits miss some key customer groups—such as inpatients, outpatients, visitors, line staff, and maintenance staff—because they are not normally represented by visit hosts. It is very important that these groups or people who have close contact with them are represented in visits.

PROVIDING TOO MUCH DIRECTION DURING VISIT

In an effort to control the outcome, a leader may attempt to ask most of the questions during interviews. In addition to the problem of focusing exclusively on "selling" ideas described previously, participants do not like to feel that their role is usurped.

MISSING OPPORTUNITIES FOR TEAM BUILDING

Teams are most effective when everyone understands the values, goals, expertise, and specific roles of others on the team. Teams are also most effective when the team understands the process and resources of the team, the nature of the final product, how the final product will be used, who will evaluate it, and by what criteria the success of the product will be evaluated. Although management consultants routinely recommend making such issues explicit at the beginning of team building, we found few visit teams that deal with these issues directly. Many teams do not even get together to discuss these issues before a visit.

NOT ATTENDING TO CREATING A COMMON LANGUAGE

Multidisciplinary design teams often speak different professional languages and have different interests and values. Designers are used to reading plans and thinking in terms of space and materials; healthcare administrators are used to thinking in terms of words and operational plans. Unless a field visit team is conscious about making links between space and operations, there can be little opportunity to establish agreement.

LACK OF AN ACCESSIBLE VISIT REPORT

Most current visits produce no report at all; some produce at least a compilation of handwritten notes. We heard a repeated problem: no one could remember where they had seen a given feature.

THE HEALTHCARE FACILITY VISIT PROCESS

The healthcare facility visit process has three major phases, divided into specific team tasks that are conducted before, during, and after a visit. These phases, along with the 13 major tasks that comprise them, are shown in Table 1.1. The process we propose is

TABLE 1.1   HEALTHCARE FACILITY VISIT PROCESS

PREPARATION

1	Summarize the design project
2	Prepare background brief
3	Prepare draft work plan and budget
4	Choose and invite participants
5	Conduct issues session
6	Identify sites—start site visit package
7	Confirm agenda and issues list
8	Complete site visit package

SITE VISIT

9	Conduct site visit

FOCUS

10	Assemble report draft
11	Conduct focus meeting
12	Prepare and distribute focus report
13	Use data to inform design

quite straightforward, but compared to most current visits it is more deliberate about defining goals, thinking through what will be observed, preparing a report, and being clear about the implications of the visit for the current design project.

Preparation

TASK 1: SUMMARIZE THE DESIGN PROJECT. In this task, the project leader or others prepare a brief description of the goals, philosophy, scope, and major constraints overview of the design project that the visit is intended to aid. It should include the shortcomings that the design project is to resolve: space limitations, operational inefficiencies, deferred maintenance, and so on.

The overview helps focus the facility visit and can be provided to the host sites to help them understand the perspective of the visit. This summary should be brief— only a few pages of bulleted items—but should clearly identify the strategic decisions the team is facing. For example, a team may be considering whether to develop a freestanding or attached woman's pavilion. It is also important to identify key *operational* questions. Focusing on design solutions too early may distract the team from more fundamental questions that need to be resolved. The purpose of the summary is to establish a common understanding of goals and constraints and to allow the visit hosts to prepare for the visit.

NOTE: *Many visits ignore this critical up-front work. Depending on the schedule and scope, the summary can be circulated to the team in advance of the brainstorming meeting.*

TASK 2: PREPARE BACKGROUND BRIEF. More than most building types, healthcare facilities have a large body of literature providing descriptions of new trends, research, design guidelines, and post-occupancy evaluations. Many design firms and healthcare organizations have this material in their libraries or can get it from local universities or medical schools. For this task, the visit organizer creates a file of a few key articles or book chapters describing the issue or facility type being visited. These are then distributed to the team, allowing all team members to have at least a minimal current understanding of operations and design.

The team leader also prepares an issues worksheet. This is a one-page form that is distributed along with the background brief to all members of the visit team prior to their first meeting. (See Figure 1.1 for a sample issues worksheet.) It encourages them to jot down what is important to them and to discuss issues with their colleagues. It works most effectively when the visit organizer adds some typical issues to help them think through the problem. Participants should be encouraged to bring the worksheet with them to the team meetings.

TASK 3: PREPARE DRAFT WORK PLAN AND BUDGET. Once the team leader or others have summarized the design project and prepared the background brief, a draft work plan outlining the major components of the field visits can be prepared. At this stage, it is important to establish a tentative budget for the visit. It is also important to make sure that the major components of the draft work plan, such as choosing visit sites and developing critical issues, match the overall goals of the organization and project. The draft work plan provides a tentative structure for the field visits, which can be modified by other team members.

TASK 4: CHOOSE AND INVITE PARTICIPANTS. The effectiveness of the team is, of course, most directly related to the nature of the participants. Field visit team members are sometimes chosen for reasons such as politics, or as a reward for good service, rather than for their relevance to the project. Visit teams are usually most successful if they mix the decision makers who will be empowered to make design decisions with people who have direct experience in working in the area or department being studied. For design firms, teams are often most successful if they include a principal and the project staff. In both of these cases, the team should combine an overall strategic view of the organization and project with an intimate knowledge of operational and design details.

ISSUES WORKSHEET
Department Level

Focus	LDRP		Name	Virginia Johnston, AIA
Date	7/15/94		Firm	King, Art & Major

TYPICAL ISSUES

Preprinted items prompt specific questions →

- · mission
- · type of facility
- · affiliation
- · off-campus services
- · main funding sources
- · nature of patient
- · list of departments
- · # beds

QUESTIONS	RESOURCE	ISSUE TYPE	
	person or item	design	operational
What finish materials have been used successfully in the LDR room?	head nurse, facilities	☒	☐
How was the need for various lighting levels addressed in the the LDR rooms?	nurse, md facilities	☒	☐
Does the layout of LDR rooms in relation to the Nurses Station work effectively?	nurses	☒	☒
		☐	☐
		☐	☐
		☐	☐
		☐	☐
		☐	☐
		☐	☐
		☐	☐
		☐	☐
		☐	☐
		☐	☐

Area to record questions and issues →

Place to identify resources →

Type of issue →

Figure 1.1 Sample issues worksheet.

TASK 5: CONDUCT TEAM ISSUES SESSION. It is usually advisable to hold a team meeting early in the visit planning process to clarify the purposes and general methods of the field visit; build an effective visit team by clarifying the perspective and role of each participant; identify potential sites, if the visit sites have not already been selected.

The issues session is often a structured brainstorming meeting aimed at getting a large number of ideas on the table. (This is particularly important during departmental and general visits and in cases where team members don't know each other.) The purpose is opening the range of possible issues rather than focusing on a single alternative.

This meeting is typically aimed at building a common sense of purpose for all team members rather than marketing a preconceived idea. An issue session also serves the purpose of making critical decisions regarding the choice of sites and identifying who at the sites should be contacted.

Each participant should bring the issues worksheet along to the meeting. The initial task is to get all questions and information needs onto a flip chart or board before any prioritization goes on. Then the leader and group can sort these into categories and discuss priorities. These categories and priorities may be sorted in the form of lists that include: (1) a list of critical purposes of the departments or features being designed; (2) a list of critical purposes of the departments or features being evaluated at each facility during visits; and (3) a list of existing and innovative design features relevant to these purposes. The critical purposes of the departments or design features at existing facilities can be charted at different spatial levels of the facilities, such as site, entrance, public spaces, clinical spaces, and administrative and support areas.

The issues session may be run by the leader or the facilitator. Because one of the purposes of this meeting is to get balanced participation, it may be useful to have someone experienced in group process run the meeting rather than the leader. His or her job is to make sure everyone participates, allowing the leader to focus on content.

This meeting may also provide an early opportunity to identify potential problems created by conflicting goals, values, or personalities on the team. For instance, a healthcare facility design project may have significant conflicts between departments or between physicians and administrators. The meeting may also allow the team members to agree on basic business imperatives and to be clear about the constraints that are of greatest importance to them, such as never having radioactive materials cross the path of patients, for example.

This meeting is successful if participants feel they can express ideas, interests, and concerns without negative consequences from other members of the team. There is no such thing as a stupid question in this meeting.

TASK 6: IDENTIFY POTENTIAL SITES AND CONFIRM WITH THE TEAM. Based on the work plan that established the visit objectives and the desires, interests, and budget of the team, the visit organizer chooses potential sites and checks with the team. If possible, he or she provides some background information about each site to help the team make decisions. Although it is rare, some sites now charge for visits.

The team may know of some sites it would like to visit, and these might have emerged in the issues session. Otherwise, there is a range of sources for finding appropriate sites to visit: national organizations such as the American Hospital Association, as well as the AIA Academy on Architecture for Health, and The Center for Health Design. Magazines are also available that discuss healthcare facilities.

Different teams pick sites for different reasons. Some may pick a site because it is the best example of an operational approach such as "patient-focused care." Others may attempt to provide a clear range of choices within a set of constraints provided by operations, budget, or existing conditions, such as "different layouts of express emergency departments" or "new, rural, patient-focused care hospitals with 150 beds."

Many visit leaders complain that the team sometimes is distracted by features outside the focus of the tour, particularly by poor maintenance. Wherever possible, it is advisable for the visit organizers to tour the site in advance of the group visit and to brief the hosts in person about the purposes of the visit.

TASK 7: SCHEDULE SITES AND CONFIRM AGENDA. For this task, the leader or organizer calls a representative at each host site to schedule the visit. The leader confirms the purposes of the visit, tells the host sites what the information will be needed before and during the field visit, and discusses who will be interviewed at the site. Healthcare facilities are sometimes more responsive to a request for a visit if they are called by a healthcare professional or administrator rather than a designer. If someone on the team knows someone at a site, that member may want to make the first phone call. Many teams also find that, if they arrange for a very brief visit, this may be extended a bit on site when the hosts become engaged with the team. When confirming the schedule for the visit with the host facilities, the visit organizer should specify that the visit team would prefer to interview people familiar with the daily operations of the department or site.

It is also important to schedule a visit when it does not interfere with the operations of the host site. While many inpatient sites find that midmorning or midafternoon is best because these times do not affect medical rounds or housekeeping, each site has its own schedule.

Healthcare administrators are usually proud of their facilities and enjoy receiving distinguished visitors. However, they often find it difficult to arrange interviews or assemble detailed information on the spot.

TASK 8: PREPARE FIELD VISIT PACKAGE. Visits are more effective if participants are provided with a package of information in advance containing information about schedule, accommodations, and contact people; information about each site, including, where possible, brief background information and plans; a simple form for recording information; and a "tickler" list of questions and issues.

1. *Prepare visit information package.* The organizers should provide participants with information about the logistics of the field visit—schedules, reservation confirmation numbers, and phone numbers of sites and hotels.

2. *Prepare site information package.* The site information package orients participants to the site in advance of the visit. Depending on what information is available, it may include plans and photos of each site; basic organizational information about the site (client name and address, mission statement, patient load, size, date, designers, and so on); description of special features or processes or other items of interest. Whereas measured plans are best, these are not often available. Fire evacuation plans can be used. Many teams find it useful to review job descriptions of staff positions for the host site, and many organizations have these readily available and are willing to share them.

3. *Prepare visit worksheet.* Facility visits are often overwhelming in the amount of information they present. It is useful for the organizers to provide the participants with a worksheet for taking notes. A sample worksheet is provided in Figure 1.2. The purpose of the checklist is to remind participants of the key issues and to provide a form that can easily be assembled into the trip report.

A successful worksheet directs participants to the agreed-upon focal issues without burdening them with unnecessary paperwork. Participants should understand the relationship between filling out the checklist and filling out the final report.

TASK 9: CONDUCT FACILITY FIELD VISIT. The actual site visit typically includes: (1) an initial orientation interview with people at the site familiar with the department or setting being investigated; (2) a touring interview where the team, or part of it, visits the facility being investigated with someone familiar with daily operations, asking questions and observing operations; (3) a recording of the site; and (4) a wrap-up meeting at the site. The interview sessions are focused on helping the team understand a wider range of implications and possibilities. If appropriate, the wrap-up session may also be used for focusing on key issues that move the design along.

NOTE: *Participants often like to speak to their counterparts—head nurse to head nurse, medical director to medical director, and so on—although everyone seems to like to talk to people directly involved with running a facility such as a head nurse. People who know daily operations are often more useful than a high-level administrator or public relations staff member.*

1. *Conduct site orientation interview.* During the orientation interview, the visit team meets briefly with a representative of the site to get an overall orientation to the site: layout and general organization; mission and philosophy; brief history and strategic plans; patient load; treatment load; other descriptions of the site. Many teams are also interested in learning about experiences the healthcare organization had with the

HEALTHCARE FACILITY VISIT WORKSHEET

Name	Virginia Johnston, AIA	Date	July 29, 1994
Site	Metropolitan Hospital	Keywords	LDR, Labor Delivery Recovery, Maternity
Area	LDR		

ISSUES CHECKLIST

Programmatic / Operational
❑ what were the general operational issues to which the architecture of the facility directly responded?

❑ how does the facility function in terms of staff and administration?

❑ how is the facility staffed?

❑ security procedures

Special Features

❑ disinfecting Jacuzzi

❑ lighting in LDR

❑ how were special issues resolved?

Preprinted summary from Issues Worksheet

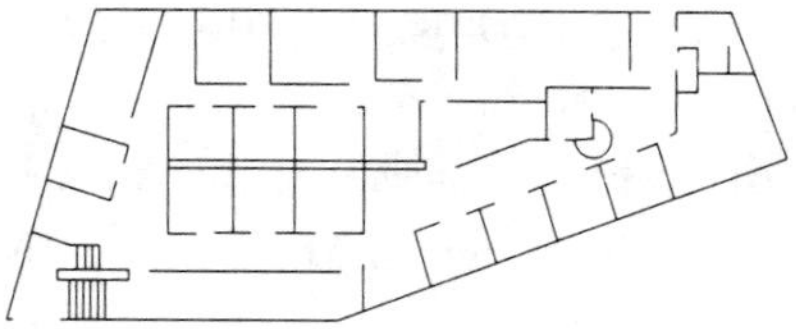

Plan and space for notes

OPERATIONAL/DESIGN ISSUES

Place to record other issues that arise during visit

Photo taken on visit

Figure 1.2 Healthcare facility visit worksheet. Form used by participants during facility site visit.

process of planning, design, construction, and facility management. What steps did they use? What innovations did they come up with? What problems did they encounter? What are they particularly proud of? What do they wish they had done differently?

2. *Conduct a touring interview.* The touring interview was developed by a building

evaluation group in New Zealand and by several other postoccupancy evaluation researchers and practitioners. In the touring interview, the team, or a portion of it, visits a portion of the site to understand the design and operations. Conducting an interview in the actual department being discussed often brings a vividness and specificity that may be lacking in an interview held in a meeting room or on the phone. One of the great strengths of the touring interview is the surprises it may bring and the option it provides to consider new possibilities or to deal with unanticipated problems. As a result, it often works best to start with fairly open-ended questions:

- What works well here? What works less well?
- What are the major goals and operational philosophy of the department?
- What is the flow of patients, staff, visitors, meals, supplies, records, laundry, trash? (Many teams actually trace one or more of these flows during the tour.)
- Can the hosts demonstrate a sample process or procedure, such as how a patient moves from the waiting room to gowning area to treatment area?
- What are they most proud of?
- What would they do differently if they could do it over?

These questions also provide a nonthreatening way to discuss shortcomings or issues that are potentially controversial. The team may then want to focus on the specific concerns that were raised in the issues session.

It is difficult, but critically important to avoid becoming distracted by idiosyncratic details of the site being visited. Often operational patterns or philosophy are more important than specific design features that will not be generalized to a new project—how equipment is allocated to labor/delivery/recovery/postpartum (LDRP) rooms in the site being visited may be more important than the color scheme, even though the color may be more striking.

Large multidisciplinary teams are particularly hard to manage during a touring interview. A given facility may have a start-of-the-art imaging department that is of great interest to the radiologists on the team but may have a mediocre rehabilitation department. In these cases, some of the touring interviews may be focused on "what the host would do differently next time."

3. *Document the visit.* The goals of the visit dictate the kinds of documentation that are appropriate. However, most visits call for a visual record, sketches, and written notes.

In most cases, it is useful to designate one or more "official" recorders who will assemble notes and be sure photos are taken, measurements made, plans and documents procured, and so on. For designer-client visits, it is often useful to have at least two official recorders to look after both design and operational concerns. However, because a team often splits up, most or all participants may need to keep notes.

It is quite rare for teams to use video to record their visit, although this seems to be increasing in popularity. Editing videos can be very costly—it may take a staff member several person-days in a professional editing facility to edit several hours of raw video down to a 10- or 15-minute length. However, this time may be reduced with the increased availability of inexpensive microcomputer-based editing programs.

If the method of creating the documentation is established in advance it can easily be assembled into a draft report.

4. *Conduct on-site wrap-up meeting.* Whereas the visit interview is focused on opening options for the team and identifying new problems and issues, the wrap-up meeting is often more focused on clarifying how lessons learned on the visit relate to the design project and how these lessons begin to answer the questions the team established. It is often useful to have a representative of the host site present at the wrap-up meeting to answer questions, if the host's time allows.

TASK 10: ASSEMBLE DRAFT VISIT REPORT.   A draft visit report may take many different formats. The simplest is to photocopy and assemble all participants' worksheets and notes, retyping where necessary. Alternatively, the organizers or a portion of the team may edit and synthesize the worksheets and notes. Although more time consuming, this usually results in a more readable report. A somewhat more sophisticated version is to establish a database record that resembles the form used to take on-site notes in a program such as FoxPro, Dbase, or FileMaker Pro. Participants' comments can be typed into the database, and sketches and graphics can be scanned in and attached. These are then provided to all participants.

Simplicity is often best; simply photocopying or retyping notes is often adequate, especially if photos and sketches are attached.

TASK 11: CONDUCT FOCUS MEETING.   Upon returning home, the team conducts a meeting to review the draft trip report and to ask

- What are the major lessons of the visit?
- What does the visit tell the team about the current project?

Unlike the issues session held early in the visit planning process, which was primarily concerned with bringing out a wide range of goals and options, this meeting is typically aimed more at establishing consensus about directions for the project.

The leader should carefully consider who is invited to the focus meeting. This may include others from the design firm, consultants, members of healthcare organization, or even representatives from the site.

TASK 12: PREPARE FOCUS REPORT. The focus report briefly summarizes the key conclusions of the visit for the visit team and for later use by the entire design team. It is an executive summary of the visit report. (The visit report may provide a number of pages of observations and interview notes.)

TASK 13: USE DATA TO INFORM DESIGN. The key purpose of a facility visit is to inform design. Whereas this can occur informally in subsequent conversations and team meetings, it is best achieved by also being proactive. For example, the team can

- Conduct an in-house feedback session about the visit
- Create a database that is usable by the design team and others
- Write a brief newsletter about the design project that includes key findings from the visit

ALLASOPHIAPHOBIA

Whereas almost everyone we interviewed felt that facility visits were valuable, it appeared to us that the way many visits were conducted carried large opportunity costs compared to how they *could be* conducted, with little additional investment. With a bit more up-front clarification of the purposes of the visit, more careful site selection, a bit more focus during the visit, and preparation of a brief report, the visits can be much more useful. Many participants recounted that the visits were more valuable where they had more opportunity to do more preparation.

It appears to us that visits are performed the way that they are because they are seldom treated as formal tasks that require planning and clear budgeting. This is perhaps because design project teams are in the process of being organized when most visits occur and the close client oversight that occurs later has not yet been mobilized. It may also be because the opportunity to see other well-run settings is inherently so compelling that the benefits of doing even more are obscured. Also, experienced professionals can often learn a great deal without the aid of much structure for a visit.

We also found what was referred to before as *allasophiaphobia*—the fear of learning in public. Individual and organizational learning is based on some simple principles: try out ideas publicly in ways that errors can be identified; be clear about assumptions and values so they also can develop; provide feedback such that the content of ideas or proposals are addressed, not the character of the person making the proposals; take action for the good of the group, not for individual or competitive gain. These ideas are part of a good facility visit and are more broadly part of effective organizational learning models suggested by organizational consultants such as Chris Argyris, Donald Schon, and Peter Senge.

However, in numerous studies where they have examined organizations in action, these consultants have found a distressing trend. Whereas most people in organizations say they do these things, when you actually examine their behavior, you find that they do the reverse. They are reluctant to try out new or undeveloped ideas because they think they might look foolish. They make statements at such a high level of abstraction that it is difficult to understand the basis of their comments. Feedback is often personal or is so general that the consequences for further development of the idea is unclear. (Often, such general feedback is well intended, as when people ease into a difficult topic, but it has the net consequence of obscuring lessons to be learned.) Organizations operate in a climate of individual competition rather than a sense of common mission.

Almost everyone we interviewed recognized the potential that a visit represents for mutual learning about new situations being visited and for further understanding the design being developed. Many of the clients particularly saw it as an opportunity to see how well the designer listens to the clients' needs. However, we also heard comments from designers such as, "If we really want to learn, we go there by ourselves before the client visit," or "The worst part of a visit is that we can't control the client." Our interviews suggested that many designers would like to carefully stage-manage their visits so that there are few surprises.

When we probed our informants, they expressed a common anxiety: their clients had hired them to "know the answer" and, by appearing uncertain, they were jeopardizing their professional roles. At least one client expressed a common view of its relationship to its designer: the client hired a designer to provide answers, not questions. Some of this anxiety is simply human nature. Few people like to have their errors exposed; it's simply nicer to be told you are correct. In addition, the pain of such feedback tends to be immediate, whereas the positive consequences are long term, and the organization improves in performance. Studies in psychology tell us that immediate punishment is usually more potent than long-term reward.

Processes such as the facility visit seem ideally suited to increasing flexibility and innovation and reducing risk. After all, it is an opportunity to see innovative facilities at a time when designs can be changed with little cost. It also provides an early opportunity to get conflicts within a design team out in the open and resolve or clarify them. But allasophiaphobia and limited experience by team members may limit this opportunity. Clients, in particular, may have limited opportunity to keep up with innovations in healthcare design and hence may enter such a process with quite fixed ideas. Unless the team has an opportunity to explore these ideas and the reasons for them, there may be little opportunity for change.

Healthcare facilities are increasingly becoming more customer oriented. Competition between facilities is increasing, and organizations see physical facilities as potential competitive advantages. In addition, many facilities are seen as "healing designs," where the layout, furnishings, ambiance, amenities, access to views, and so on, serve as therapeutic tools. Visits provide opportunities to explore such setting analytically.

Perhaps the greatest impediment to being customer oriented is that customers are seldom represented in the design process. We are all familiar with situations where a well-intentioned facility ends up being so complex that outpatients and visitors become highly stressed trying to find their way into the facility, or where the waiting experience is highly unpleasant and ambiguous. Most healthcare facilities really *do* care about customers. Nevertheless, customers are seldom represented on design teams, and few professionals have experienced facilities from a customer's perspective, so technical considerations prevail. A vivid, well-structured visit can provide clear views of these important and seldom-documented groups.

In sum, the principles underlying our facility visit process are fairly simple: be explicit about goals, objectives, and values early in the process; provide a structure that allows the team to be analytic and open to new experiences during the visit; be clear about the lessons learned after the visit is completed and make these lessons available to as large a group as possible.

Craig Zimring is an associate professor of architecture at the College of Architecture at Georgia Institute of Technology in Atlanta, Georgia. Bruce Nepp, AIA, is an architect with Anshen + Allen Architects in San Francisco. Rhonda Hillman is Chief of the Medical Facilities Management Support at the Air Force Medical Logistics Office in Frederick, Maryland.

References

Argyris, C. *On Organizational Learning.* Cambridge, MA: Blackwell, 1992.

Argyris, C. and Schon, D. *Organizational Learning.* Reading, MA: Addison-Wesley, 1974.

Senge, P. M. *The Fifth Discipline: The Art and Practice of Organizational Learning.* New York: Currency Doubleday, 1990.

Zimring, C. *A Guide to Conducting Healthcare Facility Visits.* Martinez, CA: The Center for Health Design, 1994.

2

PROGRAMMING

Rosalyn Cama, ASID

Healthcare facilities can be defined as places that administer acute, short-term, long-term, respite, hospice, ambulatory, or cooperative care. They can be inpatient facilities, traditional medical office buildings, or walk-in medical specialty clinics. With a push toward preventative medicine, wellness centers are emerging as a new architectural form (see color plate 1).

Technology and research advances will continue to change how patients are kept healthy, diagnosed, registered for admission, monitored, and treated, as well as how they recover. Most of these functions will be brought home to the family. The family will seek alternative methods of recovery and convalescence through in-home care or in a less acute facility. An aging baby boomer population also means a shift in the focus of our attitudes toward the elderly and the spaces they inhabit. As longevity increases and communicable diseases spread through our global community, delivery systems for these services will redefine and restructure the architecture of many of our healthcare interiors.

Healthcare interiors can be defined as any interior space where healthcare services are prepared and delivered to patients and their families by an active or passive, present or remote caregiver. Those spaces can be identified as interiors within traditional institutions such as

- Public lobbies
- Chapels
- Food services
- Retail services
- Community/volunteer spaces
- Administrative and staff offices
- Outpatient facilities
- Inpatient rooms
- Family rooms
- Consultation rooms

26

- Examination rooms
- Treatment and procedure rooms
- Electronic communications centers
- Laboratories
- Resource centers
- Support services
- Teaching and conferencing facilities

Healthcare interiors can also be in a hotel-like facility or in a private home (see Figure 2.1).

Many new iterations of care will emerge as the industry develops ways to deliver quality, efficient care in a competitive environment. Healthcare facilities as we know them today will change as institutions position themselves to secure more of a diminishing inpatient and growing outpatient market. The trend is to purchase or affiliate with other hospitals, develop satellite facilities, and/or merge with specialty providers to control competition.

Health-related professionals will transform their roles as services and reimbursement methods change. Competition and positioning for a limited market will cause providers to pay close attention to their physical plants. The interior consultant who

Figure 2.1 Many healthcare interiors have hotel-like qualities. Project: Rhode Island Cooperative Care Unit, Providence, Rhode Island, patient and caregivers room. Architecture: Robinson, Greene & Beretta Architects. Interior design: Rosalyn Cama Interior Design Associates, Inc., New Haven, Connecticut.

understands that the evolution of this industry is not so predictable will help to develop spaces that yield to change in a cost-effective way.

Therefore, the role of the interior designer on a project design team is to be the instrument through which that team can create interior spaces that, first, function in a manner that provides for the immediate goal and, second, allow for flexibility in this ever-changing interior environment. The success of that charge is in the initial planning and programming.

THE CLIENT'S OBJECTIVES

A project can be defined as anything from a single-room renovation that requires only finish upgrades to a large multithousand-square-foot, new construction project that requires every interior component to be planned.

The initial directive for a project can be given for a number of reasons:

- A requirement is imposed by regulatory agencies.
- An insurance provider modifies the reimbursement structure.
- An administrator views the status quo as inefficient or less competitive.
- A new program has different space or technology requirements.
- A shift in the services provided redirects space assignments.
- New equipment, technologies, or procedures redefine space.
- There is not enough space for a given task.
- The space is tired and in need of repair.
- Budgets are available for upgrades.
- A competing facility upgrades.

The most productive projects are developed as a result of strategic planning. Administrative management of a facility typically develops a plan by which its organization will function and grow for a number of years. A "mission" or "vision" is the root of this plan. Many external factors are studied regarding demographics, patient types, and reimbursement structures. An internal analysis will report strengths and weaknesses in the services provided and operational issues that support those services.

The plan is constantly reviewed to keep pace with changing internal and external factors. An analysis identifies specific issues that need to be addressed to achieve short- and long-term goals. Strategies are developed and often include issues related to space utilization.

It is important for interior designers to know their client's strategic plan. Administrators at Yale-New Haven Hospital in New Haven, Connecticut, feel it is important for every person who walks through its door to know its mission. The designer was charged with the creative task of getting the message out (see Figures 2.2 and

Figure 2.2 Incorporating an institution's mission statement into the facility design is part of the challenge. Project: Yale-New Haven Hospital, New Haven, Connecticut. Interior design/graphics: Rosalyn Cama Interior Design Associates, Inc., and Group C Graphics. Photography: Christopher Kirby Studio, New Haven, Connecticut.

2.3). Knowing this plan helps identify issues that may not seem relevant to the client, but allows the designer the ability to consult with the best interests of the client in mind. It is also important for the interior designer to be current on healthcare market trends; accreditation; life-safety, building, fire, and local codes and standards. Sources for such information include

- Professional organizations (design- and healthcare-related fields), conferences, specialty networks, trade journals, on-line services
- Manufacturers' research and design departments
- Regulatory agencies
- State agencies

Figure 2.3 Source: The American Society of Interior Designers (ASID), Washington, D.C.

IDENTIFYING SPACES TO BE PROGRAMMED

A functional program is typically developed by a medical planner (the first of many to comprise the design team) who understands the operations side of a particular segment of the healthcare market. Working with a facility's strategic plan and an understanding of current and predicted trends, the planner can create a program by which the facility will function. Simultaneously, the rest of the design team is identified and space studies are evaluated for the smooth operation of that program. Several considerations control the creative solutions that the architects can suggest:

- Site available for study
- Clients' willingness to demolish, construct, or renovate

- If renovation, then evaluation of the physical conditions (structural, mechanical, and code deficiencies) of the building for its new use
- If new construction, the town zoning and approvals
- State regulatory restrictions
- Budgets
- Interior program requirements

The interior program requirements are usually identified by the space each function requires, staffing needs, interdepartmental functions, and adjacencies required between departments and common areas. The design team should anticipate and plan for growth and change. This is all tabulated into an allotment of square footage. The interior designer, along with the client, architect, and an equipment consultant, identifies all items required for a user to function in that space. Room data sheets should be compiled for each space in the project. These sheets should then be sorted by departments or by groups of related services and then by floor, depending on the size of a project. Preliminary budgets can be created from this study to maintain the proper scope of the project.

A typical room data sheet is computer generated and formatted as the project requires. The designer records general room statistics, such as programmed square footage and actual square footage. Occupancy type and occupancy loads are also noted. Finishes are listed for each plane. Ceiling heights, special ratings, and other specifications are also noted. Building system and infrastructural data is recorded. Furniture, equipment, and fixtures are listed. Computer-aided drawings are also incorporated into the data set. This information becomes a valuable reference throughout the project.

Initial drawings identify the footprint and interior space planning of the project. This information describes graphically how the patient care delivery system will function. These early studies are usually reviewed several times with the project lead team that oversees all aspects of the project. The project lead team is comprised of any combination of the following hospital personnel:

- Administration
- Medical chiefs
- Clinical directors
- Finance
- Facilities planning and design
- Engineering and materials management
- Environmental services
- Development

In most cases, space for a new project has been determined by the time an interior designer has been retained. This should be the exception, not the rule. The designer should be included in the initial team of space and program consultants so that costly changes are avoided.

FORMULATING THE PROGRAM

The functional program is the basis of the interior design program. Rooms are divided by type and programmed for furnishings and finishes. The program documents each type of space, listing specific generic items, quantifying them, setting their dimensions, and estimating a unit and extended price (see Tables 2.1 and 2.2).

Most hospitals have purchasing agreements or belong to buying cooperatives that entitle them to specific discounts off of manufacturers' list prices. Those prices can be

TABLE 2.1 FURNITURE PLANNING/ROOMS

Room Type	Function	Furniture Items	Quantity	Unit Price	Total
13	Consult room	48″ round table	1	$360.00	$360.00
		Side chair	6	$145.00	$870.00
		2-drwr lat file	2	$315.00	$630.00
		Bulletin board	1	$ 80.00	$ 80.00
		Artwork	1	$125.00	$125.00
		Total			$2,065.00
17	Family/overnight wait	Recliners	6	$630.00	$3,780.00
		Tables	3	$200.00	$600.00
		Bulletin board	1	$ 80.00	$ 80.00
		Artwork	2	$125.00	$250.00
		Plants	2	$125.00	$250.00
		Window treatments	1	$400.00	$400.00
		Total			$5,360.00
18	Exam treatment rm	Side chair	1	$ 60.00	$ 60.00
		Task 1 chair	1	$180.00	$180.00
		Bulletin board	1	$ 80.00	$ 80.00
		Artwork	1	$125.00	$125.00
		Cubicle curtain	1	$200.00	$200.00
		Total			$645.00

TABLE 2.2 FURNITURE PLANNING/PRELIMINARY BUDGETS

Function	Room Type	Quantity	Unit Price	Total Price
SHARED PATIENT CARE/VISITOR FUNCTIONS				
Family overnight/waiting	17	1	$5,360.00	$5,360.00
Consult room	13	1	$2,065.00	$2,065.00
Exam treatment room	18	1	$645.00	$645.00
Subtotal Shared Patient Care				$8,070.00

estimated and escalated for a cost-of-living increase over the planning duration of the project. On most projects, the hospital's purchasing department or the contractor's construction manager will ultimately send the final specifications out for competitive bid. It is important to understand which items are covered in the furniture budget and which will be covered in the equipment budget. It is also important to know when a work area is to be built-in casework and covered in the construction budget and when it is to be programmed as movable furnishings.

Each room type has uniform characteristics from one facility to the next. However, special programs (such as special meals for new moms) may dictate a specific piece of furniture not typically planned for. The functional program or user reviews will quickly identify those issues. New health and safety issues, such as universal precaution requirements, will also add to the room's list. This could mean extra trash cans or gown dispensers. The type of patient population may dictate a sleep chair for a rooming-in parent or a familiar room identification sign for a disoriented dementia patient.

The Americans with Disabilities Act (ADA) has put in place requirements for all populations. Regulatory agencies are shortening the length of stay for some admissions, therefore a postpartum room may not be necessary to allow mom to recover (from delivering a baby), and a LDRP room will suffice. Furnishings in each of those spaces vary because they function differently at times. Special codes and regulatory agencies put specific requirements in place for populations, such as patients in psychiatric units. Sometimes the requirements contradict themselves, such as a psychiatric unit that services a high volume of Chinese patients. Culturally, there is a need for a hot-water dispenser in the lounge, but the state mental health codes will not allow the installation of such a dispenser. Solutions are worked out among the team.

The perceived image of a facility will also dictate a varied vocabulary of design elements from which to draw. This is important to know at this phase since pricing structures will be different. Infrastructural requirements may need to be enhanced for accessories like large art installations, fish tanks, table lamps, and so on (see color plate 2).

A medical "hotel" will be designed differently than a major inner-city trauma center. The image of a rural community hospital will be different than that of a special services facility that caters to foreign dignitaries. Specialty clinics that service different specialties on different days of the week will need universal solutions. Researching the market is important because new products are being introduced every day for the healthcare industry. Those of us who have been practicing institutional design for more than 15 years can remember a very limited resource pool. Fortunately for us, the economic downturn in the United States in the late 1980s took the emphasis away from corporate high-style finishes and furnishings and redirected creative energy toward the needs of the healthcare industry.

Drawings should confirm that special furniture arrangements work in the allotted square footage. Architects, clients, users, and interior designers should hammer out options during this phase. Discussions on what gets added and what gets dropped from the functional program should occur when new team members are added after the process begins. If the team is together from the start, then many issues are discussed early on and worked through without having to go back and rethink an approved issue.

The interior architectural image of the facility is thought through at an early phase also. This is so that the team understands the necessary structural, mechanical, electrical, or plumbing loads. Decisions are made to upgrade certain areas because of the directives dictating the project. Details are worked through in later design phases.

Similarly, finishes are programmed at this stage. Generic finishes and their history within the existing institution should be discussed with the client. Carpeting may be a terrific acoustical tool, but, if a facility is not equipped to maintain it properly, it may be a nightmare. Discussions should revolve around the life-cycle costs and maintenance of most finishes. The maintenance procedures and traffic exposed to a particular finish will cause it to perform differently. Some facilities have success with a product that was a nightmare for others. Meeting with manufacturers, educating the client to installation and maintenance procedures that will extend the life of a product, and visiting other installations that have been in existence for a while in a similar setting are good research tactics.

The best way to decide on a controversial finish is to identify a smaller renovation site in the current facility and have the product installed. Live with the product and have it undergo the facility's routine maintenance. Go back 3, 6, and 12 months later, if time permits, and evaluate the pros and cons of the generic finish or a specific manufacturer. The architects and designers should factor these discussions and tests in as they work toward a design concept that emerges in these early phases of design. Hence, the importance of early interior programming that is comprehensive in nature.

It may be determined that some of the existing furniture, fixtures, and equipment (FF&E) may be reused. At this time, a thorough inventory should be conducted of the department's existing FF&E and documented for use at a later time. Emphasis should be placed on "use at a later time," since furnishings move about in most healthcare facilities. Therefore, methods of monitoring the whereabouts of those items to be reused is essential.

Ceiling, lighting, wall protection, and flooring systems will need to be programmed with the entire design team, since many components affect other building systems. Artwork and signage systems may require additional blocking and electrical or plumbing sources. These are important components of the final project that are often forgotten. They need to be programmed early enough to be accounted for and sufficiently budgeted.

It may also be determined that a methodical approach to a project can lead to standards by which future projects are developed. For example, a new building project may lead to the renovation of the spaces left behind by the relocated departments. Those renovations may incorporate some of the same design details so that visual continuity is created throughout a facility (see Figures 2.4 and 2.5).

These early programming decisions set a budget that will become the basis from which to value-engineer later. Do allow for some flexibility since, over the life of the project, old products may be discontinued and new products added.

Interior plans should be developed in a series of working meetings where the actual users are consulted. A user can be any of the following:

- Departmental director
- Departmental employees
- Doctor/nurse/technician/clerical manager
- Patient or parent advocate
- Major donor (often for public spaces)

During these meetings, the initial program requirements should be reviewed. The user's input is discussed with the project design team and usually a representative of the client's lead team. This information is processed into a revised project program and budget that determines the approved scale of the project.

TESTING THE PROGRAM

Most product manufacturers are anxious to learn early about a project. Many are anxious to inform the design team of product development plans, since most healthcare projects span many years. A fair way to inform those who may be interested in the project is to share the early program document that specifies the generic type of

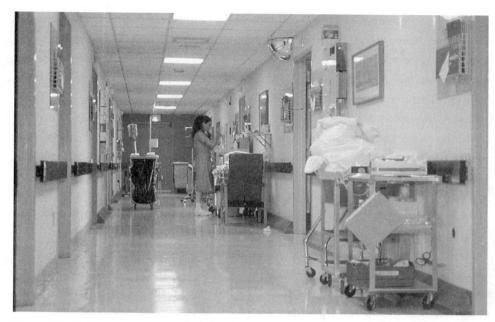

Figure 2.4   Before photo of corridors in Yale-New Haven Hospital, New Haven, Connecticut.

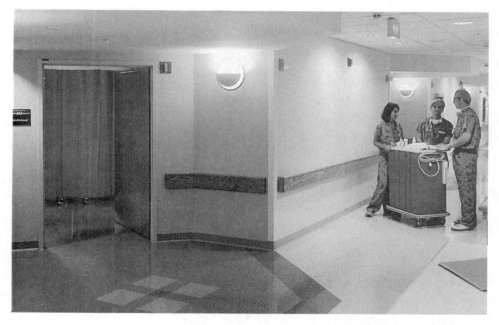

Figure 2.5   After photo of corridors in Yale-New Haven Hospital, New Haven, Connecticut, when compared to photo in Figure 2.4, underscore the importance of design. Architecture: Shepley Bulfinch Richardson & Abbott Architects. Photography: Peter Arron/Esto, Mamaroneck, N.Y.

furnishings with a budget assigned to it. Similarly, preliminary construction budgets will identify finishes and building accessories. This allows the manufacturers the opportunity to present to the specifier all products currently or soon to be in their line. These market searches then can be culled for design and functional requirements.

The design team can review submissions. Products that qualify are then evaluated by the designer, client, and end user, either by visiting existing installations, trade shows, manufacturer showrooms, or installing actual mock-ups.

Mock-ups serve two functions:

1. They verify that all program requirements will function as planned.
2. They can be developed later to serve as a training ground for staff, who may function under a new program once the new or renovated space is completed.

If the healthcare facility's planning has been carried out in an informed fashion, the program formulated carefully, and the plan executed skillfully allowing for flexibility, then the client should be set to ride the uncertain wave into the next millennium, ahead of its competition.

Rosalyn Cama is principal of Rosalyn Cama Interior Design Associates in New Haven, Connecticut.

References

Jones, W. J. "Acute Care Design: The New Generation." *Journal of Healthcare Design* 5 (1993): 33–38.

Milcare Graphics Standards. Zeeland, MI: Milcare, Inc., 1993.

Pertz, S. "Redefining Strategic Facilities Planning." *Facilities Management Journal* (November/December 1994): 29–34.

3

CODE BUSTING AND CODE REINVENTION

Barbara L. Geddis, FAIA

Code busting is both an appealing and intimidating term for most design professionals. Nearly every architect, engineer, or designer has stories about the occasional absurdity, inconsistency, or inequity of some regulatory body's imposed standard, code, or guideline. The stories range from well-known inexplicable conflicts between codes with overlapping jurisdictions to distressing tales of safety issues *caused* by regulatory enthusiasm. A design professional in Washington, D.C., recounted the story of the Washington subway system's near disaster. Someone added a warning line with tactile (translate: gritty) materials at the edge of the subway platform so that disabled passengers could feel as well as see the platform edge. A blind person tripped on the material and fell onto the track area. Sometimes well-meaning cautions imposed without testing bring unintended, disastrous consequences.

There is also the famous case of the spectacular Portland fountain of Laurence Halprin, whose rugged cascades and precipices attracted young bikers who liked the slickness for "water jumps." There were interesting legal discussions about liability and "attractive nuisances" and whether railings throughout would be safer or more dangerous. In another case, a family practice center in the Bronx, New York, has a required wheelchair ramp, with proper rails, and so on, that is becoming an ideal "jump" for roller-blading speedsters.

When it comes to overlapping jurisdictions, the recent proliferation of slightly different federal standards for handicapped accessibility (ANSI 117, ADA guidelines, and the Uniform Federal Accessibility Standards) leaves one reeling when trying to decide the proper size for an accessible toilet on any project with federal involvement. Added to this are new state codes and, in some jurisdictions, local requirements. In New York City, it is possible to have to comply with four separate and different codes dealing with accessibility.

It used to be fairly standard practice at the larger design firms to devise a pertinent codes matrix. All topics were listed on one side and the specific regulations from the relevant codes were compared across the board. Although this remains a

38

helpful exercise, it is no longer easy to construct as the number of applicable codes has mushroomed. It is thus much more difficult for even the most conscientious designer and architect to "get it right."

Cases such as these raise fundamental questions about how codes actually work in practice to protect the public's health and safety and promote the common good. Clearly the proliferation of codes and standards has made it more, not less, difficult for designers to meet their responsibility of designing safe, accommodating environments. Moreover, the literal application of code requirements has too often taken the place of common sense and good judgment.

It is part of the designer's and architect's job description to understand constraints, but also to identify possibilities; to be courageous as well as cautious. Code busting is not about circumventing inconvenient codes; it is about understanding them so well that they can be harnessed for the advancement of good design.

DEFINITIONS

Although both have an immense impact on healthcare design, there is a fundamental difference between *codes* and *standards*. Codes typically refer to nationally recognized model building codes, such as the Building Officials and Code Administrators (BOCA), as well as the National Fire Protection Association's (NFPA) Life Safety Code 101, or NFPA 101. Codes are mandatory as they are promulgated to protect the public's health and safety. Standards, though sometimes nationally recognized, include federal, state, and local guidelines developed by regulatory agencies to establish minimum and maximum design requirements for specific building types. Because of their diverse origins, standards often contain conflicts, ambiguities, and the need for interpretation.

There are five critical layers of codes and standards that have jurisdiction in healthcare design. They include life safety codes, building codes, health standards, accessibility standards, and local laws.

Life Safety

Life safety codes include both the national codes (NFPA codes) and their interpretation by state and local fire marshals. The Life Safety Code has been in existence for over 65 years. Its current name was adapted in 1966 (previously Buildings Exits Code). It is considered the most comprehensive document addressing all "factors that contribute to or center upon life safety in the event of fire."* This code is very specific about the overall design of buildings and spaces as well as the details of construction.

*Page 1.1.1, *NFPA Handbook*, 1994.

Anyone may file a written request for consideration of changes to the Life Safety Code. Specific proposals and supporting data must be referred to the central headquarters in Massachusetts. In a specific case 15 years ago, my firm requested a three-story atrium within a skilled nursing facility. Permission was ultimately granted provided we installed additional sprinkler systems on both sides of the atrium glass and met other stipulations that have since been incorporated into the code. By consulting directly with the code-writing authority, we determined what additional protections would be required to meet the intent of the code. We were thus able to incorporate a previously unapprovable design feature. Approximately every three years, NFPA 101 is revised via a long-established process of proposals, commentary, and review. The seventh edition will be published in 1997.

Building Code

Depending on the locale, this could be the BOCA National Code, the Uniform Building Code, the Southern Standard Building Code, or other model codes specific to different regions and states. What is often confusing is how to determine which edition a state has adopted. BOCA, for example, is updated every three years. It often takes states nearly that long to adopt the previous generation of the code. Thus, reading the latest codes may not be helpful. States also regularly append their own provisions or interpretations to the model codes, thus requiring the user to consult multiple documents in order to answer even simple questions.

Health Standards

Health standards can be highly prescriptive or fairly minimal depending on the state or jurisdiction. For this reason, knowledge of nationally accepted standards is almost always helpful.

From 1947 to 1984, the Department of Health and Human Services (HHS) prescribed adherence to a set of national standards for any and all healthcare projects with funding through titles VI and XVI of the Public Health Service Act. After that time, the funding having expired, these minimum requirements became guidelines. Still, these continually updated guidelines remain a very useful reference. The spirit of these guidelines is made explicit in the foreword: "These model standards are not intended to restrict innovations and improvements on design or construction techniques."

Accessibility

In all healthcare design, accessibility is a key concern. Sometimes, states and local authorities have enacted their own statutes (usually based on an interpretation of the ANSI 117 with modifications). Sometimes, ADA prevails. Sometimes, depending on the funding, Uniform Federal Accessibility Standards (UFAS) prevails (e.g., Housing and Urban Development [HUD]). Sometimes, an agency has its own exceptions. For example, the Veterans Administration has carefully documented interpretations and an exception within toilet rooms based on their own experience with disabled veterans.

My firm currently designs 100 percent of our clients' apartment doorways, bathrooms, and millwork for what we call "friendly" design. For example, we add blocking into all bathroom partitions to accommodate later grab-bar installation. As someone ages in place, needed help can be gracefully provided.

Local Laws

Local laws sometimes extend and embellish, but often contradict, the federal and state requirements. The New York City Building Code has certain regulations concerning egress that are more restrictive than any of the aforementioned codes. Some towns have sprinkler regulations far more restrictive than NFPA for healthcare and special residential occupancies. Some local zoning regulations have important distance-between-window regulations that exceed any contained in the building or fire codes.

This multiple layering of codes and standards leads to many cases of overlapping and contradictory requirements. It is most often the local and state authorities who have the responsibility to interpret and resolve any discrepancies or contradictions. However, it is the architect and designer who must identify these issues as they apply to a particular design solution. Early, proactive dialogue with the code enforcers is crucial to shaping elegant design solutions rather than compromised designs retroactively contorted by code compliance.

CODE REINVENTION

On occasion, it is not enough to merely figure out the code requirements. Sometimes it's necessary to reinvent the ground rules. My very first healthcare job in Philadelphia was to perform a life safety code analysis of a state hospital in northwest Pennsylvania, a facility that originally had eight-bed wards and private doorways to electroshock rooms. I was handed NFPA 101 and told to fix it, meet the letter of the code, and transform the place. I quickly discovered how little I knew, how much I needed to rapidly learn, and how inadequate the code was. Since then, I have become a firm believer that sometimes the codes and standards must be reinvented. The following sections describe some of the ground rules we have developed in our efforts to reinvent.

RULE 1: FIRM KNOWLEDGE. One needs to know the applicable codes and standards extremely well before taking on the task of setting new standards and seeking new ways of interpreting and applying codes. One must read and reread the language, just as though reviewing case law and extracting the critical technical finding.

RULE 2: BELIEF. One has to believe firmly in the validity and mission of codes. We do not question the authority of the regulations, but rather their specific requirements and, in some cases, the process by which they are applied. Every code has its own guiding principles which are worth reading and absorbing, especially if one is going to challenge some stricture.

RULE 3: COMMON SENSE. There is a reasonability test. If codes and standards conflict, contradict, or mutually undermine, the regulatory officials must be engaged in determining *reasonability*.

Historically, following the most restrictive code or standard was a recommended practice for many architects and designers. My firm prefers to seek the interpretation that meets the intention of the code with the least restrictive requirement. This approach demands more negotiation but allows more flexibility for innovative design. Following this simple approach has allowed us to imagine and invent new ideas about resident and patient *self-determination*—most critical in inpatient settings.

RULE 4: DIALOGUE. A design professional ought to participate in the formulation and revision of codes and standards. In a comprehensive review of the HHS standards for long-term care last year, it was fascinating to hear about the divergence of opinion of two dozen key invited professionals on revising the language of the codes. Should there be a special code for Alzheimer's? Should there be mandated standards for assisted living? I observed myself consistently choosing the fewest possible words, the clearest performance criteria, the fewest specific numerical limitations (minimum square footage, and so on), the least limiting language for design innovation, and the most words concerning purpose and intent.

RULE 5: COURAGE. New precedents are set all the time. One needs the courage to take one's knowledge and belief to the ultimate test—to set the bar higher for everyone.

Since we helped devise one of the first fully divided semiprivate long-term care rooms in 1980, I have never reconsidered or backed off the commitment to resident privacy. In the dozens of projects and room types since, we have always stayed with or exceeded the privacy level of our own prior prototypes.

RULE 6: IMAGINATION AND INVENTION. It is never a waste of time to try to imagine ways of breaking out of the box. Demapping the institutional double-loaded corridor in hospital and nursing home units still requires serious exploration. In fact, the organization of patients and residents into specialty units clearly deserves consideration for reinvention.

RULE 7: COCONSPIRACY WITH THE CLIENT. It is imperative that design professionals support and encourage their clients to seek and accept their role of leadership in setting standards, as well as the design professional's own leadership role. If a client simply requires the quickest approvable solution, the required code strategy may be quite different from the one used with clients seeking the most forward-thinking and superb solutions.

RULE 8: SELECTIVITY. It is significant to make serious choices with the client. It takes time and commitment to decide whether a small rule or a big rule will need to be waived or reconsidered.

RULE 9: LINK TO RESEARCH. Ultimately, new codes and standards will emerge from new precedents with positive outcomes for the residents. The only way to prove efficacy is to work with postoccupancy evaluation and applied research. This is the only way the state of the art will be advanced.

RULE 10: NATIONAL CONNECTION. On a local level, it is easy to be dismayed by a local fire marshall, building inspector, or a state plan reviewer. It is often immensely helpful to reach beyond the local level to what other states (and countries) are doing. I was always struck by Henry James' declaration, "We go to Europe to be Americanized." It is always immensely useful to see what other states are doing, or have done, and even to look abroad.

For example, assisted living regulations do not yet exist on a national level. Design professionals should be grateful for that. A national study in 1994 conducted by legal researchers found extreme divergence in state regulations in this rapidly evolving slot in the continuum of care.

Another curiosity is that, although inpatient areas in both acute care and long-term care are heavily regulated, ambulatory care is not. As healthcare changes rapidly, and short-term ambulatory care settings are created, life safety, infection control, and quality of life will loom larger as important design issues. There should be more and new minimal standards. For example, in designing for chemotherapy infusion spaces or treatment spaces for dialysis, there are insufficient standards on quality of ventilation, privacy, and so on. Where the codes and standards have focused for decades on institutional life, only recently has attention been paid to "day hospital" models. The many hours in clinical settings should require many of the same basic concerns.

THINGS WORTH REINVENTING

In institutional healthcare, there are certain central premises that may very well be worth reconsideration and reinvention, where the standards have become almost stifling. These include the accepted practices that

- A nurse's station/control desk must be the geographical center of any patient care floor and no more than 120 feet from any room. How is this residential?
- Corridors cannot become "rooms" and destinations in themselves and must be appropriately furnished.
- Corridor walls cannot have windows into them from the kitchens and parlors of residential units.
- Lighting levels within healthcare bedrooms have to be sufficient for reading and examination and thus seem glaring for quiet conversation and musing.
- Cubicle curtains are necessary even within "new-style" private rooms.
- The technology of life safety devices is so overwhelming, thus resulting in tremendous cost premiums, leaving little money for qualitative amenities.

There are other aspects of state standards that go unchallenged. Many state standards reference "homelike" atmosphere and self-esteem. What is often forgotten are the implications of code- and standard-driven design, including these observations:

- Handrails on both sides of a corridor are often unused.
- Toilet rooms, showering rooms, and apartment kitchens almost never have outside windows or natural light.
- Residents and patients are rarely permitted, and implicitly discouraged, to alter space or even to decorate.
- Patient care inpatient beds must have access on three sides for emergencies, thus prohibiting the resident, family, or staff from moving it around to a "daybed" location (against the wall).
- Terraces, alcoves, nooks, crannies, and pure whimsical places are considered hazardous, even dangerous.
- The very different requirements of long-term care, maternity, pediatrics, Alzheimer's disease can all be solved in the same bedroom design.
- Resident kitchen and private dining suites do not fit within the square footage maximum.
- The various regulations of ADA, ANSI, and UFAS cannot assure real accessibility and often promote institutional character.

After enlightened code busting and reinvention, we need to encourage some of the following:

- Assistive devices (grab bars) and compliant fixtures (toilets and sinks) need to be deinstitutionalized.
- Easy-to-use, soft, resident/patient room lighting designs should be an environmental attribute that can easily be manipulated.
- New bed design with headboards, footboards, and other design features that convey a hospitality or residential image.
- Bathtub/bather designs still have a long way to go.
- Really comfortable and yet attractive and affordable resident/patient side chairs need to be invented.
- Nurse call design and emergency lighting and signage need micro design attention.
- Carpet needs to live up to all the manufacturers' claims of solution-dyed, antimicrobial material.
- Seamless, elegant, and washable public floors are needed that are impervious, nonslippery, and sophisticated.
- Good-looking residential corner guards and wall protectors need to be designed.
- Residential room "front doors" that include French doors, Dutch doors, windows into corridors, and so on, need to be designed so that they will meet fire regulations.

We need to question whether magic ratios have real empirical bases, some of which have profound influence on design layouts in long-term care and acute care, including:

- Why should a 40-bed patient floor be optimal? Optimal for whom? Why shouldn't any other number (18–60) be optimal?
- Why are semiprivate and private rooms the only acceptable room type? Why couldn't four or six private rooms with private toilets share a shower room and common parlor?
- Why is 12 residents to one shower an appropriate ratio for resident/patient care?
- Why must an exam room be 90 square feet and a treatment room 120 square feet with a 10-foot minimum dimension?

SUMMARY

Code enlightenment is a fundamental responsibility of all architects, engineers, interior designers, and their healthcare clients who are seeking excellence. It will take focus, passion, and investment of time and money, as well as perseverance, to make an impact.

Seeking higher and better standards in the near future will not be such a struggle when the number of exceptionally built environments expands and that knowledge is shared.

Access to a clearinghouse of meaningful code exceptions would be useful. There are several national groups compiling information in different areas of interest. Seeking help from those who have successfully transformed a particular code or standard is very helpful.

Finally, code busting and code reinvention require careful study, experimentation, and fortitude. But, in healthcare, where the focus on the person being served can be blurred, the struggle to refocus is well worth it.

Barbara Geddis is an architect, founder, and managing partner of The Geddis Partnership in Stamford, Connecticut, which specializes in long-term care design, design for children, ambulatory care, and specialized residential settings.

References

The Alzheimer's Association. *Guidelines for Dignity: Goals of Specialized Alzheimer/Dementia Care in Residential Settings.* Chicago: The Alzheimer's Association, Patient and Family Services, 1992.

The American Institute of Architects Committee on Architecture for Health. *Guidelines for Construction and Equipment of Hospital and Medical Facilities.* Washington, D.C.: AIA Press, 1992–1993.

Association for the Care of Children's Health. *Caring for Children and Families: Guidelines for Hospitals.* First Edition. Bethesda, MD: Association for the Care of Children's Health, 1992.

NFPA. *NFPA 101, Life-Safety Code and Life-Safety Code Handbook.* Quincy, MA: NFPA, 1994.

CREATIVE, COST-EFFECTIVE DESIGN STRATEGIES

4

Kay Trimmer, AHA, IIDA

The words *low budget* should be banned from the designer's vocabulary. The key word in outstanding design has always been *creativity*. Designing to keep the bottom line as low as it can go is simply a matter of expanding one's creative thinking while disciplining the mind. An unlimited budget will eventually make design as sterile and predictable as corporate leather couches and marble walls.

Unfortunately, low-budget design has gotten a bad reputation. It conjures up pictures of institutional design, linoleum and terrazzo floors, gray- or green-painted walls, and "follow-the-line" wayfinding. It's enough to make dedicated healthcare designers shudder. The term low budget often causes a person to think *cheap* while the designer should be envisioning "challenge."

Yet, low budget does not have to be a trade-off for excellence. There really are economical ways to create beautifully constructed, award-winning "wellness" healthcare facilities. Healthcare designers must understand that there is a difference between caring for patients versus simply curing them. Designers create an atmosphere that affects the senses of patients and their families. We all wish we had more money to work with, but this creates an opportunity for us to be creative and to excel. We must remember that patients and their families judge their care by what they see, and the statement we *don't* want to hear today in conjunction with design is, "This is why healthcare costs so much." The basic needs of human beings don't change over time, only the details do.

Patients and their families who see fresh, new surroundings will experience the positive energy and begin the healing process. This also encourages productivity for staff members because they, too, enjoy the atmosphere.

The challenge of keeping costs down has several fringe benefits. First, it will please clients tremendously, which of course means referrals for new business and repeat business. Second, it will expand one's design abilities in new directions and keep the work fresh and unique. And last, it will raise one's confidence in one's ability to tackle innovative designs for each new project.

OVERALL STRATEGIES

There are many ways to create award-winning healthcare environments that are cost effective and immanently affordable. I will describe some here.

Treat your client's money as if it were your own. Use innovative new products or ideas in unique ways. It is easy for designers to reach for products that are in binders brought into the studio by manufacturers' representatives, but that is what's available to all designers. Get creative with specifications of carpet, wallcoverings, fabrics, and accessories that may take more time to research, but will make people feel happy. (Table 4.1 shows approximate costs of some furnishings.) Interrelate light, color, and textures to create interest in design by doing the unexpected. Have an artist paint a column in three dimensions that has fish on it so that, when people go to touch it, they discover it is art. In my firm's studio in Cleveland, there is a niche that is painted realistically to look like a phone booth. When someone wants to use the phone, we say, "Help yourself." If the client wants to be unique and interesting, the designer should go that one step further. See Figure 4.1 for a way to be creative with something as simple as wayfinding without spending a lot of money.

Be honest about how long the installation should last. This rule becomes critical if a master plan is being followed. This can be difficult because of lead times and unexpected occurrences. Be aware of all manufacturers' policies and procedures, and follow every order through with the representative.

It is well known that pastel shades reflect a stress-free environment for patients and healthcare workers. These colors are also less expensive to apply—only one or maybe two coats of paint are necessary; darker colors usually require at least three coats (see color plate 3).

Bring in a touch of nature with live plants, fountains, and aquariums. These items are especially helpful in reducing stress. This is not expensive if a local plant company or aquarium service is used, particularly if the owners can be persuaded to trade out some of the fee for free advertising (i.e., "Plants provided by . . ."). In addition, most aquarium services provide their clients with a bimonthly maintenance program—this gives the healthcare client a great look with no additional work. For the fountains, use inexpensive tile instead of costly marble for a great integrated design. At St. James Hospital in Chicago Heights, Illinois, my firm created a wonderful religious water fountain using a high-gloss tile that was very cost effective and has become a great fund-raiser.

Individual water walls that take the place of costly custom-built waterfalls in patient rooms, lobbies, and corridors can provide artistic stress-reducing solutions to the environment and space. They range in price from $150 to $1,500, where water-

TABLE 4.1   APPROXIMATE COST OF FURNITURE AND FINISHES

Product	Cost	Cost to Install
Wallcovering	$0.65/sq. ft. for Type II-oz. material (average) $0.35–1.50/sq. ft. (discontinued)	$0.25–.06/sq. ft.
Borders	$10–15 per spool	$0.25–.50/yard
VCT flooring (with great patterns using six colors)	$0.75–1.25/sq. ft.	
Vinyl base	$1.00–1.10/lineal foot	
Carpet base	$2.00–2.50/sq. ft. with 1.25–inch cording	
Carpet	$14–16/yard (average) $3/yard (discontinued)	$2.00–2.50/yard, depending on preparation of floor
Fiber optics	$25/sq. ft.	
Artwork (double matted; wood or metal frames; plexiglass and safety locks)	$65–100 per 20 × 40-ft. piece $1,500–25,000 special pieces	
Water fountains (with inexpensive tile)	$10,000	
Water walls	$1,500–3,000	
Aromatherapy machine	$250–1,500	
Fake fireplaces	$500–750	
Ceilings	$9/tile (painted) $1/sq. ft. (discontinued) (fire-rated, foil, and profile grid tiles are more costly)	$1.85–12.00/tile installed based on typical 20,000–40,000 sq. ft. projects

Figure 4.1 Wayfinding programs are one area in which designers can get creative without spending a lot of money. Project: St. James Hospital and Healthcare Centers, Chicago Heights, IL. Wayfinding: Aesthetics Collection. Interior design: Interior Design/Kay Trimmer, Inc., Cleveland. Mural: Denise Wey.

falls can cost $5,000 and up. With several different sizes and shapes, designs are unlimited.

Inexpensive mirrors and glass can also be used to incorporate privacy or logos. Recently, my firm faced the challenge of creating a state-of-the-art atmosphere on a budget for a plastic surgeon's office. We used sand-blasted mirrors and glass panels to simulate the silhouettes of a man's and woman's face. A water/bubble accessory sits on the counter of the patient manager's area, where the client is informed of the cost of services. The stress of receiving this information can be reduced by the relaxing bubble accessory.

Using faux finishes instead of wallcoverings is another route to saving money. Choose an artist who has the ability to take a wall and bring it to life using paint. Another idea in using faux finishes: when a wallcovering is a necessity, the designer can adapt the wallcovering design and paint a faux finish on a tabletop or other surface to complement the wallcovering. Use fiberglass or plastic mouldings instead of wood for the same look to achieve a great effect, which is most cost effective for ceilings.

Wonderful floor patterns can be created with VCT tile rather than sheet flooring. VCT tile or carpet inserts create great wayfinding. However, the use of carpet tiles cut in small pieces to simulate a design is a maintenance headache.

Figure 4.2   Fake fireplaces can help to create a cozy, homelike atmosphere. Project: St. Margaret Mercy Healthcare Center, Hammond, Indiana, LDRP unit. Interior Design: Interior Design/Kay Trimmer, Inc., Cleveland.

Fake fireplaces with gas logs can serve the same purpose as real fireplaces for a great effect. These are not limited by size, materials, or placement. The design will not be driven by the fact that it has to go in a certain place. My firm used this application in the LDRP unit at St. Margaret Mercy Hospital and Healthcare Center. It creates a cozy, homelike atmosphere for friends and family to gather in the adjacent "living room" (see Figure 4.2).

Expensive ceiling finishes are not as effective as creatively planned ceilings from a patient's point of view. It is important to give them something to draw their attention away from the matter at hand. Install two or three hand-painted ceiling tiles for a focal point that will lend a surprisingly affordable touch. The Vanderbilt House in Newport, Rhode Island, which celebrated its 150th anniversary in 1995, serves as an inspiration for creative ceilings. Its ballroom, dining room, music room, and billiard room are faced from floor to ceiling with a variety of materials that create an unparalleled richness. Few clients can afford gold leaf or alabaster, but there are many substitutes, and the presentations are endless.

Kaiser Permanente Women's Center in Beachwood, Ohio, is an example of genuine patient-focused care. Every exam room features a few ceiling tiles that are hand painted by a contract artist. People love to be in this environment. It makes a woman feel warm and cared for. My firm gets calls all the time from people asking us to do their living rooms like the waiting room (see Figure 4.3).

Figure 4.3 Walls and ceilings do not have to be a forgotten design element. Project: Kaiser Permanente, Beachwood, Ohio, obstetrics clinic waiting area. Interior design: Interior Design/Kay Trimmer, Inc., Cleveland.

Hand-painted wall art can bring the community into the wellness environment in a fun way. If the community is sports oriented, paint local sports figures on the walls along with young children at a community park. Or maybe the city has a well-known symphony, offering a different theme for the art. If the facility is involved in community affairs, use that as a theme. Many art schools and colleges offer internships for students to go to small towns to create fun art by painting murals on walls. This can be a truly rewarding experience for the hospital, community, and students. Sometimes their work can be toward their grade—the client provides the materials and a critique! Always striving for quality art with a professional artist as the supervisor is the best scenario. For those looking for the ultimate in quality wayfinding and art, there are many consulting firms that specialize in this area.

Music therapy is a tool that alters the physical and mental attitudes of patients and healthcare workers. Using an inexpensive personal audio tape player so patients can select their own music is a budget-minded solution to an elaborate sound system. Look to asking local orchestras to provide tapes as a community donation, as well as getting volunteers to play musical instruments in the lobbies. Also, a strolling violinist or guitarist is a nice touch.

Use cottage-industry people for making draperies. They are professional, less than larger firms, and take great pride in their work. However, it takes additional time on the designer's part to make sure these people know all the codes and use all the correct hardware. Use a professional installer to install the draperies and window treatments. The vast amount of choices available to a designer today make proper specifications difficult and important. Construction and performance are the two key words. It is up to the designer to teach the cottage industry what hardware and fabrics must be used to meet appropriate codes.

Design products for clients. Some manufacturers will work with designers to create a new product, pattern, or look. For example, there was nothing on the market that combined the look of residential furniture, and yet was tailored to the specific needs of Hospice of the Western Reserve, Hospice House and Headquarters, located on the shore of Lake Erie in Cleveland, Ohio. My firm decided to use one manufacturer as a single source that would listen to our client's specific needs, build the furniture, and also handle the installation. A team was created—including the client, a product designer, the product manufacturer, and the interior designer—to create a new line that was used in the patient rooms.

For this project, Hospice House needed to create a wardrobe that would secure valuables, hold clothes, house a television, store a laundry bag, and hide the dirty food tray after meals. The piece could also be used to display pictures and hold flower arrangements, giving the two-tone furniture a high residential look. The height of the piece meant that nothing would be out of reach for the resident. Ultimately, the wardrobe served several needs, proving to be very cost effective to the client. A drop-leaf table was designed to be a multifunctional piece, so that a family member could work on a computer, play a board game or have a candlelight dinner. In this case, it was very important for the manufacturer to be cost efficient, sharpen its pencils, and provide a lifetime guarantee on the products.

Using a multiuse product can also save money. For instance, there is a sleep chair from Nemschoff that my firm requested to be widened to meet the specific needs for Hospice of the Western Reserve, Hospice House and Headquarters. They obliged, and the chair was installed to serve as a patient and visitor chair during the day, then fold out for guest sleeping at night.

SPECIFICATION STRATEGIES

Here are some overall rules of thumb that will save money before a single chair or table is specified.

- Use a manufacturer that backs its products with lifetime guaranties and five-year fabric wear warranties. This will save time and money when an item needs to be replaced due to defects in the installation or in the piece itself.

- Know your local, state, and federal codes! Remember that codes can kill a design if the finished design fails to meet a local code and an alternative one has to be selected.

- Contact major manufacturers of wallcoverings, paint, furniture, flooring, and ceiling and lighting products. Meet with each one, and ask them if they are willing to work with you on the entire project and perhaps give you a better price. Some will, and some won't. But you can help them see the marketing and promotional value of being the sole supplier of that commodity for the whole facility.

- The use of patio furniture may be appropriate if it has been tested according to standards developed by the Business and Institutional Furniture Manufacturers Association (BIFMA). Make sure there are no sharp corners or legs that protrude and could be dangerous. Talk with the manufacturer about adding a second stretcher strip or brace to help strengthen the piece they already have in the line. Make sure that the piece does not have many small metal areas to clean. Find out if the manufacturer has a metal factory or department that you can work with in creating unique furniture items.

- See if the manufacturer has a new item or product it wants to place in the field. Where appropriate, check on discontinued items, since it shouldn't matter that the product will no longer be available. (Just be sure your specs are correct at the outset!) Be sure to request that the discontinued item be placed on hold for your project so it won't be sold to someone else, and request a performance bond between the manufacturer and the client.

- Look for local corporations that are either downsizing, upgrading, or redesigning. You can refurbish their panel systems and furniture rather than paying for new ones. They may even want to donate their furnishings for the tax credit as a community donation. Antique pieces can be painted and integrated into the design for unique accents.

- Don't limit yourself to one specific chair, lamp, or table. Pick three that are similar, and put them out to bid. Take the lowest bid.

- Accents that are fun and cheap can work with a theme and be as easy as using polyester clay pots for wastebaskets or wicker-looking polyester baskets for magazines. Paint an area rug on hard surface flooring. Find an antique pedestal, paint it, and place a statue on it. Hang sun, stars, moons, or other accessories on the walls. Use mobiles, or create hand-painted puzzle pieces and banners to hang from the ceiling—just be aware of the fire codes!

- Don't sit in your office and expect to come up with fresh ideas and sources year after year. Attending residential trade shows, such as the High Point Furniture Market in North Carolina, will allow you to come up with unique, inexpensive art and accessories that the client can purchase direct from the manufacturer. This will provide a unique, low-budget specification that will please the client.

- Travel and educate yourself. The reps won't always come to you—you need to go to them, especially if you want to work with them in creating a new item, pattern, or product. You are only as knowledgeable as a rep can teach you about a line. Don't say, "You have 15 minutes to show me your line." Take time and understand their product and its benefits.

- Work with art galleries and stores that may have art that hasn't sold. It's amazing how much can be found at less-than-current pricing—it may very well be the "perfect" piece!

- Have fun thinking creatively. Be open minded. Look around for unique ideas that can be integrated into the overall design for a lot less than "slick" designs that are promoted by manufacturers.

Figure 4.4 Hand-painted ceiling tiles provide a focal point for patients that is surprisingly afford-able. Project: Dr. Ronald Beech's office, Mentor, Ohio. Interior design: Interior Design/Kay Trimmer, Inc., Cleveland.

Figure 4.5 Another hand-painted ceiling tile from the same dentist's office. Project: Dr. Ronald Beech's office, Mentor, Ohio. Interior design: Interior Design/Kay Trimmer, Inc., Cleveland.

A RELAXING AFTERNOON AT THE DENTIST

If you think going to the dentist is an experience you are not looking forward to, you haven't been to Dr. Ronald Beech's office in Mentor, Ohio. After I drove 90 minutes through downtown Cleveland past two accidents, I arrived late and stressed. Pulling into the parking lot (where there was a police car attending to the accident), I said to myself, Was I supposed to have this appointment?

When I stepped into the office, I knew why I left my old dentist—his office made me uncomfortable. Dr. Beech was a progressive dentist who had listened to our ideas when my firm designed his office. The warm, soothing colors, fish tank, and hand-painted ceiling treatments immediately relaxed me. We had done the job for Dr. Beech by practicing what we preach on a budget.

While I had my teeth cleaned, the hygienist allowed me to watch a video on a TV monitor. The soft music in the background relaxed me, and I really began to focus on the health of my mouth. I wanted the mouth and smile I saw on the video. What a sales job, I thought, but I really wanted the best smile and to preserve my mouth.

After my teeth cleaning, I moved into one of the operatories. When we designed this space, we had the artist paint a fantasy scene on the ceiling (see Figures 4.4 and 4.5), which made me smile now. Next, Dr. Beech took me to another operatory that housed a CD Interactive Patient Education Oral Cam that used fiber optic technology to show me every tooth in my mouth magnified 50 times. This convinced me that I should make the fillings into jewelry that I wanted changed to white. I thought to myself, My old dentist would never believe the technology he is missing.

As I made an appointment to have my teeth whitened and bonded—spending far more money than I had planned—I decided I was worth it. It might mean a few less clothes, but I would look better with my new smile. The smile I had now was in my heart, knowing how far we've come to help reduce stress in this patient-focused world. This reduction in stress was secondary to the feeling I had about Dr. Beech and his staff, because he was the one who was truly patient focused and a real visionary in his field. I am thankful he touched my life.

The real bottom line to this story is that wonderful creative interiors can be done on a budget. It takes only a creative mind.

MAINTENANCE STRATEGIES

A key area in cost-effective design is maintenance. Over the lifetime of a facility, maintenance has probably cost clients thousands of dollars. If you can show clients up front how to save money on maintenance, you will be ahead of the game.

- Go to the maintenance department and find out what cleaning products and machines it currently uses. This will tell you which finishes, floorcoverings, and furniture you can use. If you feel the client's equipment is not up to product standards, this is the time to suggest investing in a new vacuum and possibly changing the cleaning chemicals and compounds currently in use. Work with the maintenance department. Recommend and specify only what it can maintain.

- In some cases, it may be appropriate to use vinyl rather than fabric. The new vinyls look like leather, feel like leather, and have great design touches. The only thing missing is the smell.
- Research each area for function and use. If carts and wheelchairs will be pushed on the floor, specify a material that will permit the wheels to glide easily. Employees, patients, and visitors can be at risk for injuries if the surface is not appropriate for how it will be used. Workers' compensation cases and lawsuits can be the result of an improperly placed floor surface.
- Use flip-lock cushions, removable covers, and replaceable parts. They can be reupholstered in the field.
- New-technology vacuum cleaners, vacuum bags, and cloths can greatly reduce maintenance costs, healthcare costs, and replacement of carpets. Many commercial vacuum machines are inefficient and pick up dust and throw it back into the environment. (Most asthma patients react to the particulates in the air.) A good-quality vacuum machine has two motors that can pick up 25 percent more dust than other vacuums, which means carpets are cleaned better and last longer. The newer polyethylene bags are good because dirt throwback is reduced more than with cloth bags. Airborne particulates may be reduced by 70 percent over four to nine weeks just by using these new bags. Using the DuPont Xymid fabric DustWizard cleaning cloth can eliminate many of the dust particles, translating into less time needed to clean and fewer bodies needed to do it.

All of this means several things. Carpets are cleaned better and stay cleaner longer, which extends the life of the product. Maintenance costs are drastically reduced. The environment is cleaner, which reduces spread of bacteria and viruses, leading to a reduction in employee illness and overall healthcare costs.

CONCLUSION

Designers should be constantly challenging others to reach a higher plane of design, manufacturing, and installation excellence. Sometimes the only way to get what you want may be to go out and design it yourself, or push someone else in that direction to raise the standard for healthcare design. Healthcare projects can be cost effective and attractive and can meet the needs of the patients, visitors, and staff, but only if designers choose to make them that way.

Kay Trimmer is an interior designer who specializes in healthcare. Her firm, Interior Design/Kay Trimmer, is located in Cleveland, Ohio.

IMPLEMENTATION

5

Bradford Perkins, FAIA, AICP

Most design professionals consider healthcare facility design to be one of the most complex project types. It has been estimated that a complicated building such as a healthcare facility can involve over two million yes/no design decisions. Healthcare facilities involve more client representatives, outside agency reviews, functional issues, rapidly changing technology, codes, and other design influences than almost any other building type. Even relatively small healthcare projects can take two to three years, and larger projects take from five to ten years from initial concept to completion. The designers who are successful in dealing with this combination of issues are those who understand not only the issues but also the implementation process during which these issues are resolved.

The implementation process for most healthcare facility designs can be divided into ten steps.

1. Strategic planning
2. Identification and scoping of specific projects
3. Selection and organization of the project team
4. Programming and predesign work
5. Schematic design
6. Design development
7. Construction documentation
8. Selection of the construction and installation teams and purchasing
9. Construction and installation
10. Occupancy

This chapter discusses the design team's tasks for each of these steps. Understanding all the steps—as well as the design team's potential role in each—is an essential responsibility of any design professional.

STRATEGIC PLANNING

Many healthcare facility projects are done within existing facilities or on existing campuses. Therefore, any project needs to be planned within the framework of a long-range plan. Even in new facilities, the initial building has to assume growth and change in the future.

An effective strategic plan will incorporate more than site and facility issues. It has to reflect the potential impact of changing medical practice, technology, demography, funding, and other factors that will determine the future need for and use of the facility. The role of the design professional in this initial phase can be very important.

Typically, the design professionals evaluate existing conditions, from mechanical systems to interior finishes, functional problems, code compliance, available options, and the potential cost and schedule of each major facility action implied by a potential development strategy. In most strategic plans, the facility's addition/expansion/modernization options are then evaluated against how well they help achieve the institution's key goals. Then, the facility options are prioritized.

IDENTIFICATION OF SPECIFIC PROJECTS

Once the strategic planning framework is set, the next step is to design the scope of the specific project or projects. This preliminary definition is sometimes done by the facility owner (client), but healthcare planners and design professionals often help.

The primary tasks within this step include establishing an outline program and statement of project objectives; setting a realistic schedule; outlining a preliminary project budget; and defining the professional services that need to be retained. In certain cases, this step also includes some preliminary tests of feasibility. Most healthcare facility projects must be able to balance costs and revenues in order to be feasible. As a result, clients need to have some preliminary confirmation that the project is financially feasible. All the project parameters—program, budget, schedule, and feasibility—need to be reconfirmed and refined after the full team is selected, but it is important to have a realistic outline of the project before selecting the full team.

SELECTION OF THE PROJECT TEAM

The design of any healthcare facility is a team sport. It is not uncommon for ten or more professional disciplines to be involved. They include

1. Architects
2. Healthcare planners
3. Equipment specialists
4. Interior designers
5. Civil engineers
6. Mechanical engineers
7. Acoustical engineers
8. Electrical engineers
9. Plumbing and fire-protection engineers
10. Cost consultants and/or construction managers
11. Food service and materials management consultants
12. Telecommunication consultants
13. Lighting designers
14. Physicists (for shielding of radiology equipment and related tasks)
15. Landscape architects

There are in addition to the accountants, mortgage bankers, investment bankers, attorneys, environmental consultants, traffic and parking consultants, and other specialists involved in the financing and public approval process.

The client typically focuses on the lead professionals—usually the architect, health planner, and interior designer. Selection of the remainder of the design team is often left to the lead firm or firms. The key issue, however, is to have a team that incorporates all the critical professional skills. Financial limits sometimes curtail the scope of the specialists' involvement, but the complexity of most healthcare facility projects demands that the team find a way to cover most of the specialist disciplines listed above.

The selection process for the lead professionals varies considerably, but a thorough process would include the following:

1. Research is done into firms with relevant experience.
2. A written request is sent to a "long list" of firms asking them to submit letters of interest and lists of references and relevant projects. This request would include a statement of the project objectives, an outline of the program, a schedule, and an assumed budget.
3. After a review of the submittals, four to six firms are selected for a short list and are asked to make a formal presentation.
4. In some cases the short-listed firms are asked to submit a written proposal summarizing

   • The firm's understanding of the project
   • Proposed work program
   • Proposed schedule

- Key personnel and subconsultant firms who will work on the project
- Proposed fees and expenses

Following the formal presentations and interviews, a contract is negotiated with the selected firm. In some cases, the fee is discussed only after there is a comprehensive discussion of scope, schedule, proposed specialist consultants, and other variables. The form of contract is typically based upon one of the standard AIA contract forms, but some larger healthcare institutions have developed their own standard forms.

Once the lead firm is selected, it is important that the entire team be organized. This organization must begin with the client, because only the client can

- Select the professional team
- Set the overall project goals and monitor whether they are being met
- Select—from among the options prepared by the design team—the program and design solutions that best meet the objectives
- Resolve differences and problems between team members
- Administer the contracts with the team members

Most successful projects have clients who create a clear decision-making structure and a strong team relationship with all the firms involved in the process. Some clients have even used *partnering* sessions at the beginning of a project to build the team relationships. Recognizing the importance of the client's role in this relationship, the renowned Finnish architect Eero Saarinen liked to start a project by saying to the design team, "Let's see if we can make this guy into a great client."

PROGRAMMING AND PREDESIGN

For the design team, one of the most challenging steps is the programming and predesign phase. In the past, the client would prepare a detailed statement of its requirements or program for a project during the scoping phase. Today, the increased complexity of the average project has meant that the full, detailed scope must be analyzed and defined with the assistance of the design team.

Program analysis has become a basic service for the architects, planners, and interior designers on healthcare facilities projects. Among the additional issues the design team, with the help of specialists, must define are the number of each type of space, the detailed functional requirements and dimensions of each space, equipment requirements, mechanical/electrical/plumbing and other services as needed, and the required relationships between spaces. This important initial step is discussed and illustrated in an earlier chapter of this book.

The project team also has several other tasks before design can begin. These include

- A detailed assessment of existing conditions in the project area
- Preparation of base plans showing existing conditions in structures, or a site survey, utility analyses, and soil analyses if new construction is involved
- An analysis of the zoning, building code, and other public approval issues that will influence the design.
- Special analysis of any other issues (asbestos, vibration, structural capacity, and so on) that could affect the design, cost, schedule, or feasibility of the project.

The results of the programming and related analyses are then combined into one or more preliminary concepts, an expanded statement of the project goals, and an updated project schedule and budget.

Once this material is available, several important parallel series of tasks can begin. These are the public land-use approval process, the state department of health certificate of need (CON) process (in states where a CON is required), and the financing process.

The local land-use approvals typically start with informal meetings with the municipal officials or planning department staff. They will help outline the steps in the process, identify whether any special approvals (such as zoning variances) are required, and define the information required at each step in the process. Most local approval processes for projects that involve more than renovation within an existing structure require detailed site design and schematic building design for land-use approval. On larger projects, the process may also require detailed analyses of the environmental impact of increased traffic, noise, storm drainage, and other issues before local officials give their approval. It is not unusual for the land-use approval process to take one year to complete. In many cases, the design team must take the lead in this effort.

The other key approval that begins at this point (if it is required and if it has not already been initiated during the project scoping phase) is the CON process. Many states regulate the size, cost, and other elements of health facility projects. The CON application usually consists of a detailed justification of the need for the project, a definition of the scope of the project (concept drawings, budgets, and so on), and financial analyses demonstrating its feasibility. Once this material is submitted, it is subjected to a series of reviews. In some states, these reviews can take a year or more prior to approval. In addition, most states with CON procedures also monitor the development of the design and mandate a time limit on the start of construction.

The third task that typically begins during predesign is securing the financing for the project. Few major projects are paid for from the healthcare facility's resources alone. Many involve borrowing, and most larger projects require a combination of tax-exempt bonds with credit enhancement from the federal government or some other guarantor. This process can also take more than a year to complete. During the financing process, the design team is often asked to assist in the required documentation.

Once these predesign tasks are nearing completion, it is time to start the traditional design process.

SCHEMATIC DESIGN

Schematic design is the first phase of the traditional design process. During this phase, the basic design concept is developed for all the major components of the project. The standard forms of agreement for design services provide brief definitions of schematic design as well as the subsequent phases.

The standard contractual definitions of design services are based on a theoretical process that, if it were followed, would permit the design team to move in an orderly way through the most common steps in the design, documentation, and construction of a building. This theoretical process assumes that a clear definition of the client's program exists. It also assumes that the process can progress in a linear fashion from the definition of client requirements through a series of steps—each of which results in a more complete definition of the design—until the project is sufficiently detailed to go into documentation for bidding (or negotiation) and construction.

The reality is not so orderly. Evolving program requirements, budget realities, increased knowledge of site considerations (such as subsoil problems), public agency reviews, and many other factors make it necessary to go back and modify previous steps. Design moves forward, but rarely in the clear linear fashion implied by the standard two-phase description of design.

Moreover, design rarely ends with the completion of schematic design and the next phase, design development. Most design professionals agree that design choices occur at every step of the process. In other words, building design neither starts with schematic design nor ends with the completion of the design development phase. Instead, building design is the central issue in each stage of the design team's effort from planning and programming through the traditional design phases, contract documents, and construction. The design process has been compared to a learning curve where each step exposes the design team to new opportunities, new problems, and new knowledge about the situation at hand.

Every project situation is different. Each presents a different set of requirements and limitations; a unique set of programming cultural, environmental, technological, and esthetic contexts to be considered; its own set of challenges and opportunities. Design brings to the surface the major considerations inherent in the situation. It is both a problem-seeking and a problem-solving process.

While every project has a unique combination of design influences, some of the most important are the program, the codes, the site, the constraints imposed by existing structures, the technological requirements of the systems (structural, mechanical, electrical, and so on) to be incorporated, the cost, the schedule, and—of course—the client. This list is far from complete. Moreover, in the case of healthcare facilities, almost every project has some unique requirements.

The process by which an architectural and/or interior design team—with its consultants—converts these design influences into a specific design solution varies from firm to firm. In schematic design, however, most firms begin with a period of analysis followed by a period of synthesis.

During the analysis stages, each of the design influences is studied. Often, diagrams are made of each program element, and conceptual plan alternatives are sketched. These studies in turn are analyzed to determine their potential functional, cost, code compliance, aesthetic, and other characteristics.

Thus, the formal design process begins with the architect's and/or the interior designer's analyses, understanding, and response to the basic project data. The combination of all of this information into a unified solution is the synthesis that is the core of schematic design.

Designers describe this synthesis in different ways. As architect Lewis Davis, FAIA, noted, "Very few designers—no matter how consistent their work—can trace all influences. Some are external: technology, available materials, codes, etc. Some are internal: the designer's own education and experience of the building just seen in Europe."

Some firms like to generate and test several alternatives before settling on a single approach. Others prefer to seek out a single strong idea around which they can organize the rest of the design.

But there is more than logic at work. Any experienced designer will note the importance of the nonrational, the nondescribable, and the poetic in the creation of a successful building design. At key points, judgment, taste, intuition, and creative talent take over.

Underlying this diversity of approaches, there are some common themes and design tasks. The first is an expansion of the original client's goals statement to include clear design goals. These will help in making the inevitable decisions on trade-offs of budget and quality, appearance and energy efficiency, as well as the thousands of other major decisions where competing priorities must be reconciled.

The next basic task is the development of a *parti* or basic organization for the project concept. As architect Edward Larrabee Barnes, FAIA, put it, "It is not just a case of form following function. Sometimes function follows form."

Designers also choose a design vocabulary. The vocabulary includes the essential formal or esthetic ideas that will govern the development of the design concept. Some designers develop a personal vocabulary of ideas, details, preferred materials, and so on and refine it on each project. Others approach each project as a unique problem, selecting an appropriate vocabulary to fit the problem.

As noted earlier, it is common for architects and interior designers to consider several concept solutions to a design problem. For this reason, most have developed a process for narrowing down to a single concept. In some cases, selection is based on a formal grading of a concept against the original project objectives. In others, it is an intuitive judgment based on experience. In most instances, it is a combination of both.

Beyond the first conceptual steps, however, the process becomes more complex. In all but the smallest and simplest projects, the steps that follow the concept involve a team of people. While it is true that significant projects are usually developed under the guidance of a single strong design leader, it is important to realize that not many projects have fewer than ten people involved in the decision making—architects, engineers, interior designers, specialist consultants, construction managers, public agencies, and, of course, clients. Thus, design excellence results in part from the effective management of a complex team, all of whose members contribute to the quality of the final result.

The result of all these steps is a completed schematic design. While different projects, clients, and design teams have different definitions of the completion of this phase, there are certain commonly agreed-upon objectives and products.

1. *Objectives.* The primary objective is to arrive at a clearly designed, feasible concept and to present it in a form that achieves client understanding and acceptance. The secondary objectives are to clarify the project program, explore the most promising alternative design solutions, and provide a reliable basis for analyzing the cost of the project.
2. *Products.* Communicating design ideas and decisions usually involves a variety of media. typical documentation at the end of this phase can include

    • A site plan
    • Plans for each level, including conceptual reflected ceiling plans
    • All elevations—exterior and conceptual interior elevations
    • Two or more sections
    • An outline specification
    • A statistical summary of the design area and other characteristics in comparison to the program
    • A preliminary construction cost estimate

- Such other illustrative materials—renderings, models, or drawings—needed to adequately present the concept

3. *Drawings.* These are typically presented at the smallest scale that can clearly illustrate the concept (perhaps ⅟₁₆ inch equals 1 foot for larger buildings and ⅛ inch equals 1 foot for smaller buildings and interiors).

4. *Outline specifications.* This is a general description of the work indicating the major systems and materials choices for the project, but usually providing little detailed product information.

5. *Preliminary estimate of construction cost.* The schematic design estimate usually includes a preliminary area analysis and a preliminary construction cost estimate. It is common for preliminary cost estimates made at this stage to include contingencies for further design development, market unpredictability, and changes during construction. These estimates are often developed by professional estimators or a builder selected by the client, but some design teams do their own cost estimates.

6. *Other services.* As part of the schematic design work, the design team may agree to provide energy studies, tenant-related design studies, life-cycle cost analysis or other economic studies, special renderings, models, brochures, or promotional materials for the client.

7. *Approvals.* The final step in schematic design is to obtain formal client approval. The importance of this step cannot be overemphasized. The schematic design presentation has to be clear enough to gain both the understanding and the approval of the client. Once this has been obtained, most design teams recommend that each item in the presentation be signed and dated by the client prior to the initiation of the design development phase.

DESIGN DEVELOPMENT

The objectives of the design development phase are different from those of schematic design. The primary purpose is to define and describe all important aspects of the project so that all that remains is the formal documentation step of construction contract documents.

As schedule pressures and the amount of fast-track construction have increased, some design firms have attempted to cut down or even eliminate this phase. However, there are strong design, technical, and economic arguments against doing this. Design development is the period in which all the issues left unresolved at the end of schematic design can be worked out, and this can be done at a scale that minimizes the possibility of major modifications during the construction contract documents phase. Working drawings and specifications are complex and intricately interrelated;

changes in these documents are costly and more likely to lead to coordination problems during construction.

In addition, design development is the period in which the design itself achieves the refinement and coordination necessary for a really polished work. Without this period, too many important areas of design exploration are compressed into the schematic phase or left to working drawings.

Effective design development results in the design team's working out a clear, coordinated description of all aspects of the design. This typically includes fully developed floor plans, interior and exterior elevations, reflected ceiling plans, wall and building sections, and key details—usually at the same scale as the construction contract documents. This also includes the evaluation of alternative interior finishes and furnishings. In addition, the basic mechanical, electrical, plumbing, and fire-protection systems are accurately defined, if not fully drawn. No major issues should be left unresolved that could cause significant restudy during the construction contract documents phase.

The products of the design development phase are similar to those of schematic design—drawings and specifications that fix and describe the size and character of the project, as well as any recommended adjustments to the preliminary estimate of construction cost. It is important to bring the design development phase to a close with formal presentation to, and approval by, the client.

CONSTRUCTION DOCUMENTATION

The design process does not really end with the completion of the design development phase, but the emphasis shifts to the effort necessary to have a complete, coordinated set of documents to guide the purchasing, construction, installation, and initial operations steps that follow.

The construction documents typically include drawings, specifications, contract forms, and bidding requirements. Each of these documents plays an important role.

1. The drawings provide the graphic description of the work that is to be done.
2. The specifications outline the levels of quality and standards to be met.
3. The contract forms include the actual contract, the bond and insurance requirements, and general conditions outlining the roles, rights, and responsibilities of all parties.
4. The bidding requirements—if the project is being bid—set the procedures for this process.

The professional design organizations (such as AIA and others) have model documents for the specifications, contract forms, and bidding requirements. These are good starting points, but all standard forms must be adapted to incorporate each project's unique requirements.

The largest part of this step in the process, however, is the production of a comprehensive set of drawings and technical specifications. This often takes four to six months for the large teams on many healthcare facility projects to complete. A new building or a large renovation of a skilled nursing facility or a department in a hospital can involve over 100 sheets of drawings and several hundred pages of technical specifications. Each sheet of the drawings may involve 100–200 hours of work to complete since the drawings must provide a clear, accurate dimension graphic description of the work to be done, and this drawing must be coordinated with the drawings of the other design professionals working on the same part of the project.

Experienced design professionals plan this step carefully and work to implement productivity savings. Computers, in particular, are beginning to bring some noticeable improvements in both speed and quality, but the human element is still key.

SELECTION OF THE TEAM

Once part or all of the construction documents are available, the next critical step is the selection of the builders, furniture and equipment manufacturers, and others who will provide the construction and other installed elements of the healthcare facility. Typically, the design team either manages the selection process or is an active participant with the client.

Experienced design professionals believe that, if the right companies are selected, the remaining implementation phases are straightforward. Even one bad selection, however, can make completion of the project very difficult.

There are a number of choices available. For selection of the builder, there are six major alternatives.

1. The most common is for the construction documents to be completed and put out for a bid to companies selected from a list of prequalified general contractors. The competing contractors submit lump-sum prices, proposed schedules, and other information to help in a selection. Following negotiations, the project is awarded to the contractor offering the most attractive proposal. For publicly owned projects, price may be the primary criterion, but often other clients use the bids as the basis for a negotiation to clarify cost, schedule, and other relevant factors before a contractor is selected.

2. For major healthcare facilities projects, a frequent choice is to select a contractor to work side by side with the design team. During design, the contractor provides advice on cost, schedule, and constructability issues. When the construction

documentation nears completion, the contractor provides a guaranteed minimum price (GMP) and becomes the general contractor.

3. For projects where the scope is unclear or where construction must start long before the completion of design, some clients will retain a builder to work on a cost-plus basis. Most clients do not like the open-ended nature of this method, but there are times when it is necessary.

4. A variation sometimes occurs on projects where the components such as plasterboard walls, outlets, and doors can be identified. The client may negotiate lump-sum unit prices for each component and can then choose to buy as many units as it needs or can afford.

5. An increasingly common option is *design/build.* In this alternative, the client typically retains the builder, who then hires the design team. Some clients like the simplicity and the assumed higher degree of cost control. The success of the design/build approach, however, depends upon the selection of a builder who is committed to the client's interests, since the normal quality control check provided by an independent design team is compromised. Because the design team works for the builder, it often cannot communicate quality and value concerns directly to the client. For furnishings, the equivalent is the furniture manager, who bids furniture packages within the framework of a performance specification created by an interior designer.

6. Since the 1970s, an increasingly popular option has been construction management. During the design phase, the service is similar to that described in the second option above. During design and construction documentation, the construction manager is a consultant to the client and the design team on cost, schedule, and constructability issues. Unlike the second option, however, the construction manager is a consultant to the client during construction as well. The construction manager may actually replace the general contractor, but does so on a fee basis. All of the construction subcontracts may be bid (as in the first option), but the construction manager—in his professional service form—does not guarantee the price. Once the price is guaranteed, the construction manager can no longer work solely in the client's interest—the risks are too great.

The selection of an approach, as well as the selection of appropriate companies, is important and should be carried out in a systematic fashion. Advertising for bidders and hoping the right people show up to bid is rarely enough. Most experienced design teams will research the options, identify the most qualified firms, solicit their interest, confirm their qualifications, and then limit the final proposals to the four to six best candidate firms. As is the case for many of the other steps in the process, the AIA and other professional organizations have standard forms to facilitate the process. These include prequalification questionnaires, bid forms, contract forms, and other commonly required documents. Sometimes the forms are adapted by the client's attorney to fit specific project requirements, but they are a helpful starting point.

The purchasing of interior finishes, furnishings, and equipment has some of the same options. Dealers who represent several manufacturers, or individual manufacturers, will provide fixed-price bids for furniture and/or finishes. There are also many firms prepared to provide cost-plus services with or without a guaranteed maximum price, and there are a growing number of services offering the equivalent of a design/build approach.

CONSTRUCTION AND INSTALLATION

With the start of construction and the production and delivery of furnishings and equipment, many additional companies and individuals take on major roles in the implementation process. In most healthcare facility projects, the design team is expected to provide both management and quality control throughout this process.

The management role typically includes administration of the various construction and supplier contracts; review of payment requests, change orders, claims, and related contract issues; and assistance in resolving project management issues.

The quality control role includes reviewing the work as it proceeds, reviewing contractor submissions of shop drawings and samples, issuing clarifications of the drawings and specifications, and assisting in resolving problems in the field. On healthcare facility projects, both roles can require a major commitment of the design team's time. It is not uncommon for 20–25 percent of the design team's total project effort to be spent during this phase.

OCCUPANCY

The design team's work is not complete when the facility is ready for occupancy. Virtually all clients moving into new facilities require assistance during the first few months.

The design team's task during the occupancy phase often falls into two categories: following up on incomplete construction, furnishing, and equipment issues; organizing and transferring the information necessary to occupy and maintain the facility.

Most clients will not or cannot wait until everything is complete. They often choose to move in when the building achieves substantial completion—the point at which it can be safely occupied and used. This often complicates the resolution of the open punch list items.

Occupancy also often reveals construction, furnishings, and/or equipment that does not perform as intended. Sometimes these issues (such as an underperforming air conditioning system) can be resolved with a limited amount of adjustment. Others require ongoing monitoring and additional work. Experienced design teams prepare their clients for the probability of some lingering issues and assure the clients that they will be there to help resolve them.

It is important, however, for design teams to wean clients from dependence on the design team for routine operations and maintenance. The first step in the weaning process is the collection and transfer of the operation and maintenance manuals, training information, and related information. This information should include a set of record drawings describing what was actually built. These drawings are usually prepared from marked-up working drawings prepared by the contractors. Some design teams also prepare a reference manual containing samples, supplier data, and other information on all furnishings and finishes.

CONCLUSION

These ten steps make up the process within which the design professionals must work. To properly serve most healthcare facility clients, the design team must bring expertise to each step. The design team (in conjunction with the facility's owner/sponsor) is the thread that ties all ten steps into a unified planning, design, and construction process. Thus, it is essential that design professionals be able to provide more than their particular technical service. To be effective, they must understand and be able to manage a very complex, multistep project delivery process.

Bradford Perkins is president of Perkins Eastman Architects PC—Architects, Interior Designers and Planners in New York City.

DESIGN EVALUATION	6

Mardelle McCuskey Shepley, D.Arch., Ph.D.

Building evaluations or, as they are frequently called, postoccupancy evaluations (POEs), are critical to a responsible design process. They are as essential to architecture as interviewing a client, selecting building materials, or developing construction details. The evaluation of previous experience is mandatory in many professions. It is difficult to imagine a lawyer creating a defense without examining legal precedents or a physician operating on patients without reviewing the success rate of comparable procedures. Verifying the outcome of previous design decisions enables architects and interior designers to be accountable for their decision-making process and results in a more user-responsive environment. Without this attention to evaluation, the validity of the profession may be challenged.

What are POEs? They are commonly thought of as building studies that attempt to identify the successes and failures of design decisions. According to this definition they could also be classified as architectural critiques or traditional research, but there are some distinctions. In what ways are the reviews that appear in periodicals and the awards issued by professional organizations different from POEs? How are studies that measure noise levels in a neonatal intensive care unit (NICU) or pupil dilation after viewing building facades different from POEs? Although there are overlaps between POEs, criticism, and traditional research, it is useful to distinguish between the three.

POEs have been confused with criticism by the architectural community. Zimring and Reizenstein (1981) clearly distinguish between the two. Criticism is highly personal, and its methodology is linked to subjective and historic perspectives. POEs, on the other hand, use systematic evaluation, focus on the perceptions of the user rather than the reviewer, and often involve quantitative as well as qualitative data. While it is useful to critique architectural work, it is important to acknowledge that, although a building may be well received by architectural critics, it may not be as well received by the building users (Marans and Spreckelmeyer 1982).

While most believe that a POE involves research, it is clear that evaluation may not fall neatly into a traditional research category. The question of whether there are components in the design process that meet the definition of research has been widely debated. There are those who argue that literature surveys and programming studies meet research criteria. The position of POEs is clearer. They exceed literature surveys in that they do more than reiterate existing studies. They move beyond programming in that they employ research paradigms of hypothesis testing and systematic analysis.

The ways in which a POE can be distinguished from the average research project are related primarily to its classification as a field study. Much environment-behavior research involves the manipulation of the environment by the investigator for comparative purposes. In a POE, as with many field studies, the environments are being manipulated by the users. While limited in the generality of the results, the benefit of a field study is that it is easily applied to a real environment.

Another way to define a POE is to identify its role in the context of the design process. It is most effectively used when it is included as a phase in the production of new buildings (see Figure 6.1). When an architectural or design program is initiated, it should be informed by an evaluation of the building that served as its predecessor. If the building is without a predecessor, it should incorporate the evaluations of existing

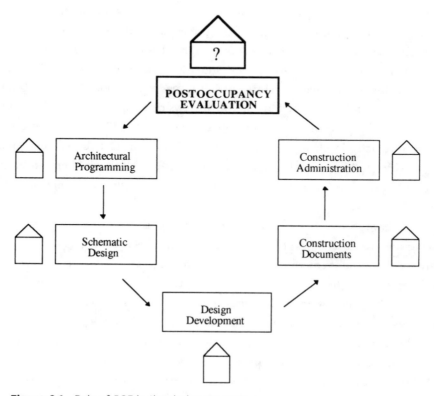

Figure 6.1   Role of POE in the design process.

prototypes. (In the case of healthcare facilities, most projects are replacement or expansion projects; the current trend is to consolidate healthcare delivery organizations rather than to give birth to new organizations.) The programming process feeds information into the ensuing schematic design, design development, construction documents, and construction administration phases. In the vast majority of design firms, the process ends here. Ideally, however, fees should be structured to accommodate a POE phase, the results of which would be utilized by the facility managers or input into a database for future projects.

WHAT ARE THE OBJECTIVES OF POE?

What are the objectives of an environmental evaluation? According to Marans and Spreckelmeyer, they are "to develop a better understanding of how the physical environment or place contributes to or impedes the goals of the individuals or groups who must operate them." Specifically, the research should attempt to clarify and supplement what is presently known about relationships between both the physical environment and its specific attributes and people's behaviors and subjective responses to that environment (Marans and Spreckelmeyer 1981).

The uses of POEs are multiple and include:

- Providing feedback on a particular building
- Aiding in the development of future designs
- Contributing to knowledge on social impact of design
- Enhancing and clarifying programming
- Lending credibility to personnel in charge of facilities
- Strengthening the designer-client relationship
- Measuring the functionality and comfort of a design with performance requirements
- Providing information that allows for fine-tuning a building
- Advising facilities of the implications of repeating design features
- Testing innovations
- Providing justification for design decisions (Zimring and Reizenstein 1981; Preiser 1994)

Identifying objectives is an important step in all activities that take place in a design firm, from functions relating to the design process to personnel management and contract philosophy. When developing a POE, objectives should be identified and prioritized as early as possible.

OVERVIEW OF POE METHODOLOGY

There are many good books and articles on POE methodology that can be applied to healthcare projects. While the following section provides an overview of some of the material published on the subject, I recommend that you consult the sources directly when formulating a study.

POEs can differ significantly in type and structure of methodology. The subjects of these studies vary in scale, building type, and building process. Regarding scale, POEs have ranged from urban communities to individual classrooms. Concerning building type, studies range from farm structures to space (NASA) environments. Regarding the evaluation of building process, studies have been done on earthquake hazard reduction, building activation, and architectural competitions.

Zimring and Reizenstein (1980) identify three dimensions that all these POEs have in common, but along which they may vary: generality of the results (a single building versus a building type), breadth of focus (the number of variables in the setting studies), and timing of application (is it for immediate "consumption" by designers, or is it to be pooled with data on other projects?).

What Methodologies Are Used in Evaluation?

In conducting an evaluation, there are multiple sources of information. In a healthcare setting, information should be sought from patients, families (and friends), medical staff, community and visitors, administration, medical staff, maintenance, housekeeping, and food services, among others (see Figure 6.2). It is also important to obtain information from the architect and designer. This information enables one to compare the designer's intentions with the building product and to elaborate upon the history of the building process and ways in which the process itself influenced the project. There are three common ways to obtain information from designers: by interviews with clients and designers, through project correspondence (particularly building programs), and through building tours with the designers (Zimring and Reizenstein 1980).

Research techniques for a POE could include unobtrusive and obtrusive measures. Unobtrusive studies are those where data is obtained without the awareness of the individuals whose response is being evaluated. A typical example is recording carpet wear to determine frequency of path use. Obtrusive measures generally require considerable awareness of the participants, as would be the case in an interview. There are benefits and limitations to each, which should be identified when an evaluation methodology is developed.

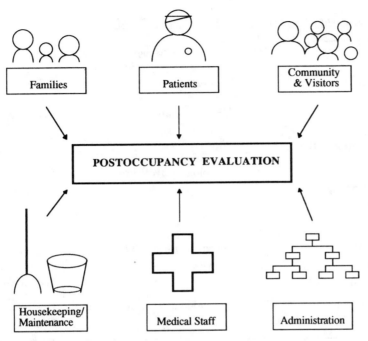

Figure 6.2 Hospital users providing information for POE.

Within this context, there are four significant means of measuring response (see Table 6.1).

1. Indirect measures
2. Instrumented recording techniques
3. Systematic observation techniques
4. Self-report methodology

Indirect measures are typically the least obtrusive, as they do not require contact with the individuals on whom the data is based. An example of an indirect measure is recording the number of times sugar bowls are refilled in a cafeteria to determine which seating locations are most frequently used (preferred).

Instrumented recording techniques are commonly used by designers in the form of video and photography. Less common is the use of hodometers (pedestrian path measuring devices) and telemeters (to measure cardiovascular response).

Behavior(al) mapping and naturalistic inquiry (Lincoln and Gube 1985) are typical *systematic observation* techniques. Behavior mapping involves the systematic recording of movement through space. Naturalistic inquiry is typified by an intense field observation and recording period followed by a structured review of the data.

Self-report methodologies are generally the most obtrusive of the four categories and are represented by direct contact with the individuals experiencing the environment via interviews, questionnaires, and drawings.

TABLE 6.1   TECHNIQUES FOR MEASURING ENVIRONMENTAL RESPONSE

INDIRECT MEASURES		INSTRUMENTED RECORDING	
Method	*Examples*	*Method*	*Examples*
Archives	Actuarial Sales records Institution protocols	Image recording	Photography Video Film
Physical aggregation	Graffiti Trash generation Energy use	Physiological recording	EEG Galvanic skin response Polygraph
Physical erosion	Path erosion Maintenance records Furniture replacement	Movement measuring devices	Telemeter Hodometer Pedometer
Demographic data	Political records	Environment recording	Dosimeter Light meter

SYSTEMIC OBSERVATION		SELF-REPORT	
Method	*Examples*	*Method*	*Examples*
Behavior mapping	Participant observation External tracking	Psychological test	Personality test Interpersonal distance
Naturalistic inquiry	Audit trail Member check	Interview	Focus groups Individual interview Guided walk-through
		Graphic	Cognitive map Self-image drawing
		Written response	Questionnaire Diary Correspondence Time log

Source: Mardelle McCuskey Shepley.

Most POEs involve the utilization of multimethodology techniques. The most common combination of procedures involves interviews, questionnaires, and physical survey (Zimring 1987).

The work of Wolfgang Preiser is highly relied upon by designers to provide methodology structure for POEs. In his recent work (Preiser 1989 and 1994; Preiser, Rabinowitz, and White 1988), he discusses three levels of POEs: indicative, investigative, and diagnostic. These levels are differentiated by the amount of time and effort available to complete the evaluation.

The objective of an *indicative* POE is to identify the major successes and failures of a project. It is usually conducted in a period of less than three days. Information that is gathered includes the evaluation of existing documentation, a walk-through, evaluation questions, and selected interviews.

An *investigative* POE requires 160 to 240 personnel hours, plus the time of support persons. The scope of this type of POE covers the details of the successes and failures identified in the indicative POE. The investigative POE is more clearly structured in that the criteria for evaluating the project are stated prior to the investigation.

The *diagnostic* POE is the most thorough of the three levels. Its objectives extend beyond obtaining information about a single building to data that can be used to design comparable building types. The diagnostic POE may take longer than a year to complete.

Good programmers should always do an indicative POE, although they may not identify it as such. It is necessary to understand a client's existing building in order to have thorough programming discussions about future buildings. Programming fees for healthcare facilities typically encompass this brief evaluation, and the results are integrated into the final program documents. In the indicative POE, certain time-consuming tasks are not required, such as consulting with the original designer who may or may not be available. It is rare that an investigative-level POE is included in the programming process.

Ogodnik (1985) also breaks POEs into three levels: a facility profile, diagnostic analysis, and special investigative studies. A *facility profile* includes a description of the facility and identification of obvious problems and successes. It involves simple methodology and acts as a source for more in-depth evaluations. The *diagnostic analysis* is a more focused multimethodological approach and offers suggestions to problems. A *special investigation* is the most complex in scope and measurement technique and may involve the comparison of multiple facilities.

WHAT ARE THE ETHICAL ISSUES?

As with other phases of design practice, it is important to be aware of one's ethical responsibilities while doing evaluations, particularly those using people as subjects. Zimring (1987) cites several ethical principles that focus on the rights of participants.

If there is any question regarding the appropriateness of a study design, an investigator can consult the "Ethical Principles of Psychologists" (American Psychological Association 1992) or contact a researcher who has conducted a comparable study. In academic settings, there is typically a human subjects review board that will evaluate the acceptability of a project. Hospitals, particularly those associated with universities, may also have their own review board that must be approached to receive approval to initiate a project.

SHOULD ALL NEW BUILDINGS BE EVALUATED?

Experts recommend that publicly funded environments and environments that have an impact on a large number of people undergo postconstruction evaluation (Friedmann, Zimring, and Zube 1978; Zube 1980). These experts also emphasize that priority be given to settings where the vulnerability of the users (such as seniors and the disabled) is notable and settings which are diverse in critical theoretical dimensions such as personal control. Healthcare facilities fall into these priority categories. Many healthcare projects are publicly funded, impact a significant number of people, deal with theoretical dimensions, and serve a particularly vulnerable population.

Researchers suggest that a sampling technique be used in order to manage the potentially large number of buildings subject to review (Garling, Book, and Lindberg 1986; Zube 1980). If all new buildings were rigorously evaluated, it would be extremely time consuming and expensive (Zube 1980). While it is cost prohibitive to do full-blown POEs on every project, architects and designers should make minor evaluations mandatory. These ministudies might entail a two-page boilerplate questionnaire that focuses on specific critical issues. It is urgent that architects and designers take steps to inform the design process and find cost-effective ways to better understand the outcomes of healthcare buildings.

Table 6.2 summarizes evaluation phases outlined by several researchers. While researchers emphasize different components within these phases, most methodologies can be broken into four phases.

1. Establishing entry
2. Designing the study
3. Conducting the research and analyzing the data
4. Disseminating the information

Keys and Wener's (1980) methodology emphasizes principles of organizational consultation, and, as a result *entry* is an important component. They describe entry as "developing a shared understanding and acceptance of the general goals of the POE." Entry is established by obtaining support from the various levels of the organization and establishing a history leading up to the decision to execute a POE.

TABLE 6.2 PHASES IN POSTOCCUPANCY EVALUATIONS

| Researcher | PHASE | | | |
	Entry	Design Study	Conduct Research	Disseminate Data
Keys & Wener (1980)z	Prehistory Needs assessment	Research planning	Data collection Data analysis	Data feedback
Marans & Spreckelmeyer (1981)	Reconnaissance Information gathering	Design	Data collection	Documentation Data analysis Dissemination
Parshall & Pena (1982)	Initiation	Preparation	Tour Discussion Assessment Conclusion	Presentation Documentation
Preiser, Rabinowitz, & White (1988)	Feasibility	Research planning Resource planning	Data collection Data management Data analysis	Report findings Recommendation Review results
Zimring (1987)	Entry Initial data collection	Respond to goals Develop strategy Sampling Design methods Pretesting Refine budget	Data collection Data analysis	Presenting information

Outline for a Minievaluation

Shibley (1985) makes the following recommendations concerning the development of a POE: know your client; begin with a simple methodology; identify various levels of application.

An individual's or firm's first few large-scale postoccupancy studies should be done with an experienced individual utilizing the wealth of information available on postoccupancy methodology design (e.g., Preiser, Rabinowitz, & White 1988; Zimring 1987). It is useful, however, to do small studies while gaining experience. The following is a recommended process for an abbreviated indicative study to initiate the notice.

1. *Entry.* One of the largest obstacles in field research is gaining access to a site for a study. Contacts leading to potential settings can be made through previous

clients, universities, or facilities who have a vested interest in the information due to an identified need.

2. *Design study.* For an initial project, the scope should be limited. Select a small setting such as a waiting room or a medications room. (It is important to remember that, regardless of the setting, ethical protocols should be followed. Individuals should not be photographed without their permission, and the limitations set by the organization providing approval for the study must be adhered to.) An interview/questionnaire technique is useful when starting out. Begin with a literature search on the setting, and identify previous POEs that have been done on similar settings (for examples, see Table 6.3). Identify two to three issues that could serve as the basis for a questionnaire or interview. These issues can be identified in an initial interview with a member of the medical staff or the facility manager (why are patients constantly getting lost?), gleaned from the literature review (does the nursing staff utilize the substations?), pulled from the architectural program (have the design objectives been met?), or identified in a building walk-through (why do patients congregate in the hallways?). Select the population to receive the questionnaire, according to the information desired. Is the most important issue patient satisfaction? Then, the questionnaire should be issued directly to patients.

3. *Conduct study.* Start with a small population and issue a one-page questionnaire (20 respondents), or conduct ten 15-minute interviews. Quantify the responses when possible and summarize and analyze the results. Data analysis for the statistically uninitiated can be minimal at this juncture, as it is confusing for those lacking experience. Friedman, Zimring, and Zube (1978) recommend that the analysis begin simply by calculating percentages and drawing graphs. For larger POEs, a specialist can be consulted.

4. *Disseminate data.* There is often a lag before the results of a study are translated into a format that can be referenced at a later date. It is important to create a summary report (less than eight pages) as soon as possible, which includes a description of the four phases and provides conclusions and recommendations.

While this minievaluation is limited in scope, the hands-on experience will aid practitioners and students in understanding the implications of POEs.

POE IN PROFESSIONAL PRACTICE

Given the proper background or experience, a variety of individuals can undertake a POE. In addition to architects, designers, and building managers, government agencies and developers also find POEs to be useful tools (Zimring and Reizenstein 1980).

TABLE 6.3   REPRESENTATIVE HEALTHCARE FACILITY POSTOCCUPANCY EVALUATION STUDIES

Author, Date	Setting	Methodology	Selected Findings
Canter, 1972	Children's hospital	Interviews, questionnaires, behavior observation	Initial conceptualizations of the design team & the structure of the team have a major influence on the final building.
Field et al., 1971	Hospital inpatient units	Semantic differential, nurse travel measurement	Of 4 hospitals, one significantly preferred when evaluating ambiance, maintenance, spaciousness, mood, & sociability. Identified typical travel times.
Harvey, 1984	Hospitals	Analyze records, interviews, questionnaires, observations	Signage confusing, exam rooms small, unstable HVAC, public corridors violated security, lack of staff brake space, inappropriate supply system.
Kantrowitz, 1993	Primary care facilities	Observation, interviews, questionnaires	Summary of critical design issues.
Kennon, Bauer, & Parshall, 1988	Teaching hospital	Tours, interviews, questionnaires	Some problems in wayfinding and building sytstems; some high lifecycle costs. Attractive & within budget.
Knight, Weitzer, & Zimring, 1978	Residence for the developmentally disabled	Observation, interviews, speech discrimination, acoustic measurements, & institutional records	Improvements in social & solitary behavior of residents, particularly in corridor scheme (reported in Zube 1980).
Lawton, Fulcomer, & Kleban, 1984	Nursing home	Behavior observation, consumer evaluation	Retardation of decline in prosthetically designed building.
Manasc & Adams, 1987	Acute care hospital	Interviews, walk-through, institutional records	Developed action plans for 27 departments.
McLaughlin, 1975	Hospital visiting & waiting spaces	Questionnaires, interviews	Provide reading lights, telephones, eating facilities in waiting areas. Warm, 'new' finishes desirable.
McLaughlin, Kibre, & Raphael, 1972	8 hospitals	Drawing records, interviews	Nursing units were the most frequently remodeled spaces. Surgery changes are usually ancillary, equipment changes impact Radiology & Laboratory.

(continued)

TABLE 6.3 *(Continued)*

Author, Date	Setting	Methodology	Selected Findings
Parshall, 1989	Teaching hospital	Questionnaires, tours, interviews	Overall organizational idea received support; some problems in orientation; image goals were met; some engineering systems difficulties.
Reizenstein & McBride, 1976	Congregate living for the mentally retarded	Observation, interviews, analysis of documents, unobtrusive measures, photography	Public & private spaces available, but more semipublic/private spaces needed. "Symbolic identification" good.
Reizenstein, Spencer, & McBride, 1978	Hospital social services offices	Observation, interviews, questionnaires	Compared old offices to program and new offices. New offices were well received.
Rivlin & Wolfe, 1979	Children's psychiatric facility	Historical analysis, interviews, systematic observations	Therapeutic environment has influence as socialization agent.
Sharkaway & McCormick, 1995	Hospital	Unobtrusive observation	Compared plan complexity, landmarks, vistas, & signage to behavior; more than half showed wayfinding difficulty when vistas & landmarks were absent.
Shepley, 1995	Children's psychiatric facility	Children's drawings, behavior data, questionnaires	Certain spaces were more conducive to negative behavior; new facility created a shift in behavior location.
Shepley, Bryant, & Frohman, 1995	Women's health center	Interviews, questionnaires, behavior mapping	LDRP units and open plan nursery met most programming objectives. Improvements were suggested.
Shepley & Wilson, 1996	Skilled nursing facility for persons with AIDS	Interviews, questionnaires, behavior mapping	Facility well received. More space for staff and programs required.
Trites, Galbraith, Sturdavant, & Leckward, 1970	Radial and linear nursing units	Behavior observation, protocol data analysis	Radial design supports nursing activities and has positive impact on subjective feelings.

(continued)

TABLE 6.3   *(Continued)*

Author, Date	Setting	Methodology	Selected Findings
Turner, Elder, & Rubin, 1977	Virus isolation facility	Analysis of documentation, interviews, observations	Project met the safety goals. Problems were the direct result of inappropriate assumptions during the design process and lack of program information.
Zeisel, 1989	Canadian hospitals	Interviews, tours, questionnaires	Reviewed multiple hospitals.
Zimring & Reizenstein, 1981	Residence for mentally retarded	Interviews, behavior observation	Double-loaded corridor design had more positive impact on residents than suites.

It has also been suggested that design schools serve as evaluation centers. The benefits of this are multiple: students receive training and learn to respect the importance of POEs; reports can be enhanced by collaboration with social scientists in other departments; universities can serve as information clearinghouses (Friedmann, Zimring, and Zube 1978). Another benefit to academic POEs is the availability of students and faculty to staff the study and access to the state-of-the-art technology available in universities. There may be some problems with university-based POEs, however. Academic POEs may be too detailed and laced with technical jargon to be easily interpreted. Kantrowitz and Nordhaus (1980) found that decision makers prefer an intermediate level of information.

WHAT ARE THE DIFFICULTIES IN DOING A POE?

Friedmann, Zimring, and Zube (1978) note that in order for evaluations to be integrated into the design process, two objectives must be met: projects must be evaluated, and the results must be incorporated into subsequent projects. It is not always possible for a firm to set the time aside to fulfill these two commitments.

Even when firms are doing POEs, it may be difficult to access the results. There are three reasons for this.

1. It is difficult to publish the results where they will be widely available.
2. An objective POE will have negative connotations, and firms may be reluctant to share the results with potential clients.
3. Design firms may lack the funding to spend the time necessary to create a rigorous methodology.

These difficulties are not insurmountable, however. Rather than publish all projects, the firm can include the results in an in-house database and consolidate them for an occasional foray into research journal publication. Regarding the stigma of a negative evaluation, projects can be published without identifying the site and still be of great benefit to the firm and the design community. Perhaps the most serious problem is the lack of funding to do in-depth studies. A thorough POE is generally out of reach for small- and medium-sized firms. It is recommended that ministudies be done on a regular basis and larger studies take place when opportunities to collaborate via joint-venture projects and university affiliations present themselves.

In short, more architecture and design firms should become involved in POEs, and the technology should be mainstreamed (Shibley 1985). Firms should seek staff with research experience or education. Several design schools are developing research-supported curriculums, and the number of doctoral students with extensive practice backgrounds appears to be increasing.

One obvious problem associated with having design firms conduct evaluations on their own buildings is their ability to be objective in light of potentially conflicting marketing goals. Even the most dedicated firm may be reluctant to produce data that might call attention to the failings of a particular project. It is also easy to unintentionally construct a questionnaire or interview that would focus on evident successes of a project rather than a representative range of issues. This is not to say that firms should avoid POEs. In addition to studies on their own projects, they can study the work of others and perhaps arrange to trade study services with other firms. If firms find that the data is too negative, then the information can be utilized in-house or be entered into a site-anonymous database for availability to others.

HEALTHCARE FACILITY POE

Healthcare POEs distinguish themselves from other evaluations due to the specific character of the type of building they evaluate. Healthcare facilities differ from other buildings in both their general and specific functional requirements. For a summary of critical performance criteria for hospitals, see Figure 6.3. Specific examples include keeping direct light from falling on isolettes in a NICU and providing enough space around a single-room maternity care bed to allow for the delivery of a baby.

In addition to critical performance criteria, there are three ways healthcare environments can be differentiated from other building types.

1. *Ability to support a full range of studies.* Healthcare evaluations can range from medical complexes the size of a small city to a nurses' substation. They can focus on administrative offices, plant operations, food service, or patient care areas (to name a few!). A hospital could be the setting for earthquake hazard reduction,

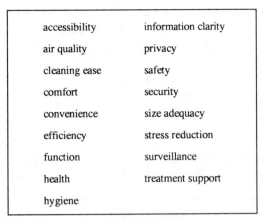

accessibility	information clarity
air quality	privacy
cleaning ease	safety
comfort	security
convenience	size adequacy
efficiency	stress reduction
function	surveillance
health	treatment support
hygiene	

Figure 6.3 Hospital performance criteria. Source: Zeisel 1989

building activation (pre- and postadjustment process to moving into a new building), or architectural competition. The breadth of functions and activities of this building type make healthcare projects unusual among building types, comparable to only a few others such as university campuses or correctional facility complexes. Table 6.3 demonstrates the variety of healthcare-related POEs.

2. *Level of complexity.* Even small hospitals differ from most other building types in terms of complexity. In addition to the variety of users, departments, and services, multiple categories of material are transported through these facilities at a high rate. Separate paths of travel may have to be identified for patients, medical staff, visitors and families, housekeeping, and maintenance. Pharmaceuticals, laboratory samples, hazardous waste, clean and soiled linen, and food must be transported efficiently. While exchanges of materials take place in most building types, the need for quick and accurate replacement of supplies and movement of patients is higher paced in healthcare facilities.

3. *Critical impact the environment has on the building users.* Appropriate adjacencies can support or impede the ability of medical staff to care for patients and save lives. Additionally it has been found that when individuals are ill they are more vulnerable to environmental influences and that the environment may impact the healing process.

While healthcare environments do not have exclusive domain over these features, they may be unique in that they entail them all.

Approaches for Healthcare POEs

Several researchers have developed evaluation methodologies specifically for healthcare facilities, three of which I describe here.

Bad..................................Good	Untidy.............................Tidy
Unpleasant...................Pleasant	Chaotic........................Orderly
Uncomfortable..........Comfortable	Messy...............................Neat
Unattractive.................Attractive	Dirty..............................Clean
Negative......................Positive	
Annoying.....................Pleasing	
EVALUATIVE	**MAINTENANCE**

constricted....................spacious	drab............................colorful
restricted space.............free space	dull................................bright
cramped.........................roomy	dreary...............................gay
SPACIOUSNESS	**MOOD**

| impersonal....................personal |
| unfriendly.....................friendly |
| unsociable.....................sociable |
| |
| **SOCIABILITY** |

Figure 6.4   Bipolar semantic evaluation. Source: Field et al. 1971.

Field et al. (1971). Field and others have developed a methodology specifically for hospitals. This HEW study focuses on techniques for measuring nurse walking behavior and semantic evaluation. The former is a mathematical construct for calculating travel time, measuring the mean nurse-to-patient distance, patient-to-patient distance, number of beds visited, total distance traveled, and total distance per patient. Bipolar categories for the semantic differential study include evaluation (ambiance), maintenance, spaciousness, mood, and sociability (Figure 6.4).

van Wagenberg and Dodd (1994). Van Wagenberg and Dodd have developed a POE specifically for evaluating the spatial organization of hospitals. They recommend a 15-step process beginning with establishing goals and formalizing the contract and ending with reporting results.

Zeisel (1989). Zeisel developed an approach to POEs for analyzing hospitals in Canada's healthcare system. It involves four phases: briefing, profile, diagnostic, and database system. The Canada hospital POEs provide information about the development of new building subtypes, such as day surgeries. However, and more important, the data is being put into a collective database for the comparison of facilities, the confirmation of successes and failures, and development of design standards.

EVALUATION CASE STUDIES

Apart from hands-on experience, the best way to obtain an overview of POEs is to review studies that have been completed. This section describes three healthcare facility evaluation studies. All were done while the principle investigator was a member of a design firm, and two involved buildings that were designed by that firm or in collaboration with another firm. In all cases, the evaluations were carried out by individuals whose current primary focus was professional practice and who either had research backgrounds or were in the process of being trained in the field of design research.

The projects represent a range of healthcare building types—a children's psychiatric facility, an HIV/AIDS skilled nursing facility, and a women's center. All three shared the following objectives:

1. The provision of guidelines for future single-room care facilities
2. Confirmation that the intentions of the designers were manifest in the final project
3. The provision of feedback about the facility to hospital administration

Children's Psychiatric Facility

In 1987, programming was initiated for the design of a new 66-bed children's psychiatric facility. This study, or series of studies, for a children's psychiatric hospital was initiated in order to provide the design team with information that would both support it during the design process and provide information for future projects. Minimal research findings, including POEs and focused research, were available to support design decisions.

ENTRY

Access to the site during the preconstruction phase was facilitated by the rapport established during the programming process. After completion of the project, support was provided for the evaluation because the psychiatric staff at the facility had an appreciation for social research and were essentially pleased with the outcome of the process. Staff went out of their way to support the evaluators, which meant donating several hours of their own time, not just for interviews and questionnaire responses, but for the data coding that was necessary to protect the identity of the residents.

STUDY DESIGN

After existing research information was digested and prior to schematic design initiation, an extensive programming process was undertaken that included multiple workshops, design charettes, and interviews. In addition to speaking with staff and administration, evaluators interviewed residents (25) of the existing children's units and solicited drawings. They used these drawings to help the children articulate their desires in a new facility and used them later for comparison purposes. Additionally, they evaluated the existing units utilizing the special incident reports generated by the staff when certain notable behaviors occurred. Information on these reports included the type and location of the behavior. The evaluators used this information to determine whether certain spaces had a significant number of negative behaviors. Special incident behaviors included absent without leave; aggression toward self, peer, or staff; alleged client abuse; sexual incidents; suicide attempts; theft; injury; possession of contraband; proper damage; fires; and complaints against the facility. Data was collected over a 12-month period and represented 266 incidents. As a result of this pilot study, the following trends were noted:

- Children seem to express negative behaviors when they are transitioning between spaces.
- Many negative behaviors take place in the time-out room.
- Accidents and aggressive acts occur with frequency in the courtyard and on the grounds.
- The dorms were the site of two of the four suicide attempts.

The new building differed from the older residential units in a variety of ways:

- The nurses station had better visibility.
- Corridors were minimized.
- Views outside were provided from most spaces.
- Single- and double-occupancy rooms were provided in lieu of dormitories.
- The entrance to each unit was strongly articulated.
- An open "popcorn" kitchen was provided.
- Finishes were relatively residential in style.

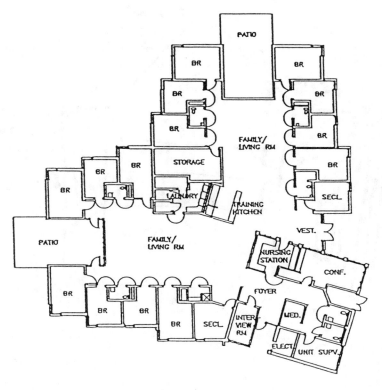

Figure 6.5 Children's facility floor plan.

A typical floor plan is shown in Figure 6.5.

CONDUCT STUDY

The formal POE took place three years after the new buildings were occupied and involved interviews, questionnaires, site observations, children's drawings, and an analysis of new special incident report data.

Interview information was gathered during a postconstruction walk-through of the new facility and from interviews summarized in local periodicals. Feedback was very supportive of the new facility, particularly regarding its residential character and the use of natural light. The site was toured, and maintenance problems were identified.

Evaluators developed the questionnaires (37) to focus on approximately 20 hypotheses related to design innovations. These hypotheses included feedback on group size, the impact of user participation in the design process, and response to the noninstitutional aesthetic. They made inquiries regarding building factors (aesthetic and functional), human factors, access to support functions, and building image. Questionnaire constructs included open-ended and focused questions, semantic differential, and bipolar response. The evaluators assigned responses numerical equivalents and analyzed them. The overall building received a "good" rating on a 1 to 4 scale. A

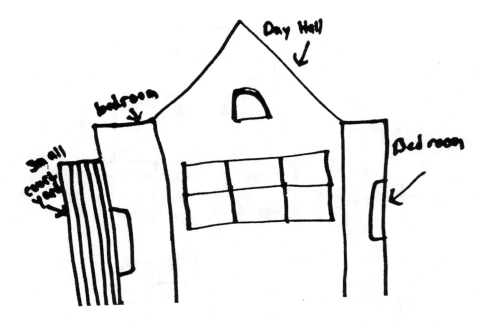

Figure 6.6   Children's postoccupancy drawing.

detailed summary is provided elsewhere ("The Location of Behavioral Incidents," Shepley 1995).

Several drawings were received from children, one of which was from a child present at the previous drawing session five years earlier (see Figure 6.6). While evaluators did not do an in-depth analysis of the drawings, they did make a comparison to the previous set of drawings to identify differences in presentation and content. They found that the post-occupancy drawings were more focused on the bedroom spaces and were clearer and more organized.

Regarding the special incident report, the hypothesis that the incidents would be relocated was confirmed—transitional spaces were no longer locations of high levels of incidents. The number of incidents did rise in the patient rooms, where supervision was limited; however, the staff still supported the use of private and semiprivate rooms over dormitories. Regarding other hypotheses, there was a significant drop in incidents just prior to and immediately after the move. This is consistent with the hypothesis that there is a "honeymoon effect" associated with the occupancy of a new building.

As a result of this study, the following design recommendations were made:

- While patient clusters of 11 may be appropriate, these groups need to be separated from one another to eliminate the domino effect that occurs if there is a loud incident in a cluster.
- Staff and residents prefer single-occupancy and double-occupancy rooms over dormitories to enhance privacy; however, some additional supervision may have to be provided to offset the number of negative incidents.
- Floor plans should eliminate hallways and unsupervised entries when possible.

DISSEMINATE DATA

This study was given to the designers of the project, presented at conferences, and published in a research journal. The format attempts to appeal to both researchers and designers by following the American Psychological Association (APA) format and includes design guidelines in the conclusions section.

Women's Center

Single-room maternity care centers have become the predominant model for new birthing centers. The facility that is the setting for this study was one of the first of its kind, and the designers were aware that it would serve as a model for facilities to come.

The setting is a 48-bed addition to an existing 400-bed hospital. Completed in 1991, half of the patient rooms are dedicated to single-room maternity care, also referred to as LDRP (Figure 6.7). Other building functions include: surgery, administration and support, antepartum testing, and neonatal intensive care.

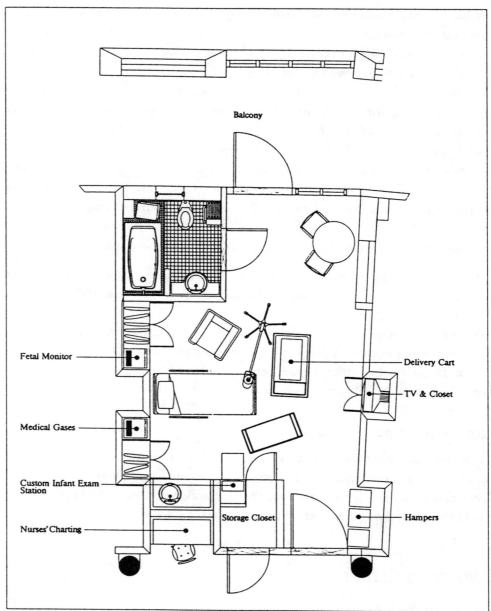

Balcony

Fetal Monitor

Delivery Cart

TV & Closet

Medical Gases

Custom Infant Exam
Station

Storage Closet

Hampers

Nurses' Charting

LDRP ROOM

Figure 6.7 LDRP floor plan.

ENTRY

A staff member of the firm that designed the project led the evaluation team, and a report was already established with the hospital. Administration was supportive of the study and encouraged staff to participate.

STUDY DESIGN

The evaluation team used questionnaire, interview, and behavior mapping techniques. Twenty-two of 28 questionnaires were returned. Administration preselected respondents according to amount of experience. Respondents represented various levels in the organization, including nursing staff, physicians, and support staff. No patients participated in the study. The hospital manages its own patient survey that, while not directed at the physical environment, provides information about satisfaction with the experience at the Women's Center. The questionnaire asked 218 open-ended and directed questions, addressing both building and human factors and focusing on four departments: surgery, neonatal intensive care, birthing, and administration/support.

Team members interviewed eight representatives of these four departments as part of the postoccupancy study, most of whom had participated in the programming process. The interviews lasted 45 to 60 minutes in focus groups. Evaluators used the results of the questionnaires to structure the interviews.

Two behavior mapping studies took place, one designed to evaluate the success of the decentralized charting stations, the other to measure the time that nursing staff and others were able to spend with babies in the NICU in the open plan. These studies were pilot efforts, whose primary intent was to focus on specific issues that were of high priority in the programming phase.

CONDUCT STUDY

The questionnaire responses suggested that the new building was well received, particularly in the area of aesthetics. This was important relative to the original directives of the design team, which included the objective of creating an environment expressing hospitality aesthetics rather than a high-tech ambiance. However, some problems became apparent relative to the maintainability of the residential-appearing finishes. As with all three of the projects presented here, patient spaces received a more favorable response than staff spaces. The LDRP concept was supported by 100 percent of the respondents, and suggestions were made regarding the improvement of room storage and lighting. The NICU was the best-received department of the four departments reviewed. The response was very supportive of the open-plan design (there are no dividers between baby stations) and flexibility. In the surgery suite, an additional operating room was requested (one was eliminated during a cost-reduction phase), but the recovery room received high marks for the natural light (there are skylights in the room) and high visibility for supervision. Administration was described as having limited space, but the ambiance of admissions and waiting was appreciated.

Specific suggestions regarding the design of the LDRPs were made during the interviews with staff members. It was recommended that

- More storage be located along the footwall to allow access to supplies during a delivery.
- More work surface (a fold-down table) be provided in the LDRP.
- Lighting be increased in the family alcoves.
- Larger hallway charting areas be provided.
- More durable flooring be considered in patient rooms. Regarding flooring, wood was used and, while aesthetically pleasing, involved additional maintenance. The carpet in the NICU, on the other hand, was greatly appreciated for its acoustical and residential qualities, in spite of increased maintenance needs.

The behavior mapping study at the nursing station identified some conflicts in the use of the small central nursing station—some of the activities that were supposed to take place in the hallways were still taking place in the central nursing station. This occurred because, as a rule, nursing staff tend to use nursing stations for social interaction, and the staff that had originally decided to decentralize nursing were no longer at the institution to encourage substation activity. Regarding the NICU, time spent with babies was recorded and will serve as a benchmark for a subsequent study that was initiated in the fall of 1995 in another facility.

DISSEMINATE DATA

The results of this study have been presented at conferences and are published in detail (Shepley, Bryant, and Frohman 1995). The architect reviewed the results and made suggestions regarding the significance behind some of the outcomes. A copy has been made available to the hospital.

SNF for Persons with AIDS

As our culture and its requirements change, the built environment follows. To keep up with these developments, it is necessary to do POEs on new building prototypes. In the case of healthcare environments, the need is extremely pressing—appropriate environments can support the care of patients and may even have prosthetic value. Facilities for persons with HIV/AIDS fall into the category of new building types for which there is a great demand. Unfortunately, there is little research available to support an informed design process for such facilities. In order to provide new information on this building type, a POE was done of a new, freestanding skilled nursing facility (SNF) for persons with AIDS.

ENTRY

Unfortunately, some of the building types that would benefit most from POEs are also the most precarious in terms of carrying out an evaluation. Environments where people are vulnerable are difficult to access, as it is particularly important to protect the privacy of the users. Fortunately, the administrators and staff at a new facility for persons with AIDS had been intimately involved with the design process for that facility and were fully aware of the possibilities of a supportive environment. When it was recommended to them that a POE be conducted at their site, they were extremely cooperative, knowing that their facility was a model for future facilities.

STUDY DESIGN

This POE and the previous one at the Women's Center were completed during the same time frame, utilizing similar methodologies. Unlike the previous POEs, however, this project was not designed in the office of the evaluators.

The facility, which was well received by the architectural community, is a 35-bed SNF with a separately licensed adult day health program. Both functions were analyzed as part of the project. A typical floor plan is shown in Figure 6.8.

Prior to initiating the postoccupancy study, the POE team conducted a literature survey. Although little hard data is available, several articles have been written about potential design guidelines for this population, utilizing information about other healthcare settings. This information was summarized, together with ideas generated from the personal experience of the evaluation team.

The study began one year after occupation. As with the Women's Center, three methodologies were used: questionnaires, interviews, and behavior mapping. Unlike the Women's Center, researchers were able to distribute questionnaires and obtain interviews from patients and not just from staff.

Twenty-six individuals responded to questionnaires. Staff questionnaires included approximately 200 open-ended and focused questions. Researchers limited patient questionnaires to two sides of a single page, so as not to overly burden the patients. Questions were generated based on the qualities of the new environment that were distinct or innovative relative to its predecessors, such as the impact of the residential environment and the extensive use of outdoor space. Other questions came from issues raised in the literature, such as whether an AIDS facility should be segregated or integrated into other care facilities. The results were subject to statistical analysis.

Fifteen individuals were interviewed during the postoccupancy process, including four adult day health clients. Residents were not interviewed because researchers thought it would be inappropriate to intrude on their privacy. The staff interviews lasted 45 minutes to an hour and were held in an administration office. Day health clients were interviewed a maximum of 20 minutes each in the multipurpose room.

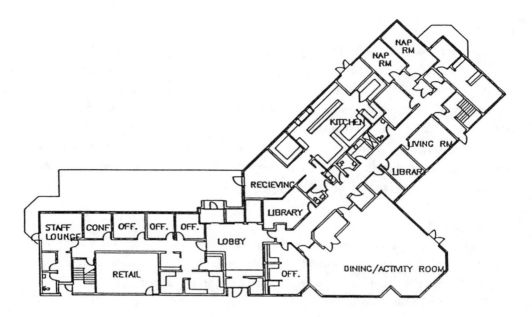

FIRST FLOOR PLAN

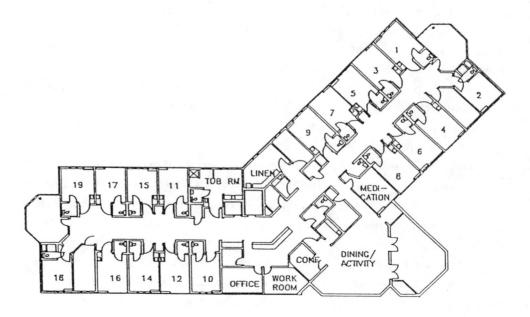

SECOND FLOOR PLAN

Figure 6.8 Floor plan for facility for persons with AIDS.

In response to the strong emphasis on outdoor spaces in the building program, researchers conducted a short behavior mapping study to evaluate the utilization of the largest of the outdoor patios. The purpose of this pilot study was to test a procedure for observing behavior patterns in this passive outdoor space and to identify potential issues for a more detailed study. A nonparticipant observer made observations every five minutes from 10 A.M. to 2 P.M. The observer noted locations of people on a floor plan, as well as whether they were smoking or using a wheelchair.

CONDUCT STUDY

According to questionnaire responses, the building was well received. The facility received an overall rating of 2.16 on a scale of 1 to 4 (1 = excellent, 4 = poor). The building was rated higher in patient areas than in staff areas for two reasons: during the programming process, residents were given the highest priority; the group originally contracted to operate the facility underestimated the amount of staff space required. The most significant problem identified in the questionnaire was lack of space. This was thought to be largely due to the exceptional popularity of the programs, leading to overcrowding. Another significant response was that patients and staff alike strongly supported the stand-alone facility over a facility that would be integrated with other diagnoses.

The interviews corroborated the four questionnaire responses: the overall building was received positively; patient spaces are more adequate than staff spaces; lack of space is a significant problem; and freestanding facilities are preferred. Additionally, interviewees emphasized that outdoor space is important and that residential finishes, although aesthetically appropriate for this environment, are difficult to maintain.

Due to the brevity of the behavior mapping study, the results must be viewed with caution. There were some important conclusions that are intuitively supported, however. Separate areas should be provided for smokers and nonsmokers, and temperature and weather control are important if the space is to be accessed year-round. Researchers found that activity was greatest immediately before and after lunch, when the patio was warmest (the study was done during the spring in a temperate climate) and when the largest number of clients were there to participate in the lunch program. The study also noted that clients found the standard patio furniture to be a little difficult to see (pale colors blended into the pavement) and that the color contrast and comfort of the furniture should be taken into account in outdoor furniture specification. The most important outcome of this portion of the evaluation was the finding that the outdoor space is used regularly, although this study was not of sufficient duration to quantify the exact need.

A detailed summary of the results of this study are published elsewhere (Shepley, Wilson 1996).

DATA DISSEMINATION

This report was circulated to both the head administrator and director of the facility, the former of which provided feedback and corrections. It has been presented at the annual conference of the Environmental Design Research Association and is currently being considered for publication in an architectural research and planning journal. As with the other POEs described here, it addresses both standard research issues and design guidelines.

FUTURE FOCUS OF HEALTHCARE FACILITY POEs

There are various suggestions regarding appropriate directions for design evaluation of healthcare facilities, including the following:

- Designers should use minievaluations iteratively during the design process. Identical questions could be issued before and after completing a building to see if previous concerns have been addressed. Additionally, a series of POEs could occur over the lifetime of the building to confirm its appropriateness as a prototype in light of inevitable social and technological changes. This would also help facility managers to quantifiably identify needs and judge them against requests for space changes.
- It would be a great service to the design community if these studies could be compiled at a common location. If studies are more standardized, it will be possible to consolidate the data in a common databank (as is being done with the Veteran's Administration and the Canada hospital system) and make the information available to designers.
- Evaluations need to be feasible financially for design firms (Friedmann, Zimring, and Zube 1978). This may have to happen in steps. Experience in evaluation should be flagged during project acquisition interviews and described as a benefit of contracting with a firm. Small studies should be accounted for in the fee structure, and larger studies should routinely be proposed during contract negotiations. Firms are stretched by tight fee structures, and lack of support for evaluation studies will continue to plague the process until the public is made aware of the impact of informed design on the quality of healthcare delivery.
- The gap between theory and application needs to be bridged (Friedmann, Zimring, and Zube 1978). Studies must be designed to be readily interpreted by practitioners, and professional ethics should demand that the information be sought out and used.

- Databanks need to be established for evaluation information (Friedmann, Zimring, and Zube 1978). Universities and public agencies are most prepared to serve as repositories for POE information and should take up this challenge. More rigid systematization will support the compiling of data.
- Researchers conducting studies need to expand their focus on evaluating whether the original policies are appropriate rather than whether the policies have been implemented (Zimring 1987).

POE TRENDS

The previous section described a wish list for the future of POEs that may or may not be fulfilled. Certain positive trends have been observed by researchers and practitioners, however.

1. *Growth in the number of evaluations.* With the push toward an informed design process, it is likely that the importance of POEs will be strongly felt in the future. As a result, they may become a more integral part of programming for all designers.
2. *Standardization.* Bechtel (1989) foresees a time when, due to fee limitations, POEs become more standardized and less encumbered by the customization associated with social science techniques. Preiser (1994) and Zeisel (1989) advocate for standardization in support of replicability. In addition to making the information available, this would allow for verification of the generalizability of the results.
3. *Shift in focus.* Another welcome trend in POEs has been the shift in focus from designer needs to client needs (White 1989). One possible reason for this is that the fragile state of the economy over the last two decades has forced many owners and designers to focus on the essentials of a project (e.g., the basic needs of the users).
4. *Practitioner participation.* Farbstein (1989) has noted an increase in the number of practitioners involved in POEs. Zeisel (1989) has observed the emergence of a researcher/practitioner professional. The design profession has left its postmodernist roots and is reconciling itself to a more socially responsible, informed building product.
5. *International institutionalization of POEs.* Growth in the POE industry may be occurring as evidenced by the institutionalization of POEs in some countries and the increase in the number of firms engaging in this activity. There is no quantitative demonstration however, that more support is being given to these studies (Zeisel 1989).

6. *Spread to new building types.* More and more building types are becoming settings for evaluation studies (Zeisel 1989). Due to the importance of healthcare facilities, it is likely that they will remain the focus of many studies.

7. *Higher-quality information for clients.* Zeisel (1989) cites evidence that POEs are being used to provide clients with better and broader information. Studies are being communicated more effectively, and higher-impact POEs are appearing (Zeisel 1989).

CONCLUSION

If students are given the opportunity to understand the significance of folding evaluation into the design process and if professionals are reassured of the utility of such studies, postoccupancy evaluations will become a natural part of the building process. It is inevitable that this information will enable us to build better healthcare environments for the diverse group of people that utilize them.

Mardelle McCuskey Shepley is a registered architect and assistant professor at Texas A&M University. She is also the associate director of the TAMU Center for Health Systems & Design.

References

American Psychological Association. "Ethical Principles of Psychologists and Code of Conduct: Reports of the Association." *American Psychologist* 47 (1992): 1597–1611.

Bechtel, R. B. "Advances in POE Methods: An Overview." In *Building Evaluation,* edited by W. F. E. Preiser. New York: Plenum Press, 1989.

Canter, D. "Royal Hospital for Sick Children." *The Architect's Journal* 156, no. 36, (1972): 525–564.

Farbstein, J. "Advances in Post-Occupancy Evaluation Applications: An Overview." In *Building Evaluation,* edited by W. F. E. Preiser, New York: Plenum Press, 1989.

Field, H., Hansen, J., Karalis, C., Kennedy, D., Lippert, S., and Ronco, P. *Evaluation of Hospital Design: A Holistic Approach.* Boston: Tufts-New England Medical Center, 1971.

Friedmann, A., Zimring, C., and Zube, E. *Environmental Design Evaluation.* New York: Plenum Press, 1978.

Garling, T., Book, A., and Lindberg, E. "Spatial Orientation and Wayfinding in the Designed Environment: A Conceptual Analysis and Some Suggestions for Postoccupancy Evaluation." *Journal of Architectural and Planning Research* 3, no. 1 (1986): 55–64.

Harvey, J. "Post-Occupancy Evaluation: Do You Meet Users' Needs?" *Dimensions in Health Service* 61, no. 6 (1984): 12–13.

Kantrowitz, M. and Associates. *Design Evaluation of Six Primary Care Facilities for the Purpose of Informing Future Design Decisions.* Martinez, CA: The Center for Health Design, 1993.

Kantrowitz, M. and Nordhaus, R. "The Impact of Post-Occupancy Evaluation Research: A Case Study." *Environment and Behavior* 12, no. 4 (1980): 508–519.

Kennon, P. A., Bauer, J. S., and Parshall, S. A. "Evaluating Health Care Facilities" (Part I). *The Journal of Health Administration Education* 6, no. 4 (1988): 819–831.

Keys, C. and Wener, R. "Organizational Intervention Issues: A Four-Phase Approach to Post-Occupancy Evaluation." *Environment and Behavior* 12, no. 4 (1980): 533–540.

Knight, R. C., Weitzer, W. H., and Zimring, C. M. *Opportunity for Control and the Built Environment: The ELEMR Project.* Amherst, MA: The Environmental Institute, University of Massachusetts, 1978.

Lawton, M. P., Fulcomer, M., and Kleban, M. H. "Architecture for the Mentally Impaired Elderly." *Environment and Behavior* 16, no. 6 (1984): 730–757.

Lincoln, Y. and Gube, E. G. *Naturalistic Inquiry.* Beverly Hills, CA: Sage Publications, 1985.

Manasc, V. and Adams, J. "Post-Occupancy Evaluation by Hospitals." *Hospital Trustee* 11, no. 5 (1987): 5–7.

Marans, R. W. and Spreckelmeyer, K. F. *Evaluating Built Environments: A Behavioral Approach.* Ann Arbor: Institute for Social Research & Architectural Research Laboratory, The University of Michigan, 1981.

Marans, R. W. and Spreckelmeyer, K. F. "Measuring Overall Architectural Quality: A Component of Building Evaluation." *Environment and Behavior* 14, no. 6 (1982): 652–670.

McLaughlin, H. P. "Post-Occupancy Evaluation of Hospitals: What One Such Evaluation Produced." *AIA Journal* 63, no. 1 (1975): 30–31.

McLaughlin, H. P., Kibre, J., and Raphael, M. "Patterns of Physical Change in Six Existing Hospitals." In *Environmental Design: Research and Practice,* edited by W. Mitchell. Los Angeles: University of California, 1972.

Ogodnik, T. M. "The User of Space Programming and Post-Occupancy Evaluation." *World Hospital* 21, no. 4 (1985): 58–61.

Parshall, S. "A Hospital Evaluation: The Problem-seeking Method. In *Building Evaluation,* edited by W. F. E. Preiser. New York; Plenum Press, 1989.

Parshall, S. and Pena, W. M. *Evaluating Facilities: A Practical Approach to Post-Occupancy Evaluation.* Houston: CRS Sirrine, 1982.

Preiser, W. F. E. "Towards a Performance-based Conceptual Framework for Systematic POEs." In *Building Evaluation,* edited by W. F. E. Preiser. New York: Plenum Press, 1989.

Preiser, W. F. E. "Built Environment Evaluation: Conceptual Basis, Benefits and Uses." *Journal of Architectural and Planning Research* 11, no. 2 (1994): 91–107.

Preiser, W. F. E., Rabinowitz, H. Z., and White, E. T. *Post-Occupancy Evaluation.* New York: Van Nostrand Reinhold, 1988.

Reizenstein, J. E. and McBride, W. A. *Designing for Mentally Retarded People: A Social-Environmental Evaluation of New England Villages.* Ann Arbor, MI: University of Michigan, Architectural Research Laboratory, 1979. (Cited in Friedmann, Zimring, and Zube 1978).

Reizenstein, J. E., Spencer, K. R., and McBride, W. A. "Social Research and Design: Cambridge Hospital Social Services Offices." Unpublished manuscript, Harvard University School of Design, Cambridge, 1976 (Cited in Friedmann, Zimring, and Zube 1978).

Rivlin, L. and Wolfe, M. "Understanding and Evaluating Therapeutic Environments for

Children." In *Designing for Therapeutic Environments: A Review of Research,* edited by D. Canter and J. Canter. New York: John Wiley, 1979.

Sharkaway, M. A. and McCormick, M. "Wayfinding in Complex Healthcare Environments: Linking Design to Research." In *Twenty-Sixth Annual Conference of the Environmental Design Research Association: Proceedings,* edited by J. L. Masar, P. Grannis, and K. Hanyu. Oklahoma City: EDRA, 1995.

Shepley, M. M. *Methodologies for Measuring Spatial Perception.* Ann Arbor, MI: University of Michigan, 1995, in press.

Shepley, M. M. "The Location of Behavioral Incidents in a Children's Psychiatric Facility." *Children's Environments* (1995, in press).

Shepley, M. M., Bryant, C., and Frohman, B. "Validating a Building Prototype: A Post-Occupancy Evaluation of a Women's Medical Center." *Journal of Interior Design* (1995, in press).

Shepley, M. M. and Wilson, P. *Designing for Persons with AIDS: A Post-Occupancy Evaluation at the Bailey-Boushay House,* 1996, in press.

Shibley, R. G. "Building Evaluation in the Main Stream." *Environment and Behavior* 17, no. 1 (1985): 7–24.

Trites, D. K. and Galbraith, F. D. "Influence of Nursing-Unit Design on the Activities and Subjective Feelings of Nursing Personnel." *Environment and Behavior* 2, no. 3 (1970): 303–334.

Turner, G. E., Elder, J., and Rubin, A. "National Cancer Institute's Emergency Virus Isolation Facility: A Case Study for Developing a Methodology of Post Occupancy Evaluation." Washington, D.C.: National Bureau of Standards, Institute for Applied Technology, Center for Building Technology, 1977.

van Wagenberg, A. F. and Dodd, E. M. *Post Occupancy Evaluation Methodology for Assessing Spatial Organization of Hospitals.* Unpublished paper, Eindhoven University of Technology, The Netherlands, 1994.

White, E. T. "Post-Occupancy Evaluation from the Client's Perspective." In *Building Evaluation,* edited by W. F. E. Preiser. New York: Plenum Press, 1989.

Zeisel, J. "Towards a POE Paradigm." In *Building Evaluation,* edited by W. F. E. Preiser. New York: Plenum Press, 1989.

Zimring, C. M. "Evaluation of Designed Environments: Methods for Post-Occupancy Evaluation." In *Methods in Environmental and Behavioral Research,* edited by R. B. Bechtel and W. Michelson. New York: Van Nostrand Reinhold, 1987.

Zimring, C. M. and Reizenstein, J. E. "Post-Occupancy Evaluation: An Overview." *Environment & Behavior* 12, no. 4 (1980): 429–450.

Zimring, C. M. and Reizenstein, J. E. "A Primer on Post-Occupancy Evaluation." *American Institute of Architects Journal* 70, no. 13 (1981): 52–58.

Zube, E. H. *Environmental Evaluation.* Monterey, CA: Brooks/Cole Publishing, 1980.

II

PRODUCTS

7

CEILINGS

James F. Mathis

For far too many years, the ceiling seemed to be the poor stepchild of health-care design. It was often considered nothing more than a functional necessity, receiving whatever remained in the design budget after the balance of the facility had been carefully furnished.

But, as research emerged linking patients' attitudes to the total environment, the ceiling began to take its rightful place on the design agenda. Today, ceilings are considered design opportunities, incorporating both form and function. They can, and should, complement and enhance the interior. After all, patients spend a great deal of time on their backs, and the ceiling is the predominate feature within their viewing range.

One of the reasons for ceilings' metamorphosis has been the advent of a whole new generation of products, grid systems, and installation techniques. The challenge for the design professional is to explore all the possibilities and then select the ceiling that best meets the requirements of a particular space in terms of design, quality, and performance.

CEILING TYPES

The commercial ceilings industry consists of three major types:

1. Metal ceilings
2. Gypsum board and plaster ceilings
3. Mineral fiber and fiberglass acoustical ceilings

Metal ceilings fall into four categories: functional, decorative, metallinear, and open cell. They are more popular in Europe than in North America.

Gypsum board (drywall) or plaster ceilings are smooth-surfaced ceilings often used to create a clean, monolithic visual. There are various installation methods, including black iron and metal furring systems. Compared to the other ceiling types, drywall ceilings are neither acoustical nor easy to access.

Acoustical ceilings are the most commonly used ceiling systems in healthcare facilities in the United States because of their combination of aesthetics, acoustics, and accessibility to the plenum.

ACOUSTICAL CEILINGS

Acoustical ceilings are offered in two forms: panels and tiles.

Panels

The most common acoustical ceiling system consists of either 2' × 2', 2' × 4', or 4' × 4' acoustical panels suspended in a metal grid. Depending on the manufacturer, other panel sizes are also available. The 2' × 2' panel is currently the most popular size because it is easier to handle and less costly to replace than its larger counterparts.

Acoustical panels are made from either a mineral fiber-based material or fiberglass. Both types are offered in lay-in and tegular versions. Tegular panels feature a reveal or exposed edge that is visible below the plane of the grid (see Figure 7.1).

In terms of relative costs, standard lay-in panels are the most economical, followed by tegular edge panels, and then decorative panels that feature either a pattern or another finish, such as wood, on the surface. (Metal ceilings, whether decorative or functional, comprise the next level of cost.)

Tiles

Acoustical ceilings are also available in 12" × 12" tiles that are installed in a concealed grid system. Tiles are often used in areas where a more monolithic look is desired in the acoustical ceiling and where accessibility to the plenum is not a major concern.

Very little "drop" space is needed to install tile. In general, the concealed grid systems used for tile need only a 3-inch clearance, while the exposed grid systems for panels need a 7-inch clearance.

Acoustical tile ceilings are more difficult to access than acoustical panel ceilings. However, if access is required, there are concealed grid systems that provide this feature. The most common is a downwardly accessible system in which any tile not resting on an exposed flange can be removed by pulling downward with a specially designed knife. Depending on the grid system, some upward accessibility is also available.

Figure 7.1 Popular tegular-panel edge details include (clockwise, from bottom right) square, beaded, stepped, and chamfered. Photo: Armstrong World Industries, Inc., Lancaster, Pennsylvania.

If using tile, remember that pattern matched ceiling tiles do the best job of integrating tile to tile. The result is an acoustical ceiling with excellent joint-hiding abilities that give it the appearance of a real one-piece ceiling.

Grid Systems

The grid systems that hold suspended ceiling panels in place are usually constructed of steel. Main tees are 12 feet long, while cross tees are usually 2 or 4 feet long. Aluminum grid systems are available for use in high-humidity applications.

The three most common types of grid systems are $^{15}/_{16}$-inch exposed tee, $^{9}/_{16}$-inch exposed tee, and $^{9}/_{16}$-inch bolt-slot system.

In addition to these standard systems, a number of decorative or specialty grid systems are also on the market. These systems give designers the opportunity to create unique ceiling effects by adding detail to the space.

For example, one system offers a combination of colors in a unique double-line grid

Figure 7.2   The three-dimensional PVC facings on this decorative grid system match or complement the edge detail of the acoustical ceiling panel the system supports. Photo: Armstrong World Industries, Inc., Lancaster, Pennsylvania.

design. This allows designers to either accent or match other interior finish colors in the space. It also gives the visual of a slotted grid system without actually having one.

Another system transforms the grid into an architectural design element by either matching or complementing the edge detail of the acoustical ceiling panel it supports. The effect is attained through the use of a three-dimensional, extruded PVC facing that is factory applied onto the steel grid elements (see Figure 7.2).

TEXTURE AND COLOR

Texture provides a means of adding interest to an acoustical ceiling through nuances of light and shadow.

There are a number of options available, ranging from soft, fine textures that offer an unobtrusive appearance and a sense of expansiveness to a room to boldly textured surface designs that add an extra dimension to a room's overall appeal.

Another way of achieving dimension is to use deeply scored acoustical ceilings. These geometric ceilings work together with a narrow grid system to help create a monolithic appearance.

Many of the acoustical ceiling panels and tiles on the market today are available in a variety of standard colors to help add warmth to a space. Custom colors are available by special order but many require a minimum order quantity and added lead time.

In addition, multitone or variegated paint finishes are now available to add even more depth and character to a ceiling and to match the intricate, multicolored effects that are popular in healthcare interiors.

Acoustic Performance Indicators

A quiet environment helps promote healing. As a result, the acoustic performance of a ceiling is an important consideration. In general, mineral fiber ceilings are good sound absorbers and fairly good sound barriers. Fiberglass ceilings are usually excellent sound absorbers and poor sound barriers. Performance in these areas is generally indicated by two values—the noise reduction coefficient and the ceiling attenuation class.

NOISE REDUCTION COEFFICIENT (NRC)

The NRC is a measure of the average sound absorption of a material. It represents the amount of sound absorbed by a material when the sound is incident from all directions. It is also averaged over a frequency range representative of speech.

NRC values range from 0.00 to 1.00. An NRC of 0.50 means the material absorbs 50 percent of the sound that strikes it; an NRC of 1.00 means it absorbs 100 percent of the sound. Ceilings with NRCs between 0.50 and 0.70 are considered good sound absorbers. Those with an NRC of 0.85 or higher are considered excellent.

CEILING ATTENUATION CLASS (CAC)

The CAC (previously called ceiling sound transmission class [CSTC]) is a measure of the sound transmission loss of a ceiling and plenum combination. It is a single number in decibel units that represents the loss in sound level as it is transmitted through a ceiling, into the plenum above the ceiling height partition, and back through an adjacent ceiling (e.g., from one patient room to an adjacent patient room).

CAC values range from 15 to 45. Ceilings with CACs of 30 to 35 are considered good sound barriers; those with CACs of 40 and higher are considered excellent.

OTHER PERFORMANCE INDICATORS

There are a number of other physical performance indicators to consider in addition to acoustics. Two of the more important are

1. *Light Reflectance (LR)*. This is a measure of the percentage of light striking a surface that is reflected and not absorbed. LR values range from 0.00 to 1.00 and

indicate the minimum percentage of reflection. For example, an LR of 0.75 means at least 75 percent of the light striking a surface is reflected.

2. *Flame Spread Rating.* This indicator of a material's surface burning characteristics indicates how quickly a flame will spread across the face of a ceiling panel. The information is expressed by a Class A, B, or C designation according to guidelines contained in ASTM E 1264. Class A signifies the highest class (slowest rate of flame spread).

CODE REQUIREMENTS

When specifying ceilings, it's important to fully understand all the code requirements of a space because building codes can sometimes limit choices of ceiling systems. Designers must check all local and national codes that apply, especially

1. *Fire.* Determine what level of fire resistance is needed. For example, in some corridors and public spaces, fire resistance is a must. When dealing with fire resistance ratings, remember that they apply to a floor/ceiling or roof/ceiling assembly *in its entirety.* Components such as the ceiling panels or grid system are not assigned an individual fire resistance rating.

2. *Seismic.* This is another issue to deal with, especially on the West Coast and Zone 4 areas. Where they exist, seismic codes usually require a more complicated installation system, which can limit the type of ceiling.

If design professionals have questions concerning code compliance, physical performance parameters, installation, and so on, most acoustical ceiling manufacturers offer a technical assistance hotline. That number can usually be found in the manufacturer's literature.

THE RIGHT CEILING

Once design professionals are familiar with all the technical aspects, determining the optimum ceiling for a particular area of a healthcare facility will depend greatly on matching the characteristics of different ceilings with the needs of the space. To help in that process, the remainder of this chapter takes a look at the primary requirements for ceilings in a variety of healthcare spaces, from main lobby to therapy room and cafeteria to consultation room.

Lobbies

Lobbies tend to be upscale when it comes to ceilings and other interior finishes. The reason is simple: they are the feature areas that give both patients and visitors their first impression of the facility. As a result, aesthetics is usually the key consideration in selecting ceiling materials, followed by acoustics and durability.

When it comes to first impressions, it's important to know the image the hospital wants to portray. Is it a high-tech image with a highly sterile look? Or, is it a soft, warm image with a highly decorative look? Either is acceptable today.

Regardless of the direction chosen, the ceiling should be able to pick up the theme of the space. The ceiling should also integrate well with the other interior finishes, including the floorcovering, wallcovering, fabrics, mouldings, and so on.

When it comes to design, a number of developments have occurred within the acoustical ceiling industry that can help add character, originality, and personality to lobbies and other high-visibility spaces. The first is the introduction of a system called Metaphors that offers the unique visual of a coffered ceiling but with the acoustical performance, accessibility, and installation ease of lay-in panels (see Figure 7.3). The ceiling is created by simply installing a coffer in the grid system and then placing an acoustical ceiling panel in the crown of each coffer.

The second development is the advent of decorative, custom ceiling systems that offer hundreds of design possibilities using standard ceiling panels. One such concept is built around three standard carved panel configurations: corner panels that feature a pattern along two perpendicular sides, border panels that feature a pattern along one side, and accent panels that feature a pattern in one corner. By linking the panels together, designers can create an almost endless array of ceiling layouts. This development, made possible through computer technology and state-of-the-art manufacturing equipment, has had a wide-ranging impact on contract interiors. Designers can now echo corners, highlight functional areas, and create focal points (see Figure 7.4).

Yet another development is made-to-order fixture openings that incorporate the same edge pattern as the panel itself, thereby producing a level of detail not previously possible in acoustical ceilings. The square or circular openings are centered in each panel and created at the factory to eliminate the need for field cutting. The openings allow designers to continue a chosen edge detail around high-hat light fixtures, sprinkler heads, speaker grilles, air diffusers, and other HVAC openings.

Another increasingly popular way of providing an upscale visual to a standard acoustical ceiling in lobbies and other high visibility spaces is to accent it with drywall around the perimeter. In the past, stud and track had to be installed to the deck above to obtain this effects. Today, however, there is a new installation system called *drywall furring* that allows the drywall to be attached directly to the acoustical

Figure 7.3 The Metaphors ceiling system offers the unique visual of a coffered ceiling with the acoustical performance, accessibility, and installation ease of lay-in panels. Photo: Armstrong World Industries, Inc., Lancaster, Pennsylvania.

ceiling's grid system. Unlike traditional stud-and-track perimeters, which must be installed *before* the acoustical ceiling, the new system permits the perimeter framing to be installed *at the same time* as the acoustical grid system. This results in lower costs, less time, and improved quality assurance of the finished installation. Typical applications include drywall surrounds, drop soffits, and return soffits.

It's important to note that drywall furring applications are full-module installations, meaning that the ceiling panels, or modules, remain uncut. This results in a better look, smoother transition between the ceiling and wall, and improved integrity of the entire ceiling.

Patient Rooms

There are two philosophies concerning ceilings in patient rooms. Some designers prefer drywall ceilings because of their ability to perform as a sound barrier and

Figure 7.4 By linking the panels of decorative or carved custom ceiling systems together, designers can echo corners, highlight functional areas, and create focal points. Photo: Armstrong World Industries, Inc., Lancaster, Pennsylvania.

thereby increase privacy between rooms. Others prefer acoustical ceilings because of their ability to perform as a sound absorber and thereby decrease noise levels within each room.

Patient privacy from room to room is dependent to a large degree on the partition system between the rooms. If the partition does not run slab to slab, designers need to be concerned with the CAC value of the ceiling, and drywall may be a better option. Use of drywall, however, will result in reverberation noise within the room.

If it is more important to absorb the noise in the room and create a quieter atmosphere, then an acoustical ceiling is the better option. An acoustical ceiling will also provide the accessibility the staff may need to get to oxygen and other lines that run through the plenum.

If an acoustical ceiling is used in a patient room, one of the key considerations is the type of hardware to be installed. It's important to know how elements such as the curtain track and lighting are going to interact with the ceiling. For example, a tegular ceiling is a little more difficult to use in patient rooms because of the need to space the curtain track away from the grid. A lay-in ceiling is often the better choice.

Therapy Rooms

The choice of acoustical ceilings in therapy rooms depends on the type of therapy that takes place in the room and on whether water is present. Rooms in which the humidity level is expected to be high because of the presence of water or for other reasons usually require the use of "sag-resistant" acoustical ceilings—ceilings that can withstand relative humidity up to 90 percent and temperatures up to 90°F.

Sag-resistant ceilings are also good choices for areas where air conditioning may be interrupted from time to time or completely shut off for long periods of time. They are also needed in air conditioned areas where doors are opening frequently, allowing warm air to enter and causing temperature fluctuations.

From an aesthetic point of view, most humidity-resistant panels are fine fissured and available in either lay-in or tegular versions. For a slightly more upscale look, there are panels that offer not only a high degree of sag resistance but also a scored, grid-hiding visual.

For areas such as indoor pools, saunas, and whirlpools, where corrosive chemical fumes may be present in addition to high temperatures and high humidity, ceilings that can withstand 100 percent humidity are desirable. Usually offered in nonperforated and perforated versions, the perforated variety will provide acoustical control, a common concern in indoor pool areas.

If the room will house a gymnasium type of physical therapy, such as that in which a ball is thrown, durability becomes the main ceiling concern, although acoustics should also be addressed because of noise control. If the activity within the room is mainly a one-on-one type of therapy, then acoustics may be the primary concern.

Food Service/Food Preparation

Food service areas can range from formal dining rooms at assisted living facilities to fast-food cafeterias at a hospital. Each has its own design and ceiling requirements.

Formal dining areas require a combination of aesthetics and acoustics. A wide array of panels is available to meet this need, including some specifically designed with these types of settings in mind. An example is Armstrong's Classic Motifs line. These fine-textured, sculpted panels offer acoustical control, ornamental plaster-like designs, a variety of colors, the accessibility of lay-in panels, and significant installed cost savings compared to decorative plaster or tin-pan ceilings. Classic motif patterns range from Art Deco to Art Nouveau.

When it comes to cafeterias, one of the questions that needs to be asked is, "Does the hospital want to create a warm, comfortable space where people will sit and linger, or does it want to create a fast-food type of facility?" The answer will determine what type of ceiling to use. If the administration wants to move people through the facility quickly, perhaps a little "colder" ceiling should be used. If it's a place to sit and linger, then a "warmer" ceiling is the choice.

Food preparation areas have entirely different ceiling requirements; namely, scrubbability and dirt and germ resistance. Many municipal departments of health and sanitation require that ceilings in food preparation areas have a nonperforated, cleanable surface with a nonreveal edge. To meet these requirements, as well as the most stringent U.S. Department of Agriculture (USDA) sanitation codes, most designers use vinyl-covered gypsum board ceilings in these areas. If an acoustical ceiling is used, vinyl laminate or Mylar-faced panels are a good choice because they provide acoustical control in addition to cleanability and sanitation.

It's important to note that the areas over cafeteria serving lines and salad bars are considered food preparation areas and may require USDA-approved ceilings.

Laboratory/Pharmacy

The choice of ceilings for use in a laboratory can range from standard lay-in ceiling panels to very stringent "clean-room" ceilings depending on local codes. It's important that design professionals look into local codes to determine if clean-room conditions are required and, if so, to what level.

Clean rooms are defined by class. A Class 10 clean room will contain less than ten particles per cubic foot. (A particle is counted if it is larger than 0.5 microns.) A Class 10,000 clean room will contain less than 10,000 particles per cubic foot. The higher the class, the lower the level of cleanliness.

If an acoustical ceiling is used to meet clean-room requirements, the panels are usually vinyl faced (unperforated) or Mylar faced. Both are suitable for use in Class 100 clean-room applications when a closed cell gasket is applied between the grid and panel. In many cases, the grid used in clean rooms is made from aluminum and is either 1.5 or 2 inches wide. The wider grid is needed to accommodate any high-efficiency particulate air (HEPA) filters that are used in the room.

When choosing a ceiling for a pharmacy, also check local codes. Some codes may consider a pharmacy to be a laboratory and require clean-room conditions. Other codes may consider it simply a retail space and permit any type of ceiling.

Examination/Procedure Rooms

As in the case of laboratories, the choice of ceilings in examination and procedures rooms is often dictated by the level of cleanliness required either by local codes or by

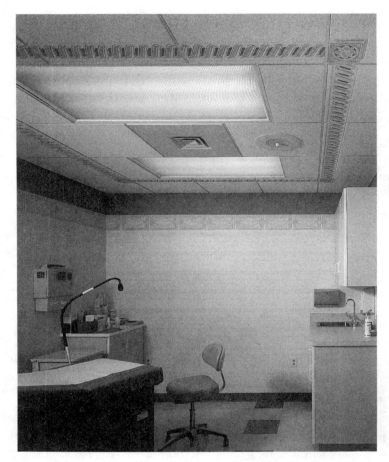

Figure 7.5 As evidenced here by the use of carved, field-painted panels, if the prime concern is acoustics in an examination or procedure room, the range of ceiling choices is wide. Photo: Armstrong World Industries, Inc., Lancaster, Pennsylvania.

the healthcare facility's administration. If clean-room conditions are required, the range of ceiling choices is narrow. If they are not required, you need to determine if clean-room features are still, in fact, the prime concern or if acoustics are more important. If the latter is the case, then the range of ceiling choices is wide (see Figure 7.5).

When dealing with procedure rooms, be aware that operating rooms are a special case. Most codes require that an epoxy-painted monolithic finish be used in these spaces. As a result, plaster or gypsum board is usually the preferred ceiling in operating rooms.

Geriatrics

When dealing with the elderly, it's important to be concerned with glare and hot spots. Try to eliminate hot spots by using as much ambient or up-lighting as possible.

This type of lighting requires more highly reflectant ceilings. As a result, choose ceilings with high light reflectance values. In fact, the higher the light reflectance value, the better.

Pediatrics

In children's areas, the ceiling is a great visual plane on which to create a distraction for patients as they lie in bed. One simple option is the use of mobiles. Another is the use of carved acoustical ceiling panels that incorporate a series of whimsical patterns. Themes, from Armstrong, features a collection of patterns ranging from falling leaves to railroad cars, all of which offer a warm and welcoming visual over the bed (see Figure 7.6). The panels can be field painted to incorporate color and accents.

One note of caution when working with pediatrics: make sure the range of patient ages is known. Most pediatric units are based on the procedures performed rather than on the actual age of the patient. As a result, some of the patients in pediatrics can be as

Figure 7.6 The Themes collection features a variety of carved ceiling panel patterns ranging from falling leaves to railroad cars, all of which provide a warm, welcoming visual over a bed. Photo: Armstrong World Industries, Inc., Lancaster, Pennsylvania.

old as 19 or 21. If a space is going to house older pediatric patients, don't choose juvenile images.

Consultation Rooms

Consultation rooms, along with grieving rooms, meditation rooms, chapels, and similar types of spaces, require a higher level of acoustical control than other spaces. That's because the purpose of these rooms is to provide privacy, and acoustics is therefore the prime concern. To achieve proper acoustic control, ceiling panels should have an NRC of 0.65 or higher.

Corridors

Acoustic performance is also important in corridors in order to maintain a quiet atmosphere in the patient area. In some facilities, corridor plenum heights may be at a minimum. If this is the case, there are downwardly accessible acoustical ceiling panels available that do not need special tools for removal. Armstrong's Cassettes ceilings, for example, have hidden edge details that allow the panels to move laterally for easy removal.

Office/Administrative Areas

Acoustics and aesthetics are both important in administrative areas, although cost will also play an important role. In general, the cost of a ceiling goes up as the aesthetics go up. Regardless of aesthetics, the NRC should be 0.55 or higher to obtain a proper level of acoustic performance.

Service Areas

Most healthcare facilities don't want to use much of their design budget on service areas. Consequently, economy is usually the key here. However, because of the nature of the space, ceilings in service areas are usually subject to frequent plenum access, and damage resistance should be another key factor.

Along these lines, it's important to determine maintenance needs not just in the service areas but throughout the facility. If it appears that the maintenance staff is going to be fairly hard on the ceilings, take durability into account as a key factor, along with acoustics, aesthetics, and cost. In these cases, recommend damage-resistant ceilings. They generally cost a little more than standard ceilings, but, in the long run, the added durability will more than offset the added cost.

CONCLUSION

The ceilings used in healthcare facilities are as diverse as the facilities themselves. Ceiling selection, however, is not necessarily a difficult process. Once the inherent needs of a particular space are known, and once both the technical (acoustics, sanitation, and so on) and aesthetic needs that must be met by the ceiling in that space are known, review the products offered by various manufacturers to determine the range of choices available.

In some cases, final ceiling selection will be easy. In others, design professionals may have to compromise needs somewhat to obtain the desired results. In all cases, however, they should be patient focused. If you think of yourself as a patient as you design, it's hard to go wrong. The right choices, from floor to ceiling, will not only calm patients but also comfort visitors and improve staff working conditions.

James Mathis is manager, architectural building products design, for Armstrong World Industries in Lancaster, Pennsylvania.

8

FURNITURE

Tama Duffy, ASID

In 1986 when I started on my first major project in healthcare, I was fortunate to be working with the Mayo Clinic in Rochester, Minnesota. The Mayo Clinic is an international facility known for quality care and also for the quality of its interior environments. I learned much from that project that I still use today in determining appropriate product applications. One of the first discussions I was involved in with the Mayo Clinic was about its waiting room chair.

First developed in 1954, the Mayo Chair was designed to accommodate a wide variety of patient sizes and medical conditions, to provide comfort for the long waiting periods, and to provide ease of maintenance. In 1968, the chair was modified with aesthetic upgrades and less expensive construction techniques, and the leg finials (initially a part of the chair leg to protect them from the floor buffers) were removed.

When I became involved with the project, discussions had already started between Robert Fontaine, director of environmental design at the Mayo Clinic, and Christopher Murray, a designer working for the furniture manufacturer, David Edward, Inc., on what was to become the 1988 version of the Mayo Chair. Alterations now appropriate for the 1988 version of the chair included modifying the wood species from an oiled walnut wood to a hardwood easier to maintain and finding new construction techniques that could reduce the chair costs. Design considerations too important to eliminate were the very same considerations established in 1954: open back and sides for cleaning, eight-way hand-tied springs in the seat cushion for comfort and aesthetics, wider seat depth and width for added comfort, and sloped seats and arms to accommodate the wide range of body types, ailments, and the elderly (see Figure 8.1).

The Mayo Chairs designed in 1954 are still in use today at the Mayo Clinic. In considering furniture appropriate for healthcare, it appears that the basic needs and requirements for furniture have not changed. There is still a need for furniture that is maintainable, comfortable, and affordable. Throughout this chapter, I will discuss several of the products available and appropriate for use in healthcare facilities.

122

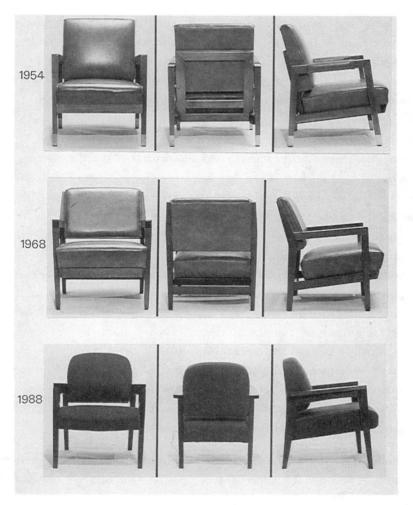

Figure 8.1 The Mayo Chair, which has had two redesigns since 1954, was designed to accommodate a wide variety of patient sizes and medical conditions, provide comfort, and allow for easy maintenance. Photo: Mayo Foundation, Rochester, Minnesota.

SEATING

The majority of furniture required for the healthcare environment is for seating, and the one criteria that all manufacturers and end users agree upon is the need for durability. In discussions with numerous seating designers and manufacturers that produce products specifically for healthcare, I've found that many of their design requirements are similar. Everyone has chosen a slightly different approach on how to accomplish these requirements, but the universal list of requirements seems to always contain the following ten items.

1. *Replaceable components.* Provides end users with the ability to replace or repair furniture right at their facility; eliminates the need to provide loaner furniture while waiting for repairs and prolongs the life of the chair.
2. *Recoverable seats.* Allows soiled or damaged upholstery to be replaced in a matter of moments, eliminating seats being unavailable for use.
3. *Slightly higher seat heights.* Provides a more upright seat while still keeping users' feet on the ground.
4. *Slightly firmer seat.* Creates stability and allows users to exit the chair more easily.
5. *Shortened seat depths.* Because of the chair's higher and firmer seat, a shorter seat depth is created, providing a comfortable yet firm seating surface. This prevents sinking into a seat that would be difficult to exit.
6. *An open area under the front part of the seat.* Provides a space where users can firmly plant their feet when standing.
7. *Arms with grips that extend beyond the front of the chair seat.* Provide support and can be pulled or grasped to lift oneself out of the seat.
8. *Cushions covered with an antimicrobial moisture barrier or built with a closed cell foam.* Prevents liquids from penetrating the cushion and allows for the covering to be replaced while keeping the cushions intact.
9. *Seat cushions built with a combination of springs and/or dense foam.* Provides a long-lasting, comfortable seat built for heavy-duty use.
10. *Open spaces between the seat and the back.* For maintenance and cleanability, allows crumbs and dirt to be easily cleaned from the chair.

The following five manufacturers have seating products that meet these requirements and have additional products appropriate for the healthcare environment.

Kusch + Co.

A 55-year-old company, Kusch + Co. is a leading supplier of healthcare furniture in Germany and, since the 1970s, has been supplying a large quantity of products for North America. Sixty percent of its products are used in social/cultural facilities, the other 40 percent in corporate facilities. First producing wood chairs in the late 1930s, Kusch + Co. started engineering steel furniture in the late 1960s. Knowing that the social facilities in Germany expect to use the chairs that they purchase for anywhere between 15 and 25 years, Kusch is well aware of the need for durable and dependable furniture. "Less than one percent of our products need maintenance," states Winfried Hornig, Kusch's export manager. The company's wood chairs are produced using triple doweling, compressed double tenon, and different densities of foam for the seat

Figure 8.2 Cleanly designed, Kusch + co.'s products appeal to patients, staff, and visitors. Photo: Kusch + co, Huntington Station, N.Y.

cushion. To increase its products' durability, Kusch's wood is finished with a flame-retardant, water-soluble lacquer.

Hornig explains that the products produced by Kusch + Co. are created for three groups of people: patients, staff, and visitors. Its product line ranges from lounge chairs and high-back, fully upholstered patient chairs with ottomans to small and playful wood stacking chairs. The products of Kusch are cleanly designed and appeal to a great number of end users and designers (see Figure 8.2).

The company also produces a table line compatible with its lounge and patient chairs. The coffee, lounge, and end tables are available in a variety of sizes and heights. The wood finish used throughout its product line is resistant to alcohol and water.

The company starts its involvement with its products at the onset of production. The company dries its own lumber and even produces its own chrome plating and powder coating finishes. Its diverse product lines have many options available—arms, armless, high back, polypropylene shoes for the legs, different foam densities, and veneers of ash, oak, or beech.

The wood primarily used in Kusch's products is beech. This wood is readily available in Germany; it is hard, cuts precisely, does not split easily, is durable, and has a very light consistent color throughout. The light color of the beech wood has been a successful design element in producing Kusch's chairs. Kusch's lighter colors and furniture with slightly eased corners perform well and are readily accepted in healthcare environments. The company believes that good-quality products require good money to purchase, so it does not cut corners on details and construction.

Health Design

Health Design is a division of Brayton International, a Steelcase Design Partnership Company. When discussing Health Design's entry into healthcare, Michael Shields, vice president of product design and development, explains that a large university medical center came to Brayton executives about four years ago and asked them to manufacture specialized seating for healthcare. Because of this, Brayton created Health Design and entered into the healthcare market, introducing various seating lines in June 1992. Focusing its efforts on lounge/waiting area seating, its new products provided specifiers with a multitude of new design options. Known for its clean lines and quality office seating, Brayton's healthcare product line introduction was of the same quality and design image. Health Design strives to blend design with functional requirements.

Since the introduction of its products, Health Design has continued to create new designs and recently introduced another new seating line in 1995, this time focusing on seating for patient rooms. Collaborating with the design firm of Fahnstrom & McCoy, Health Design created a design brief for a high-performance patient chair that could be easily serviced and is built from components. The Progeny series (see Figure 8.3) meets this design criteria and is created from a welded steel frame chassis onto which a variety of components can be added. If components are damaged, replacement or reupholstering is quite simple.

Shields noted that no specific structural standards existed for healthcare seating. So Health Design, along with other manufacturers, has agreed to manufacture its products 20 percent over Business and Institutional Furniture Manufacturers Association (BIFMA) industry standards. BIFMA set the standards that exist for product safety and durability standards and prescribes exact application, equipment, and performance standards for every test in each product category. This ensures that each manufacturer's testing for compliance with BIFMA standards applies the same basis for evaluation.

Three chair styles are available in Progeny—contemporary, transitional, and traditional. Health Design uses maple as the hard wood accent for its Progeny line and the corresponding lounge tables. It feels that the open-pore oak, used by most other furniture manufacturers, is not as suitable for healthcare as the closed-pore maple.

The steel chassis is available in two sizes for patient room uses. Added to the chassis are a variety of elements that not only can change the look of the chair, but

Figure 8.3 The Progency series high-performance patient chair features a number of replaceable components. Photo: Health Design, a division of Brayton International, a Steelcase Design Partnership company, High Point, North Carolina.

have motion device options, such as rocking or gliding. This chair series was designed to allow facilities to create a continuous aesthetic for patient rooms and into all other spaces in the medical facility.

The Children's Furniture Company

The Children's Furniture Company's mission is to create children's furniture that enriches and enlivens the lives of children. Its product line is applicable for kids ranging from 2 to 11 years in age. All of its products have nontoxic finishes, and the company's aniline-dyed colors are not a stain or a paint, so the wood grain is visible through the color.

The company's philosophy is to give children choices and allow them to use their own imagination. Its products are created to attract and stimulate while at the same time to calm and soothe children. A furniture piece especially suited for healthcare waiting areas is the Magnetic Sand Table (see Figure 8.4). This play table, designed by Harry Loucks, design director at the Arkansas Children's Hospital, has a vacu-formed plastic tray that contains the glass bead "sand." This tray is sealed, preventing any spills. Individual or multiple children can sit at this table and move the cars around in the sand. The cars have magnets and are moved by the magnet hand pieces that the

Figure 8.4   The Magnetic Sand Table is a maintenance-free "toy" designed for children's waiting areas that requires nothing to be put away. Photo: The Children's Furniture Company, Baltimore.

children manipulate from under the table. It is virtually a maintenance-free "toy" designed specifically for waiting children, requiring nothing to be put away.

Children's Furniture Company's collection of chairs and tables are fun and inspiring. The leaf chairs, as described by company president Christopher Murray, are "more than something to sit on. The chairs were designed with botanically correct leaf shapes that teach about the environment as well as encourage the imagination of both children and adults alike."

ADD Specialized Seating Technology

The design of the chairs from ADD take a totally new approach to seating structure. Encouraged by his think-tank California surroundings of the 1970s, Roger Leib, president, built furniture as a hobby early in his career. His first concept of seating, combining aluminum, Plexiglas, and foam, earned him a double-page spread in *Industrial Design* magazine. Continuing to develop new structures and forms, his first

Figure 8.5 The Warren Chair's innovative structure and rocking motion became an immediate hit with patients and hospital staff. Photo: ADD Specialized Seating Technology, Los Angeles.

big opportunity came from the American Hospital Supply. Shortly thereafter, in working with Cedars-Sinai Medical Center, Los Angeles, the Warren chair was developed.

The Warren chair (see Figure 8.5), introduced in the early 1980s, received many design awards and captured national attention. With the attention came ADD's growth. This growth went hand in hand with the chair's development, and its innovative structure and soothing rocking motion became an immediate hit with patients and hospital staff alike.

In addition to structural innovation, Leib explains that ADD's goal in its patient room chair design is to "get patients out of bed sooner and keep them out of bed longer. This is because patients who are up and out of bed tend to heal faster. Bedridden patients typically cost more to care for and are more demanding than patients who are out of bed and in a chair." Since the bedridden patient is static, codes require hospital staff to rotate the patient every two hours, which takes time and money. By moving the patient to a chair with dynamic capabilities, healing is actually accelerated by the body being upright and moving.

The moving sensation that occurs while seated in the Warren chair (and other

ADD patient chairs) mobilizes upper respiratory fluids and helps the healing process. Facility end users and family members have commented that Alzheimer's, upper-thoracic surgery, and maternity patients are particularly comforted by this movement. The patented front-cantilevered construction of the ADD chairs keeps the front part of the chair static so as not to create under-thigh pressure when the chair rocks backward. The rocking movement is created from the structure and shape of the seat and the support. (In typical rockers, the rocking movement compromises circulation to the legs, which, in turn, can cause a patient to fall when exiting.) The chair is also designed not to create any crevices that might crush fingers or pinch legs.

The seat support is created through the use of a cleanable, durable, and breathable woven vinyl fabric. This support seat cycles the body weight through the rocking motion and reduces the seated load per square inch by not allowing the user's weight to remain concentrated in one area.

Patient, visitor, and companion chairs are available in a variety of heights and sizes, allowing facilities and designers to specify chairs most appropriate for patient types (i.e., elderly women in long-term care facilities would be more comfortable in the Petite Warren). The chairs are also available with base varieties—metal and wood.

Leib currently has received 22 patents, most of them "utility" as opposed to simple design patents. His most recent is a utility patent for a unique structural system employed on ADD's new beam seating. This structure allows long spans of chairs to literally float, reducing the number of support legs and allowing ease of floor maintenance. Continually intrigued by engineering, structure, and innovation, ADD Specialized Seating Technology's commitment to healthcare furniture is to create "products that support the therapeutic process."

Nemschoff Chairs

Leonard Nemschoff, chairman of the board for Nemschoff, is no newcomer to the healthcare industry—the company's first healthcare project was completed in 1957. The first product developed for healthcare by Nemschoff was a geriatric chair. At that time, Leonard states, "The word 'geriatric' was an unknown." But, due to a research project in Peoria, Illinois, Leonard started producing geriatric chairs. In addition to patient comfort, his first concern was the need for a durable wood finish. At that time, spilled medicine was one of the biggest problems in healthcare facilities. So Nemschoff developed a finish lacquer that withstood not only medicine spills, but rigorous cleaning with bleach. Today Nemschoff, continually researching new products, is testing various water-soluble finishes. These water-soluble finishes produce no toxic vapors during the manufacturing process.

Nemschoff, a manufacturer of furniture specifically designed for healthcare, has numerous appropriate products. In this section, I will focus on its specialty chairs. These chairs are often selected by healthcare providers. In fact, the company's Sleep-Over chair won a Nightingale Award at the 1994 Seventh Symposium on Healthcare Design, receiving recognition for excellence in innovation and design. Nemschoff chairs are designed for specific end users, and a tremendous amount of research and product testing takes place before solutions are determined.

The SleepOver chair was designed to be two things—a patient chair and a sleeper chair. "One of the goals for this chair was for the sleeping surface to be flat enough to allow you to sleep on your stomach," states Mark Nemschoff, president/CEO. The chair has a 72-inch sleeping surface that is produced by pulling the seat cushion forward and pushing a button that allows the back to lie flat. The surface is not only flat, it is also comfortable and designed within a chair footprint of only 32 inches wide 31.5 inches deep.

The dialysis chair has an upright position and two reclining positions and also can be easily adjusted to infinite positions all the way to the Trendelenburg for medical emergencies. (The Trendelenburg position is one that lowers the level of the shoulders to below the level of the knees.) Due to the need for dialysis patients to occasionally receive CPR (which would be performed in the Trendelenburg position), this chair has a support bracket attached to the back of the chair that gives the chair stability and eliminates the risk of the chair, and thus the patient, from tipping over backwards.

Nemschoff's line of Prísto treatment chairs has the same seating positions as the dialysis chair. In addition, the company also offers several attachment devices that allow staff to hang side tables, IV support, tray tables, drainage bags, and blood-drawing tables from the treatment chairs. The treatment chairs can be used in multiple areas within a medical facility: preadmission testing, blood drawing, blood transfusions, chemotherapy, preoperative testing, and postoperative recovery. And, with the recent shift from inpatient to outpatient care, treatment chairs are taking the place, in many cases, of stretchers.

Nemschoff has also developed a children's treatment chair, Kids Kare (see color plate 4). Kids Kare has the same quality and durability as the adult treatment chair, but it is scaled smaller for children. Kids Kare is 21.25 inches wide by 35 inches deep and is designed for children between 5 and 12 years of age. The push bar on the back of the chair allows for infinite positioning. The footrest elevates automatically as the chair reclines and also slides forward and backward to support children's feet. The chair was created in cooperation with Texas Children's Hospital and was developed to increase the child's sense of security and well-being.

Nemschoff offers a lifetime warranty. The company warrants all of its products against defects of material and workmanship under normal use and service for the life of the product. Nemschoff also has a unique system called the Nemschoff Engineering and Manufacturing Archive Specification, or NEMAS. This system allows users the ability to replace any part that is current or has been discontinued from the standard line, because the engineering and manufacturing of all product parts have been archived.

CASE GOODS AND NURSE STATIONS

In addition to seating, healthcare facilities also have a need for case-good storage spaces, most typically bedside cabinets and wardrobes. Nurse stations require very flexible and reconfigurable components. Similar to seating, these furniture pieces also need to be cleanable and durable. When selecting furnishings to meet these needs, it is extremely important to understand the client/user requirements in order to choose appropriate products. The following three manufacturers produce durable products.

Milcare Inc., a Herman Miller Company

First started in 1971 as Health/Science, a Division of Herman Miller, Milcare was the first manufacturer to introduce new concepts in hospital materials and logistic management. Basically addressing "everything on wheels," it quickly had to resolve issues of durability and maintainability. The company's Co/Struc product line, a system of carts and storage units, allows facilities to move supplies from storage and restocking areas directly to the end users through the use of mobile storage units filled with interchangeable shelves and drawers (see Figure 8.6). All of the Co/Struc components are cleanable and made of durable injection molded thermoplastic. Co/Struc, due to its interchangeable parts, is also used in pharmaceutical and laboratory areas. With the addition of gravity-fed drawers for pharmacy picking stations, black resin tops for lab counters, and floor-supported modules to keep microscopes stable, Milcare continues to develop new state-of-the-art products for all of these areas.

Combining Milcare's knowledge of materials management and healthcare environments, its nurse station addresses many important concerns of nursing practitioners. Rated as the number one nurse station in the Nurse Station of the Future Symposium (a survey of facility users compiled by Perkins & Will in 1994), Milcare's nurse station clearly met the facility user needs for flexibility and efficiency (see Figure 8.7). Although the planning, design, and location of nurse stations is currently changing, there will always be some type of work area near patient rooms that will require access to technology and products to organize patient information, which Milcare's components can fulfill.

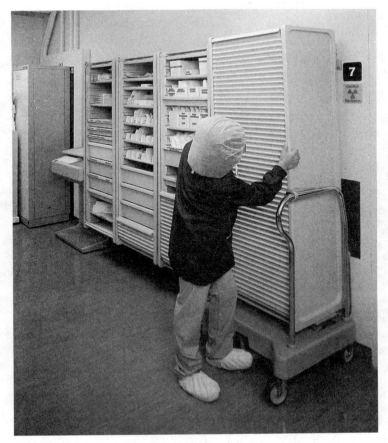

Figure 8.6 Co/Struc is a system of carts and storage units that allows staff to move supplies from storage and restocking areas directly to patients through the use of mobile storage units filled with interchangeable shelves and drawers. Photo: Milcare Inc., A Herman Miller Company, Zeeland, Michigan.

A few of the Milcare nurse station components of particular interest are

- "Dura-tiles" (painted metal tiles created to provide durability and cleanability)
- Heavy-duty, reinforced work surfaces designed with special under-counter structure to support up to 400 pounds of equipment
- Monitor shelves angled to provide users ergonomic comfort
- Floor gaskets at the base of panels to seal the panel to the floor and eliminate the accumulation of dust and dirt under the panels
- Hospital-grade, hard-wired electrical base conduit with special grip connections due to the sensitivity and importance of keeping all monitors connected when the workstation is bumped by passing carts
- A variety of drawer pulls designed to accommodate personnel with arthritis and limited grasping abilities

Figure 8.7 Facility users rated Milcare's nurse station number one for its flexibility and efficiency. Photo: Milcare Inc., A Herman Miller Company, Zeeland, Michigan.

Through research, Milcare found that many design professionals wanted some of their nurse stations to have a custom look. To support this request, Milcare developed a method to install its product behind a custom millwork facade. This flexibility allows designers to create an image appropriate and unique for each medical facility and at the same time utilize Milcare's componentry behind the facade. In discussing new products, Peggy Leven, product/market manager for Milcare Inc., explains that its research is very customer driven. Milcare solicits input from focus groups, spends a lot of time in the field, and researches trends in the healthcare marketplace. This information helps Milcare determine what new products to pursue.

Milcare has helped many facilities create "virtual operating rooms." Milcare's mobile case carts are packed in central sterile areas with the tools and supplies needed for each surgeon. As a surgeon schedules surgery, these case carts are moved up to the scheduled operating room on Milcare's transport carts. The case carts are moved from the transport carts onto a mobile track mounted on the wall outside the sterile operating corridor. The case carts, packed with the supplies and hanging on this mobile wall track, are then pushed along the wall into the sterile area. The transport carts are returned to central supply and do not enter the sterile areas; thus dirt collected on the transport cart wheels is not carried into the sterile areas. Through this system of moving supplies, operating rooms can be utilized by many surgeons for many different procedures. The system is just another example of how Milcare creates greater flexibility for facility users and designers.

Nemschoff Chairs

Nemschoff starts its case good manufacturing by drying its own lumber to a 7-percent core moisture content. Due to the extreme abuse its products receive, Nemschoff feels that consistently dry wood is crucial in the making of its case goods. Its products, including wardrobes, dressers, and bedside tables, are all manufactured using dry construction techniques.

The base construction of the company's case goods are solid oak, oak veneer on a plywood core, or veneers/laminate over a 45-pound particleboard. These various solids allow for Nemschoff to produce products within different client budgets, while still maintaining a high level of quality. The products are available with edge options of solid oak, post-formed plastic laminate, or heavy polyvinyl chloride (HPVC).

Nemschoff's solid wood drawers are created using a five-sided dovetail construction with metal runners. Nemschoff can supply these extremely durable wood drawers with a solid plastic drawer liner as a moisture barrier. Vinyl-clad drawers are also available. The vinyl material is applied over a medium-density fiberboard core and is sometimes preferred by end users because of its cleanability.

David Goodlund, vice president of commercial sales, explains Nemschoff's plastic drawer option and why the company offers it. "Many facilities request a wood exterior due to image concerns, but want to purchase a plastic drawer because of cost constraints. The plastic drawer withstands 90 pounds of pressure and is cleanable. This drawer reduces the overall cost of the item, while still providing the facility with a very durable product." These drawers can be installed with a tamperproof drawer runner that does not allow the drawers to be removed. Nemschoff supplies many psychiatric facilities with this model due to their additional safety requirements. Should the plastic drawers ever break, replaceable drawers may be purchased at a small price and replaced in the field.

The bedside cabinets are always manufactured with a vent in the back of the cabinet, creating a moisture-free unit (see Figure 8.8). Additional options for the bedside cabinets include tops manufactured with a solid material such as Du Pont Corian, poured urethane edges, and the drawers or doors furnished with soft plastic pulls. All of these options allow a facility end user or designer the ability to design products to meet the facilities' own specific needs.

Figure 8.8 Nemschoff's bedside cabinets have many design options, for example, a vent in the back to eliminate moisture. Photo: Nemschoff Chairs, Sheboygan, Wisconsin.

Steelcase Inc.

Steelcase Inc. is focused on "the business of furniture within the healthcare facility," states Lois McCardell, product manager for Steelcase Inc. Steelcase has focused on the work environment for decades, and it has taken this knowledge into the healthcare marketplace. Applying its knowledge of how people work, Steelcase's InterAct Modular Systems provide work areas applicable to healthcare environments.

InterAct is a freestanding system based on core units, not panels, that allows accessories and dividers to sit on top of the unit. To protect people and objects from sharp dangerous corners, InterAct was designed with curved angles and rounded shapes. The front facade of the InterAct units provide vertical light elements encased in an impact-resistant plastic column cover. These vertical lights provide night lighting and give a certain aesthetic image (see color plate 5). The freestanding modules facilitate areas for stand-up charting, interaction with visitors, observation of patient monitors, and work on computers, as well as providing easy access to charts and vertical surfaces to post schedules—all the tasks of medical and support staff.

The design of the nurse station units meet the ADA code requirements for work-surface accessibility, are easy to assemble, are constructed with limited seams, and have desk-height electrical receptacles that are fed from power brought into the units at the base.

Steelcase Inc. currently has added several new components due to user requests: Du Pont Corian work surfaces, charting systems that mount to the top of workstations, monitor supports with a movable shelf, and horizontal paper storage trays. Its storage trays and shelves have wonderful colorful labels that clip onto the units, making labeling a breeze.

Steelcase Inc. will be supplementing its InterAct product line shortly with bumper guards that attach to base units and electrical enhancements. The company plans to specifically teach end users how to use its products. User information is the cornerstone of Steelcase's product development.

CALIFORNIA TECHNICAL BULLETIN 133

One additional furniture element to be aware of is the California Technical Bulletin 133. The CAL 133 is widely recognized for establishing the standards for fire safety in furnishings. This bulletin requires furnishing assemblies to pass fire tests and is now required by many states other than California. By containing the spread of fire, the compliant furnishings are potentially lifesaving devices, especially in healthcare facilities where many people will require extra time to exit a facility in an emergency. When selecting furnishings for healthcare environments, it is important to get the CAL 133 testing results from the manufacturers. Keep in mind that this test requires that the complete, finished product be tested together. So, even though fabric manufacturers might state that they pass CAL 133, the fabric still needs to be tested on the actual product on which it will be upholstered before it can actually pass the requirements for CAL 133.

CONCLUSION

Hopefully, this chapter has removed some of the mystery behind healthcare furniture and the products made specifically for this industry. It must be noted that this review has just brushed the surface of the many manufacturers providing furniture for healthcare applications. Other manufacturers to contact for information include G2 Healthcare Furniture, Haworth Inc., Hill-Rom, Kimball Healthcare Co., Krug Furniture Inc., LA-Z-Boy, L-U-I Corporation, Midmark Corp., Sauder Manufacturing Company, SMED International Tuohy, Wieland Furniture, and Wilkahn, Inc.

There are many reasons why these product selections require special attention: Healthcare facilities are open 24 hours a day with multiple end users. Most have maintenance standards that at times require products to endure cleaning solutions of 100-percent bleach. Many environments are completely sterile. Products used in healthcare facilities are under the constant abuse of being crashed into by carts and equipment.

Thomas DeBoer, healthcare specialist for Haworth Inc., indicates that over $800 million is spent each year on furnishings for healthcare facilities. Given this large amount of spending, additional research and new technologies will probably continue to be directed toward new products. As competent professionals, designers should continue to ask manufacturers and users a lot of questions on how they will use the furniture, to evaluate the furniture at test sites, and to look for new and innovative ways to solve the needs of the healthcare client—the patient.

Tama Duffy is a principal with Perkins & Will in New York, New York.

EDITOR'S NOTE: *See Appendix A for the names and addresses of the furniture manufacturers mentioned in this section.*

9

CARPET

Richard Radke

When interior designer Kathy Burton, ASID, of The Bower Partnership in Rockville, Maryland, specified carpet for a 32,000-square-foot, three-story addition to the Shady Grove Adventist Hospital in Rockville, she was looking for a floorcovering product that would convey "a very comfortable, nonclinical and home-like environment" while being able to withstand the "wear and tear of hospital traffic."

Burton specified several styles from The Harmony Group, a collection of woven-interlock, solution-dyed, nylon products from Mohawk Commercial Carpet for the hospital's Education Conference Center, Admitting Department, and Maternal Child Health Unit (see Figure 9.1). The carpet, in combination with light-colored residential-style wallpaper, oak furnishings, soft lighting, and valance drapery, led several labor and delivery patients to remark that the noninstitutional setting was "nicer than the rooms at home!"

Clearly, Burton was successful in her attempt to humanize a clinical environment and evoke a healing ambiance for patients while meeting the budgetary, performance, and maintenance needs mandated by the facility staff and administration.

One of carpet's many advantages is its ability to soften interiors and contribute to the healing environment in tangible ways. A carpeted interior provides visual comfort, reduces noise, and gives both actual and visual warmth to the environment. These factors are prime motivations for specifying carpet, but they aren't the only reasons. In this chapter, I will cover various aspects and advantages of the role of carpet in healthcare settings. A brief overview of the market will be presented. I will also look at the benefits of carpet from the perspective of the patient or visitor and those qualities that facility administrators favor. I will also discuss the performance attributes of carpet, providing details on antimicrobials, carpet construction, life-cycle costing, dyeing methods, and other factors that must be considered for a carpet product to perform successfully. I will give tips on smooth installations and, finally, discuss maintenance and its critical role in keeping carpet clean and great looking.

Figure 9.1   Several Zeftron (by BASF) ZX solution-dyed, nylon, woven-interlock products from Mohawk Commercial Carpet's Harmony group provided the aesthetic and performance features needed for this healthcare setting. Project: Shady Grove Adventist Hospital, Rockville, MD. Interior design: Bower Partnership. Photography: Anne Gummerson Photography, Baltimore.

OVERVIEW

According to economist Clifford Neely, editor of the *October Consultants,* the healthcare sector accounted for about 10 percent of the 340 million square yards of commercial carpet sold in North America in 1995. That means that about 31 million square yards of commercial carpet were specified for hospitals, nursing homes, mental treatment facilities, and drug and alcohol rehabilitation settings. Of this figure, replacement carpet demand accounted for slightly over 27 million square yards, with about 4 million square yards installed in new construction.

A survey of over 50 healthcare facility managers conducted by *Floor Focus* magazine showed several preferences for floorcovering products specified for different areas within a hospital (see Table 9.1). Nylon carpet is the workhorse in this market, comprising the majority of installed product. Although polypropylene and wool are also considerations, only nylon possesses the resilience and performance attributes to

TABLE 9.1 FLOORCOVERING PRODUCT PREFERENCES IN HOSPITALS

Hospital Area	Carpet (%)	VCT (%)	Sheet (%)	Other (%)
Lobbies/waiting rooms	75	10	0	Carpet tile—5 Terrazzo—5 Slate—5
Hallways	66	24	0	Carpet tile—5 Terrazzo—5
Operating rooms	0	14	52	Rubber—29 Terrazzo—5
Patient rooms	24	24	38	Carpet tile—9 Terrazzo—5
Doctors' offices/nurses stations	66	10	10	Carpet tile—10 Terrazzo—4
Emergency room	0	23	58	Rubber—15 Terrazzo—4
Childrens' areas[a]	28	24	26	Carpet tile—4 Terrazzo—4
Elderly care*	53	23	4	Carpet tile—4 Terrazzo—p4

[a] 12 percent had no separate pediatric or elderly care units.
Source: Williamson-Powers, Co., (1994).

stand up to consistent buffeting from foot and rolling traffic as well as the onslaught of harsh cleansers necessary to maintain a sterile environment. For healthcare, "the only acceptable yarn system is advanced generation continuous filament nylon," stresses Anthony King, Axcess Marketing Group President (King 1994).

Designers generally specify densely tufted level-loop, textured-loop, or cut-loop styles for durability and because they ease rolling traffic from carts, wheelchairs, and gurneys. Colors like blue, green, and rose have been named as favorites that provide a psychological lift and mask stains or soil (Williamson-Powers 1994). Yellow and gold-bronze shades are also emerging trends in office and common areas of hospitals and healthcare settings (Wise 1994).

PATIENT'S PERSPECTIVE

Many benefits afforded by carpet positively affect the attitude and comfort of patients and visitors to hospitals, long-term care facilities, ambulatory centers, and rehabilitation centers. These benefits are discussed in the following sections.

Aesthetics

As the anecdote opening this chapter illustrates, no other floorcovering offers a more homey atmosphere than carpet. With traditional hospital settings leaning toward a more residential feel and a growing number of life-care and rehabilitation centers emerging, carpet is a big factor in providing a transition from home to homelike healthcare, treatment, and extended living environments. Carpet's physical characteristics of a soft, yet sturdy, pile helps to evoke a more friendly, inviting feeling to a setting that traditionally provokes tension and apprehension. "It's important to provide a clean, noninstitutional, positive, and uplifting environment for patients, their families, and staff," designer Burton stresses.

"Carpet has a lot of properties that we need to change the environment," says Marcie Shrom, owner and president of Interiors Management Group, based in Wilmington, Delaware. "It's warm, and it feels better. But you must specify it with an eye toward performance."

In addition to physical comfort, design options with carpet are virtually endless. Whether you want to achieve a classy, patterned look for a hospital lobby, a cozy feel for a life-care facility, or a cheerful environment for a children's treatment center, carpet can help you meet your goals.

Color

One of the hallmarks of carpet is the color it brings to the environment. With the wide array of yarns available today, designers can choose from an almost endless selection of solids and heathers to produce a custom look for a hospital.

Care should be taken when selecting color. In addition to the styling considerations of the project, the hue of local soil or dirt, plus anticipated staining agents, should be considered. A healthcare facility located in an area surrounded by Georgia clay, for example, would benefit from a red-toned carpet that is patterned and hued to mask tracked-in dirt and mud.

Shrom notes that, when it comes to color, she selects carpet first. "I choose a carpet I can mix with a variety of textures to add interest," she says. "I prefer multicolors so I can change insets and select colors from the carpet to coordinate with furnishings, while keeping a sense of continuity throughout the facility. To maintain the color scheme and visual consistency, we will develop an average of three carpets to be used throughout. You don't have to have 95 carpets in a facility to have 95 colors to work with."

Standard lines offer color and style security for a facility that will have ongoing renovations or construction. For this reason, Shrom avoids custom colors. "I prefer standard colors that will remain in the line and can be used as the project develops over the years," she says.

Acoustics

Have you ever dropped a metal saucepan on a hard-surface floor? Most likely it made quite a racket as it clattered and clanged to the floor. It may even have dented or damaged the floor's hard surface. If you had a similar mishap on a carpeted floor, a low-decibel, cushioned thud was probably all that resulted.

No other material does double duty as a floorcovering and an acoustical aid. Carpet absorbs ten times more airborne noise than any other floorcovering and as much as other types of standard acoustical materials (Carpet and Rug Institute 1994). Transmission of sound in the immediate area is reduced, as is noise transmitted to floors below. This is an important consideration when rolling carts are employed as a matter of course in healthcare environments.

Better acoustics mean a quieter environment for patients on the mend and for hospital staff. Hospital administrators will also appreciate the fact that specifying carpet can reduce costs, since it eliminates the need for separate acoustical flooring treatments (Carpet and Rug Institute 1994).

Safety

Related to the acoustical benefit in carpet is the safety afforded by a soft-surface floorcovering. Remember the saucepan you dropped in the preceding scenario? Imagine, this time, that you've dropped a glass of juice or a ceramic cup of coffee. It's not likely that either of these vessels would survive a fall on a hard-surface floor. Drop a fragile object on a carpet, and chances are that it will escape unharmed, eliminating dangerous shards, slivers, and splinters that could injure a patient.

In addition, because carpet is absorbent, it captures spilled liquids or other slippery substances. Of course, it's important to clean spots and spills as soon as it is practical to avoid staining and possible microbe production in the fibers and the backing. In the meantime, however, there isn't as much of a chance that a person will slip and fall because of a liquid spilled on a carpeted surface as there would be with a spill on a hard-surface floor.

Carpet also helps create a safer and more secure environment for vision-compromised or Alzheimer's patients by reducing glare that results from light reflecting off hard-surface floors. Reflections on shiny floors may confuse these patients, predisposing them to tripping and falling. Carpet creates a smooth, nonreflectant surface that can be a boon to perceiving distance for the sight-impaired patient.

In addition, identifying an area or wing in a facility with a broad expanse of distinctively colored carpet may help patients navigate their way around their temporary home. The Alzheimer's Association found that patients recall colors better than numbers, so using carpet to color code rooms or other living areas can assist these patients in finding their way independently around their environment (Wise 1994).

By specifying carpet, design professionals can help save a healthcare facility from broken equipment, injured patients, and lawsuits accompanying injury liability.

Comfort and Warmth

The cushioning properties of carpet's pile, which make it acoustical and safe, also contribute to comfort underfoot. The dense pile, with or without a cushion underlayment, reduces fatigue for hospital staff who must be on their feet for long hours. This soft support also increases the appeal for carpet in children's play areas.

Carpet is also an efficient thermal insulator—the denser the pile, the greater the insulation. Table 9.2 shows the thermal resistance of some common materials. In a hospital environment, one in which patients may well be barefoot, the physical warmth afforded by carpet can change the experience of walking down corridors from cold to cozy.

TABLE 9.2   THERMAL RESISTANCE OF COMMON BUILDING MATERIALS

Building Material	R-Value $(Hr. - ft^2 - {}^oF/BTU)$ per inch
Copper	0.00037
Concrete	0.10
Plywood	1.25
Carpet	2.4
Fiberglass insulation	3.2

Source: CRI.

PLEASING THE PURCHASER

There are other advantages to carpet that the public may not perceive or care about, but end users do. The hospital administrator is concerned with "maintenance and long-term appearance in use," says King. "His hot buttons are cost containment and marketing perception" (King 1994). As in other aspects of the design, end users want to invest wisely and then make sure that the investment performs for a long time—six to ten years in the case of carpet. There are several elements that contribute positively to a project, which I will discuss in the following sections.

Performance

Performance should be the first consideration, even surpassing aesthetic criteria. Correctly specified and properly constructed carpet has the ability to enhance the environment and perform in a variety of ways that please staff and administration.

To ensure that the product performs properly, be sure it's appropriate to the area. Carpet is a versatile product, but the Carpet and Rug Institute (CRI) advises against carpet in areas subject to excessive or frequent spills, like emergency and operating rooms, trauma and recovery areas, or labs. Pamela Blyth, president of the American Society for Healthcare Environmental Services in Durham, North Carolina, likens working in a hospital to working in a small-scale city. "There are so many different areas in the hospital and they all have different needs and different characteristics. There's never going to be any one carpet, or one floor type or one anything. If you are going to talk color, talk in terms of med surgeon units or psych units. If you're going to talk about maintenance, talk in terms of the cafeteria versus the newborn nursery, because it's going to be very different," she says (Williamson-Powers 1994).

This is where technical choices about fiber type, dye method, construction, stain resistant properties, and sanitary considerations come in. Shrom cautions against giving too much attention to style and not enough to the technical aspects of the project. "It is certainly important to use style and design to help create a healing environment," she says. "But one of the mistakes designers make is to apply a generic healthcare spec to any healthcare project. You have to look at the specific needs of a space: Who will be using it? What will they be doing in the space? What materials and equipment will be in use? Those are the kinds of questions you need to ask yourself before you specify any aspect of the space, especially the carpet."

The traffic classification systems utilized by some fiber manufacturers will assist you in selecting a product that meets the traffic level you anticipate for your project. For instance, BASF Corporation's Performance Certification system classifies commercial carpets made from its branded Zeftron® nylon yarn into three categories.

- Class I: Moderate commercial traffic—approximately 500 daily foot traffics.
- Class II: Heavy commercial traffic—approximately 500–1,000 daily foot traffics.
- Class III: Extra-heavy commercial traffic—over approximately 1,000 daily foot traffics.

BASF Corporation's Performance Certification System rates the finished carpet in terms of appropriateness for traffic level. For instance, a carpet with a Class I rating that is intended for installation in an administrative area is not designed to perform well in a Class III entryway or lobby that is subjected to over 1,000 foot traffics a day. Use these kinds of guidelines to help select the proper product for the location.

Life Cycle/"Use Life" and Comparative Costs

Although price came in behind durability and appropriateness to area in the health-care facility manager survey, it is still a key consideration (Williamson-Powers 1994). And it's another area where carpet excels.

"Carpet is a most cost-effective surface," states Shrom. "You can contribute a great deal to the healing environment in terms of acoustics, and a wide range of colors with carpet. Depending on the needs of the space, you can specify a 28- to 30-ounce, level-loop, multicolored, heat-set, solution-dyed product for $18 to $21 a yard, providing a great value for the end user."

"Initially, vinyl composition tile appears to be very inexpensive to buy and install," Shrom continues. "However, generally six to seven coats of high gloss are required. In the case of a really penetrating stain, the layers need to be stripped back anyway, which is costly and time consuming."

To assess the comparative cost of floorcoverings over time, specifiers need to evaluate the variety of costs, including product price, installation, predicted life of product, maintenance, labor, and maintenance equipment repair and upkeep associated with different types of floorcoverings.

Carpet costs can be deceiving—a higher initial cost for the product can be offset by a lower financial outlay in terms of maintenance labor, time, and equipment. The CRI notes that "repair costs on vinyl cleaning equipment are higher than the repair costs of carpet maintenance equipment. The cleaning equipment associated with vinyl floor cleaning involves higher-speed moving parts and thus more equipment repairs."

Hiding, Resisting, and Removing Stains

Stain-hiding features of a particular carpet are another key consideration for facility managers. In fact, durability and stain-hiding features number first in importance among the facility managers (Williamson-Powers 1994).

Stain-hiding, resistance, and removal properties, as well as special stain-fighting technologies that may be engineered into the carpet or fiber, have a lot to do with fiber, color, and patterning choice. To begin with, it's important to evaluate what kind of stains may happen in a facility. What color are they? Where may they occur? When planning color or pattern, choose styling that will mask discolorations or stains with texture, hue, or pattern. To avoid compounding the problem with tracked-in soil, position walk-off mats in entrances and elevators.

One highly successful stain-removal system is Zeftron® 2000 nylon from BASF. The nylon fiber manufacturer guarantees that stains resulting from spills can be removed from commercial carpets made of Zeftron® 2000 solution-dyed nylon for a period of ten years from date of carpet purchase, or BASF will replace the carpet in the affected area. The guarantee also applies to stains that are removed using bleach-based solutions. A combination of leading-edge solution-dye technology, paired with a BASF-approved stain protector and fluorochemical finish, allows the manufacturer to offer this effective system.

Duracolor® MD (Lees Commercial Carpets) also offers a stain-removal system based on patented yarn-dyeing technology and engineered specifically for healthcare applications. Lees claims the carpet offers permanent resistance to 99 percent of common stains, most of which can be removed with water and a mild detergent. The product, which is tufted of DuPont Antron® Legacy, is also resistant to fading due to sunlight and bleach-based cleansers (see Figure 9.2).

Interface Flooring Systems (IFS) offers a stain and soil release system on its Performance Broadloom six-foot-wide commercial carpet products. It is based on Prokekt2® (IFS), a stain-blocking and soil-release enhancement process, along with DuraTech® (DuPont) soil and stain resist treatment. IFS says that most stains will clean up with water and cleaning solutions.

Recyclability and Solution-Dyeing

Today, environmental considerations are an important part of commercial carpet specifications. Many brands of commercial carpet for healthcare now offer a recycling option at the end of their useful life. Recycling carpet has several advantages for the

Figure 9.2 The carpet tile installation in the Arkansas Children's Hospital reception area in Little Rock features a Duracolor product constructed of DuPont Antron Legacy nylon from Lees Commercial Carpets. Photo: Lees Commercial Carpets, Greensboro, North Carolina.

environment and the facility because

- It diminishes the drain on natural resources by minimizing the amount of carpet waste in landfills.
- It reduces the need to extract raw materials for the manufacture of carpet and other plastic products from natural resources.
- It projects a positive image of the facility to the community.
- As legislation to reduce landfill waste evolves, it may become more cost effective for the end user to recycle carpet than to pay to have used carpet carted away to landfills.

There are several methods of recycling. The technique employed in the Partnership for Carpet Reclamation program, instituted by DuPont, depends on post consumer carpet being collected, consolidated, sorted, and shipped to DuPont, where the fiber component of the carpet is used in a number of products, such as asphalt and plastic reinforcement, carpet cushion components, or fuel for steam or electric generators in the manufacture of carpet.

Another type of recycling, called closed-loop recycling, is employed by BASF Corporation. In *6ix Again™ Recycling Program for Commercial Carpet* (named after the type of nylon BASF produces—nylon 6), BASF converts its Nylon 6ix™ fiber from used commercial carpet back into its original raw material, a polymer called caprolactam. From this caprolactam, first-quality Nylon 6ix fiber is extruded for commercial carpet, thus reducing the burden on natural resources. This cradle-to-cradle approach can produce new carpet fiber from old carpet. The process is continually renewable—like nature itself—so that, when carpets made from the recycled fibers reach the end of their useful lives, they too can be recycled into new carpet fiber again and again, without loss of quality.

Another area in which to exercise environmental conscience is in the selection of dyeing methods for healthcare carpets. Conventional dyeing methods, like piece, beck, and yarn dyeing, use significant quantities of water for processing.

Solution dyeing, on the other hand, is a method of dyeing carpet fiber as it is being produced. In the case of solution-dyed nylon for example, pigment is added to the molten polymer. The resulting fiber is dyed *in solution,* so the color is locked into the fiber as a permanent physical characteristic. This process is not as water intensive as conventional dyeing methods, plus it offers the added advantage of imparting a high degree of colorfastness to the fiber. In healthcare settings, where harsh chemicals, diluted bleach solutions, and sunlight are present, specifying a solution-dyed fiber for healthcare carpet is both a pro-environment and long-term performance choice. "I think all carpet should be solution dyed, since, at the very least, everybody spills coffee," Interiors Management Group's Shrom says.

Solution-dyed fibers employed in healthcare settings can be either nylon or polypropylene. Generally, nylon is selected for its outstanding wear characteristics and resilience.

CARPET CONSTRUCTION

Carpet construction directly relates to carpet performance. There are several factors to consider in this section: manufacturing methods, factors affecting performance, backing, and dyeing methods. The need for antimicrobials and moisture barriers will also be examined.

Manufacturing

Although there are several ways to manufacture carpet, the most common method in use today is tufting. Tufting machines are similar to sewing machines, except that the single needle is replaced by rows of several hundred needles that stitch rows of pile yarn tufts through a fabric called a primary backing. For healthcare applications, this backing is generally synthetic polypropylene (Wise 1994).

Along with traditional tufting and weaving machines, state-of-the-art tufting equipment helps provide enhanced aesthetic or soil-hiding effects. For instance, the Computerized Yarn Placement (CYP) loom from Tapistron International provides precise computer-controlled placement of colored yarns to achieve a woven effect. The Super-Velvaweave machine from Tuftco combines different pile heights—in cut or loop piles—to create texture and patterns. The Precision Cut-Uncut (PCU) equipment from Card-Monroe enables intricate patterns to be achieved. When deciding on patterns, however, it is important to choose a style that will not cause confusion to vision-impaired individuals.

Weaving is a method of manufacturing carpet that joins face and backing yarns simultaneously to produce a total product and results in a heavy, firm fabric with a high strength owing to the interweaving of the face and backing yarns. A latex backcoating is generally applied to add stability. Although a generally more costly process due to longer production time, weaving can also achieve beautiful and intricate patterning. A variety of weaving styles offers a choice of effects. For instance, a simple velvet loom can produce plushes, friezes, loop, multilevel-loop and cut-and-loop styles; the Wilton loom is a modified jacquard that creates intricate patterns; the Axminster loom can produce a wide range of patterns, mostly in cut-pile textures (CRI 1992).

Mohawk Commercial Carpet also offers a technique known as *woven interlock,* which combines knitting and weaving technology (see color plate 6). The resulting carpet features an "independent-loop" construction that is able to spring back from foot or rolling traffic with great resilience. Due to the nature of the interlocking structure, edge ravel or zippering cannot occur. In fact, all Mohawk woven interlock products are backed by a ten-year texture retention warranty and a lifetime guarantee against edge ravel and zippering.

Fusion bonding is a technique that implants yarns into an adhesive-backed coating. A cut-pile texture is then achieved by slicing two parallel sheets of face-to-face carpet down the middle of the pile. This method, expertly employed by IFS, is frequently used for tile.

These manufacturing methods produce a number of different piles. Loop piles have both ends of the yarn anchored in the backing. Level-loop piles can result in a smooth, sturdy surface for foot and rolling traffic, while multilevel loops offer interesting texture to the fabric.

Cut piles are produced when the tops of these loops are cut, leaving individual tufts. Cut-pile carpets are recommended for lower traffic areas such as administration and office areas. Saxonies and friezes are variations on cut piles—a twist is added to the yarn before the carpet is constructed, resulting in a textured surface. Cut-loop piles combine both loops and cut yarns for textural and sculpted effects.

Factors Affecting Performance

One of the key factors affecting performance in carpet is the density of the pile. This is because a higher-density carpet exposes less of the fiber's surface to soiling, at the same time preventing soil from penetrating into the carpet. In addition, tightly packed fibers prevent layover and traffic patterning. Generally, the more face yarn in the product, the better it will perform. Yet, the more fiber in a carpet's pile, the more expensive that carpet becomes. Therefore, to be cost effective, specify a low, dense pile for the best value and performance. The following formula will help you determine the density coefficient of a carpet.

$$\frac{36 \times \text{pile yarn weight (in ounces per square yard)}}{\text{Pile height (or pile thickness) in inches}}$$

For instance, the density coefficient of a loop-pile carpet of 28 ounces pile weight and a pile height of 0.156 inches would be figured this way:

$$\frac{36 \times 28}{0.156} = 6,461$$

Keep in mind that, as a bare minimum, Class III traffic conditions require a coefficient of 5,000 ounces per cubic yard, but a higher coefficient will provide better performance (CRI, *Floorcovering,* 1995).

In tufted carpet, the number of rows of tufts per inch (gauge) across the width of the carpet and the number of stitches per unit length of each tuft row also affect density. For instance, a ⅛-inch gauge carpet would have 8 tuft rows per inch, a ¹⁄₁₀-inch gauge carpet would have 10 tuft rows per inch, and so on. To determine gauge in a woven carpet, divide the pitch by 27 inches.

Yarn size, measured in a unit called *denier* for bulked continuous-filament yarns and in *cotton count* for staple fibers, also affects density. Denier is the weight in grams of 9,000 meters of yarn; a high number means a large denier or coarser the yarn. Cotton count is an inverse measure, which counts the number of 840-yard skeins of yarn in one pound. Therefore, the finer the yarn, the higher the cotton count (CRI 1992).

Fibers and Yarns

A wide range of fibers and yarns are used in commercial installations, but, for healthcare, nylon is the most commonly used fiber due to its resilience, abrasion resistance, wearability, and reasonable price.

There are two types of nylon, both petroleum based: *nylon 6,* made from a polymer called caprolactam, and *nylon 6,6,* made from hexamethylene diamine and adipic acid. There has been a great deal of controversy in the last few years, attempting to pit one type of nylon against the other and to identify one type as superior. Both types of nylon offer superior wear and performance characteristics, and, properly constructed into well-specified carpet, either is a good choice for healthcare installations.

Olefin, or polypropylene, can also be used, but only in areas that are not subject to high degrees of traffic, since this fiber lacks the wearability and resilience characteristics that nylon possess. Polypropylene is a solution-dyed fiber, so it is stain resistant and fade resistant. It also generates low levels of static electricity and is less costly than nylon.

Wool is a lush fiber, with natural fire-retardancy characteristics. However, its high cost tends to restrict its use to executive or accent areas (Wise 1994).

Yarns made from these fibers can be either bulk continuous filament (BCF) or staple yarns. Staple fibers contain short fibers that give a natural appearance, but may fuzz more readily than BCF. Therefore, BCF yarn is the fiber of choice for healthcare use (Wise 1994).

Dyeing Revisited

In the previous discussion of solution-dyed nylon, it was revealed that this predye method rendered the fiber nearly impervious to fading, or bleaching, and facilitated stain removal. These reasons help make solution-dyed nylon one of the best carpet fibers to use when the possibility of staining is imminent.

There are other methods of predyeing fibers that can provide beautiful aesthetics and acceptable performance, although they generally are not as colorfast as solution-dyed nylon. When selecting a dyeing method, carefully analyze the needs of the area, including propensity for spills and stains. These other methods include the following:

- *Stock dyeing.* In this method, the color is applied after the fiber is extruded, but before it is spun into yarn.
- *Yarn dyeing.* A conventional dyeing technique that applies color to finished yarn, this includes *skein dyeing* in which small packages of plied, heat-set yarn, called skeins, are dyed; and *space dyeing,* which is a method of applying different colors to a length of yarn, creating interesting accents when tufted into a finished piece of goods (CRI 1992).

Postdyeing methods apply color to the finished carpet. These processes do not have the colorfast properties of solution-dyed yarns or even specially engineered yarn-dyed products. These techniques are best used in areas where the chance of staining, soiling, and fading is very low. Postdyeing methods include the following:

- *Piece or continuous dyeing.* Color, generally solid, is applied from an aqueous dye bath to unfinished carpet. Interesting looks can result when multidye-level yarns are used. These yarns have a variable affinity to the dye bath, which can result in patterned and tone-on-tone looks.
- *Printing.* Color is applied, often in a pattern, after the carpet is tufted, and most often on cut-pile carpet (CRI 1992).

Besides color, density, and yarn size, yarn twist also can add bulk, texture, and improved performance to a carpet. Heat is used to set the "crimp" or the "twist" in carpet yarns, most often in cut pile products.

Mixing carpet dyed by several methods in one installation may contribute to cleaning confusion on the part of the maintenance staff. To avoid this problem, consider specifying the same dye method for all carpet throughout the facility, or specify a very detailed maintenance plan to address the cleaning needs of differently dyed carpeting.

Backing—Moisture and Microbes

In tufted products, a secondary backing—made of natural jute or woven polypropylene material and applied to the finished goods in addition to the primary backing—enhances the dimensional stability of the carpet. Synthetic rubber latexes are the most frequently used backcoating and laminating compounds; they help to secure the tufts in place, prevent fuzzing, and add dimensional stability. Unitary-backed tufted carpets have a chemical backcoating with no secondary backing and are best suited to glue-down installations. The finished weight of a tufted carpet includes all backing materials, latex, foams, and finishes, as well as the face yarns (CRI 1992).

Some carpet mills apply a moisture-resistant backing to carpets intended for healthcare applications. As part of its Performance Broadloom carpet system, IFS offers a thermoplastic barrier that, together with chemical seam welding, creates an impermeable shield against moisture. Lowe's Carpet Corporation's new vinyl-backed system of six-foot and modular carpets also uses a chemical weld to seal out moisture and discourage growth of mold, mildew, and bacteria.

Another method of insuring a sterile environment and fighting malicious microbes is to apply an antimicrobial agent to face fibers and backing. Gary Youngberg, vice president of marketing for Lowe's Carpet Corporation explains that carpet latex in backing and adhesives creates a nourishing environment for bacteria and fungi. The mill's Enviroguard system in the carpet face yarns, backing, and adhesive forms a one-two-three punch against microorganisms, bacteria, and fungi.

IFS has developed InterSept, a proprietary antimicrobial that inhibits the growth of a broad spectrum of gram-positive and gram-negative microorganisms. InterSept, which is a patented nonvolatile treatment incorporated into the molecular structure of the backing system on both carpet tiles and Performance Broadloom, works by damaging the cellular walls of bacteria and fungi so they are unable to reproduce. This destroys their ability to colonize and inhibits the development of microorganism-induced odor. Antimicrobial protection is also extended to the carpet's face yarns.

Duracolor MD (Lees) adds Bioguard, an antimicrobial designed to help foster a hygienic healthcare environment.

Conductive Carpet

Sixty-eight percent of facility managers that specified carpet in healthcare settings feel that it was important for the carpet to have antistatic properties for use around sensitive electronic equipment (Williamson-Powers 1994). Uncontrolled electrostatic discharge can reroute proper electronic impulses within a computer, resulting in "soft" failure such as incorrect data entry or a computer running haywire through its program. A sufficiently high discharge can cause hard failure, resulting in actual damage to expensive medical equipment.

Static electricity generation is affected by a number of variables, including relative humidity (dry air encourages greater static production), type of flooring material and base floors, composition of shoe soles, and even gender. (Women typically generate more consistent static electricity levels than men!)

Static tolerances must extend beyond simple antistatic treatment for personal comfort. Antistatic carpets prevent the generation of static above 3500 volts, making the environment less shocking for humans. Conductive carpets typically prevent generation of static above 2000 volts, which helps protect static-sensitive equipment.

The key to preventing electronic equipment from damage, however, is the ability of conductive carpet to dissipate static charges through the conductive fibers imbedded in the face yarn into a conductive backing. BASF Corporation offers a Conductive Carpet Limited Lifetime Warranty that ensures that the Zeftron nylon carpet, when installed and maintained according to BASF guidelines, will not generate static above 2,000 volts, when tested by industry procedure AATCC 134. In addition, the face of the carpet will have a minimum resistivity (resistance to the flow of electricity) of 1.5×10^5 ohms, and a maximum resistivity of 1.0×10^8 ohms, when evaluated in accordance with NFPA 56A test method. Plus, the static decay rate for a Zeftron nylon conductive carpet is two seconds or less, so stray electricity will be managed and dissipated before it can adversely affect electronics. Performance Broadloom by IFS also includes static-dissipating material as part of the fiber and backing.

A note of caution: beware of topically applied static-controlling agents. Besides being susceptible to rapid walk-off, some types can cause carpets to soil at an accelerated rate.

REGULATIONS AND REQUIREMENTS

Carpet specified for healthcare projects must pass a number of federal standards, particularly those pertaining to flammability. In addition, other federal regulations may impact your spec. The following sections will give you a sample of what to expect.

Flammability

In addition to building code and local fire code requirements, all carpets manufactured for sale in the United States are required to pass two distinct federal standards. The first—Federal Standard FF1-70, specified by the Consumer Product Safety Commission (CPSC)—measures the carpet's tendency to ignite from a source of flame dropped onto its surface. If the flame spreads more than three inches from point of ignition, or if more than one of eight samples does not pass the test, the specimen fails and cannot be legally manufactured for sale (CRI 1992).

The second federal standard is called the Flooring Radiant Panel Test, which applies only to carpets used in corridors and is a recommendation where automatic sprinkler protection is not provided. (Carpet applied in rooms is regulated by FF1-70.) The flooring radiant panel test measures the lowest intensity of radiant heat that causes a carpet to spread flame over its surface, otherwise known as *critical radiant flux*. A high level of critical radiant flux (roughly meaning that it takes more heat energy for a carpet to spread flame over its surface) of 0.45 watts per square centimeter is suggested within exits and corridors of health care facilities. The flooring radiant panel test has been adopted by the following codes and agencies:

- Basic Building Code of Building Officials and Code Administrators International, Inc. (BOCA)
- Standard Building Code of Southern Building Code Congress International, Inc. (SBCC)
- Life Safety Code of the National Fire Protection Association (NFPA)
- Uniform Fire Code of the International Conference of Building Officials (ICBO)

- American Society for Testing and Materials (ASTM) (test identified as ASTM E-648; for NFPA, test identified as NFPA-253)

Other fire-related regulations and tests include a smoke-generation test—the National Bureau of Standards Smoke Density Chamber, referenced under NFPA-258 and ASTM E-662—and a test for combustion toxicity. The ASTM test is intended for use in research and development and not as a basis for ratings for building code purposes (CRI 1992). Nevertheless, some agencies use this test data to evaluate carpet in relation to smoke generation.

In 1989, New York State mandated that carpet installed in commercial buildings must meet the requirements of that state's Uniform Fire Prevention and Building Code, Article 15, Part 1120—Combustion Toxicity and Regulations for Implementing Building Materials and Finishes Fire Gas Toxicity Data File. To comply with this regulation, products must be tested and registered concerning combustion toxicity, chemical content, and flooring radiant panel (CRI 1992).

Americans with Disabilities Act

In 1992, the ADA was instituted to ensure that individuals with disabilities have access to a wide range of locations and services. Compliance with ADA requires rendering ground and floor surfaces along accessible routes stable, firm, and slip resistant, with securely attached carpet. Other ADA recommendations for carpet regulate pile thickness and construction, treatment of exposed edges, and changes in level of over 1/4 inch (CRI, *Carpet Primer,* 1995).

General Services Administration (GSA)

When specifying carpet for government healthcare facilities, special requirements may be needed. The GSA and HUD, which also oversees the Federal Housing Administration (FHA), both publish carpet specifications and standards.

When working on government projects, reference the "Technical Requirements for Carpet, Carpet Tile and Carpet Cushion" (available from GSA), and UMD-44d, a bulletin that requires all carpet in the FHA market to pass a carpet certification program and be certified by a HUD-approved administrator (CRI, *Carpet Primer,* 1995).

INSTALLATION

Two criteria are key in installation—seaming techniques and ventilation during the installation. Timing for the installation is critical to minimize disturbance in healthcare settings, while providing adequate time for ventilation during and after installation.

Most healthcare installations of broadloom carpet will be via the direct glue-down method. This method is more suitable for rolling traffic and ramp areas, provides durable seams, reduces possibility of seam peaking, and is less expensive than stretch-in over cushion. Care should also be taken to locate seams in the lowest traffic areas and to provide proper transitions between surfaces, such as carpet and vinyl flooring. The direct glue-down method must be performed over a clean, dry, level subfloor. A stretch-in installation over cushion may be specified if the subfloor is uneven and in need of patching and if the area is not located on ramps or isn't subject to critical traffic stressors like rolling carts (Wise 1994).

Some mills offer specialized methods for rendering an installation seamless to reduce the opportunity for microbe accumulation in the backing or the subfloor. Carpet seams can be chemically or heat welded. Lowe's Carpet Corporation and IFS both offer broadloom systems that can be welded for seamless installation.

Thirty-two percent of facility managers prefer adhesive-free installation to combat odors generated by the adhesives (Williamson-Powers 1994). Some carpet mills, such as IFS, offer virtually adhesive-free installation systems. IFS offers "virtually glue-free" installation of its Performance Broadloom products since the high degree of dimensional stability in the backing reduces the need for a traditional amount of adhesive (see Figure 9.3). Other systems employ a dry adhesive applied to a scrim which is rolled onto the floor atop which the carpet is installed. Still others use a mechanical bonding system created by the interaction of hook tape on the floor and a loop scrim on the carpet backing (CRI, *Carpet Primer,* 1995).

Carpet tiles that are applied in a free-lay method also reduce the need for adhesive. However, adhesive manufacturers today have developed low-emitting adhesives (adhesives without a solvent base) that can ensure higher indoor air quality when used in combination with the CRI guidelines for installation (see Figure 9.4). The CRI guideline, "Standard for Installation of Commercial Textile Floorcovering Materials," CRI 104, can be obtained directly from the CRI.

Adequate ventilation is critical to a glue-down installation. The majority of facility managers indicated that proper ventilation was key to eliminating odors from adhesives and helping to ensure good indoor air quality (IAQ) (Williamson-Powers 1994). To minimize emissions and maintain good IAQ, the CRI recommends the use of low-emitting carpet products, trim, and accessories, combined with fresh-air ventilation achieved by opening doors and windows, using exhaust fans, operating ventilation systems at full capacity, and segregating air circulation of the renovation area from the remainder of the building for 48 to 72 hours. After the installation, the carpet should be vacuumed to eliminate fibers loosened during installation, and fresh-

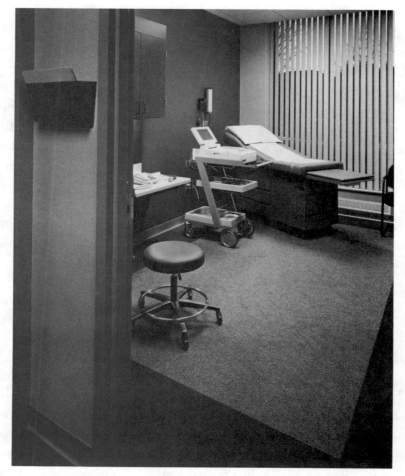

Figure 9.3 Quantum Plus carpet that is fushion bonded of solution-dyed Zeftron 2000 ZX nylon by BASF provides physical warmth and comfort in this examining room at St. Elizabeth's Hospital in Lincoln, Nebraska. Photo: Interface Flooring Systems, Inc., LaGrange, Georgia.

air ventilation continued at normal room temperatures for 48–72 hours to dissipate any lingering odors (CRI, *Carpet Primer,* 1995).

INDOOR AIR QUALITY

With the rise of *sick building syndrome,* along with a variety of other ailments and illnesses being tied to IAQ over the last decade, furnishings suppliers have focused a lot of attention on maximizing the quality of indoor air. Much of the IAQ problem has been tied to poor ventilation, reduced air flow, and improper maintenance of ventilation systems. Yet, manufacturers of building materials, like carpet manufac-

Figure 9.4 Carpet testing program label. Photo: Carpet and Rug Institute, Dalton, Georgia.

turers, have adjusted methods and materials in their products to reduce any offending substances to below acceptable levels.

A majority of the facility managers feel that carpet is among the safest materials in any room in terms of its toxic emissions (Williamson-Powers 1994). In fact, carpet ranks as the lowest emitter of volatile organic compounds among a variety of building products.

To further ensure carpet's safety as an indoor building material, the CRI, in cooperation with the Environmental Protection Agency (EPA), completed a Carpet Policy Dialogue process in late 1991. Also participating in this process was the American Lung Association, CPSC, and 19 other consumer, environmental, labor, government, and industry groups. As a result of this dialogue, the CRI developed a voluntary program to test emissions from carpet. This program is called the CRI Indoor Air Quality Carpet Testing Program.

The presence of the CRI IAQ Carpet Testing Program green label on showroom carpets, manufacturer literature, and presentation folders means that the labeled carpet does not exceed the established emission levels of total volatile organic compounds, styrene, and 4-phenylcyclohexene (4-PCH). A test for formaldehyde is also included to show, definitively, that this substance is no longer used in the manufacturing of carpet. Product types are retested periodically to be sure that they continue to fall within CRI emissions guidelines. In addition, a Consumer Information Label also lists commonsense guidelines for the installation of new carpet (CRI 1994).

In addition to the matter of toxic emissions, carpet has been unfairly targeted as an aggravating factor in allergic reactions. In fact, when properly maintained, carpet can trap allergens, dust, and microorganisms and hold them safely until destruction by antimicrobials or removal by vacuuming. Frequent and routine vacuuming, preferably with a high-efficiency particulate filter bag (less than one-micron filtration) will reduce the amount of airborne particles that could be spread into the air if mopped on a hard-surface floor (Wise 1994).

Commonsense procedures also prevail. If a person is particularly sensitive to airborne particles or chemical odors, it would be best to isolate that person from the cleaning or installation process until the area can be ventilated with fresh air.

MAINTENANCE—THE KEY TO PERFORMANCE

Maintenance is a natural conclusion to this discussion of carpeting for healthcare. No matter how carefully you've specified low-emitting, well-constructed, and properly hued and patterned products, and regardless of the fact that you have installed them according to strict guidelines, carpet has not yet been known to be able to maintain itself! It will take a planned schedule of cleaning procedures, instituted by on-site staff or a contracted cleaning service, to keep the carpet investment looking good and providing excellent performance.

There are two components to maintenance that can be thought of as emergency treatment and long-term care. Emergency treatment consists of quick measures needed to address spots, spills, and stains from food, medications, or other agents. Immediate action is critical here, even with carpets engineered for easy stain removal. The fiber producer or carpet mill can advise you on specific measures you can take to remove specific stains. General rules to remember are: avoid overwetting the stain, and blot—don't rub—the stain.

To provide a quick system of stain response, one facility manager of a 650-bed private hospital in the Midwest has instituted an "OOPS Hotline"—a telephone extension for hospital personnel to use only when something has been spilled. Maintenance personnel are then dispatched immediately to the site to sop up the stain (Williamson-Powers 1994).

Long-term carpet care involves a regular and routine plan of maintenance. Begin with preventative maintenance by installing walk-off mats in entrances, elevators, and other areas where traffic becomes concentrated. It's a good idea to vacuum these areas even when soil is not visible, just to prevent buildup of dirt and soil.

A majority of healthcare facilities use a contract cleaning service to execute a cleaning plan, although on-site staff can provide excellent results. Interiors Management Group's Shrom prefers working with the facility's own cleaning personnel. "Typically, on-site staff are flexible and willing to learn how to maintain specific products." she says.

Regardless of the type of cleaning service provided, a routine cleaning schedule needs to be planned, appropriate to the area. A minimum maintenance recommendation from the CRI is as follows:

- High traffic—vacuum daily
- Medium traffic—vacuum twice weekly
- Light traffic—vacuum weekly

These are general recommendations. Only careful analysis of traffic patterns and rates of soiling in the facility will determine proper maintenance scheduling.

In terms of equipment, a heavy-duty wide-track vacuum cleaner may be used for large open areas to reduce time and labor costs. An industrialized version of the domestic upright vacuum cleaner is also an essential maintenance tool. Preferably, it should have a hose and wand attachment for cleaning under heavy furniture; otherwise, a canister-type vacuum may also be needed. Both vacuum cleaners should have powerful suction, high-efficiency filter bags, and adjustable brushes or beater bars to bring imbedded dirt to the surface.

Restorative maintenance should also be planned for the facility. This includes periodic thorough cleaning by one of several methods:

- *Absorbent compounds.* A minimum-moisture method in which a dry absorbent compound is applied to the carpet pile. After the compound has remained on the carpet for a short time to allow the soil particles to bond to it, the compound and attached soil is removed via vacuum cleaning.
- *Absorbent pad.* Otherwise known as "rotary bonnet," in this method, detergent is applied to the pile and mechanically agitated. An absorbent pad, made of bath-mat-quality cotton terry cloth for best results, is used to absorb the solution and soil particles.

- *Dry foam.* This is a minimum-moisture method in which a cleaning foam is applied to the fiber. Suspended soil and foam are subsequently extracted by wet vacuuming.
- *Hot-water extraction.* In this method, hot water and cleaning solution are injected into carpet fibers under high pressure. The solution, soil, and residual moisture should be immediately extracted to avoid overwetting and to reduce drying time.
- *Rotary shampoo.* Shampoo is injected into the carpet through specially designed brushes. Some machines are capable of extraction; others may require an additional wet vacuum step to remove soil and shampoo solution (CRI, *Carpet Primer,* 1995).

Take care when selecting detergents. A detergent or cleaning agent that dries to a sticky or oily residue will attract soil to the carpet fibers. A better choice is a detergent that dries to a powder or fine flake—this can be vacuumed away with ease.

SPECIFICATION CHECKLISTS AND TIMELINE

This section summarizes the preceding sections and provides a quick reference checklist of elements important to the specification. All recommendations are courtesy of the CRI.

CONSTRUCTION AND PERFORMANCE SPECIFICATIONS

1. Construction type (tufted, woven, fusion bonded)
2. Gauge or pitch
3. Stitches or wire per inch
4. Pile or wire height
5. Pile fiber
6. Yarn ply, count, and heat set
7. Pile yarn weight
8. Color
9. Texture
10. Backing materials
11. Backcoating type and weight per square yard
12. Finished total weight per square yard
13. Ease of maintenance
14. Stain resistance
15. Antimicrobial treatment
16. Conductive capacity
17. Resistance to fading from light or harsh cleaners
18. Use life of product

INSTALLATION SPECIFICATIONS

1. Type of installation: glue down, tackless, and so on. Evaluate and determine:

   - Load and nature of traffic (foot traffic, wheeled carts, and so on)
   - Type and condition of subfloor
   - Prestige level desired (cushion adds to luxurious feeling underfoot)
   - Dimensional stability
   - Budget

2. Cushion type and grade, if required
3. Installation procedures and accessories
4. Certification that materials meet federal, state, and local government ordinances
5. Delivery and installation schedules
6. Carpet maintenance

GOVERNMENT SPECIFICATIONS AND REGULATIONS/FEDERAL REQUIREMENTS*

1. GSA Technical Requirements for Carpet, Carpet Tile, and Carpet Cushion
2. Textile Fabric Products Identification Act
3. Consumer Product Safety Commission: FF1-70; 16 CFR 1630 flammability requirements for all carpet (Federal Fabric Flammability Act)
4. Flooring and radiant panel test method for carpet installed in corridors: ASTM E-648 or NFPA-253–flammability requirement for regulated areas only
5. Americans with Disabilities Act, section 4.5—Ground and Floor Surfaces

SPECIFICATION TIMELINE/NEW INSTALLATIONS OR RENOVATIONS

120 DAYS BEFORE OCCUPANCY:

1. Write specifications for carpet and installation.
2. Request proposals.

90 DAYS BEFORE OCCUPANCY:

1. Review proposals.
2. Check references of carpet companies and installation contractors under consideration.
3. Select company; place order.
4. Prepare maintenance plan under the guidance of the manufacturer.

*These acts, requirements, and tests may regulate carpet installation in a facility—check to make sure what regulations are applicable to your project.

60 DAYS BEFORE OCCUPANCY:

1. Confirm that order was placed with the mill; confirm shipment date from mill.
2. Schedule delivery, arranging for holding site.
3. Confirm installation date.

30 DAYS BEFORE OCCUPANCY:

1. Check correctness of shipment; carpet style, color, pattern, and dye lot.
2. Check for manufacturing defects (manufacturers will not replace carpet once it is installed).
3. Complete all other construction prior to installation to protect new carpet.
4. Have carpet installed observing CRI 104 guidelines for installation.
5. Ventilate during installation to protect IAQ.
6. Review punch list on site with mill representative.

PUBLICATIONS TO OBTAIN

The following literature is available from the CRI, P.O. Box 2048, Dalton, GA 30722, 800/882-8846:

1. *The Carpet & Rug Institute's Carpet Primer.*
2. *Standard for Installation of Commercial Textile Floorcovering Materials,* CRI 104.
3. *Carpet & Indoor Air Quality in Commercial Installations: A Guide for Specifiers & Designers* (brochure).
4. *Covering the Future: Environmental Stewardship of the Carpet and Rug Industry* (brochure).

SUMMARY

Today's commercial carpet is a well-engineered product designed to enhance the healing environment of a wide range of healthcare facilities. Through a combination of construction, performance, and specialized features, carpet contributes to the value of the installation. With careful specification and planning for installation and maintenance, carpet will be an investment that hospital patients, staff, and administrators will enjoy for many years to come.

Richard Radke is a senior contract specialist with BASF Carpet Products Group in Atlanta, Georgia.

References

Carpet and Rug Institute. *The Carpet & Rug Institute Specifier's Handbook.* Dalton, Georgia, 1992.

Carpet and Rug Institute. *Floorcovering Products for Schools.* Dalton, Georgia, 1995.

Carpet and Rug Institute. *The Carpet & Rug Institute's Carpet Primer.* Dalton, Georgia, 1995.

Carpet and Rug Institute. *Carpet & Indoor Air Quality in Commercial Installations: A Guide for Specifiers & Designers.* Dalton, Georgia, 1994.

King, A. "Healthcare for Fun and Profit." *Commercial Carpet Digest* 4 (March 1994).

Williamson-Powers, C. "The FOCUS '94 Health Care Survey: What Facility Managers Think About Flooring." *Floor Focus* 27 (January/February 1994).

Wise, O. "Carpet Choices for Healthcare Facilities." *Journal of Healthcare Material Management* (July 1994): 34–39.

10 LIGHTING

Jules G. Horton, FIALD, FIES

T he quality and quantity of light in a built environment has a decisive psychological effect on occupants and visitors of all ages, healthy and sick alike. Since people under stress react more strongly to environmental variables, healthcare facility design should strive to satisfy the often contradictory needs of patients, medical personnel, maintenance workers, and visitors. The needs for each of these groups can be summarized as follows:

- *Patients* fall into many categories, but the principal categories are ambulatory and bedridden patients. The former need good lighting for reading in their rooms and in lounges; corridors should stimulate the desire to move around. Bedridden patients should be able to change lighting at their beds in accordance with their conditions and preferences.
- *Medical personnel* fall into many occupational categories, such as surgeons, other medical doctors, nurses, lab technicians, and so on. Their work has varying lighting requirements, but what they have in common can be summarized as the need for good task visibility, freedom from glare, and adequate contrast in the field of vision to assist concentration and minimize visual fatigue.
- *Maintenance workers* perform better when their tasks are not needlessly complicated by too many types of light fixtures and lamps. The ease (hence speed) of relamping means fewer fixtures out of service.
- *Visitors* to a healthcare facility stay for a limited time, but the way they feel about the care their loved ones receive can be greatly affected by the *feel* of the place. Cold, monotonous lighting, evoking the vague but somehow pejorative term *institutional,* can increase their anxiety, which, in turn, may be passed on to patients.

Healthcare facilities are inherently expensive to build and maintain. They are subject to many safety codes and contain a great deal of complicated, expensive equipment and systems that often become obsolete in a relatively short time due to technological

Color Plate 1: Wellness centers, such as this outpatient waiting area at Hasbro Children's Hospital in Providence, Rhode Island, are emerging as a new architectural form.

Architecture: Shepley Bulfinch Richardson & Abbott Architects.
Interior Design: Rosalyn Cama Interior Design Associates, Inc.
Photography: Jean Smith, Cambridge, Massachusetts.

Color Plate 2: Art installations, plants, water fountains, and other accessories may call for enhanced infrastructure requirements.

Project: Hasbro Children's Hospital, Providence, Rhode Island, main lobby.
Architecture: Shepley Bulfinch Richardson & Abbott Architects.
Interior Design: Rosalyn Cama Interior Design Associates, Inc.
Photography: Robert Miller, Great Falls, Virginia.

COLOR PLATE 4: Kids Kare treatment chair, which has the same quality and durability as its adult counterpart, was developed to increase children's sense of security and well-being.

PHOTO: Nemschoff, The Healthcare Furniture Specialists, Sheboygan, Wisconsin.

COLOR PLATE 3: Pastel shades are less stressful for patients and staff and require fewer coats of paint.

PROJECT: Hospice of the Western Reserve, Cleveland, Ohio.
INTERIOR DESIGN: Interior Design/Kay Trimmer, Inc., Cleveland.

COLOR PLATE 5: InterAct Modular Systems is a freestanding system based on core units, not panels, that allow accessories and dividers to sit on top of the unit.

PHOTO: Steelcase Inc., Grand Rapids, Michigan.

COLOR PLATE 6: Color point, a style from Mohawk Commercial Carpet Group, is constructed of solution-dyed Zeftron® 2000 ZX nylon using Mohawk's woven interlock process.

PHOTO: Mohawk Commercial Carpet, Atlanta.

COLOR PLATE 7: In a modern healthcare environment, cubicle cloth can be a multicolored dobby, jacquard, or warp print that is specially designed and selected for an area, such as maternity, pediatrics, surgery, or geriatrics.

PHOTO: DesignTex, Inc., New York City.

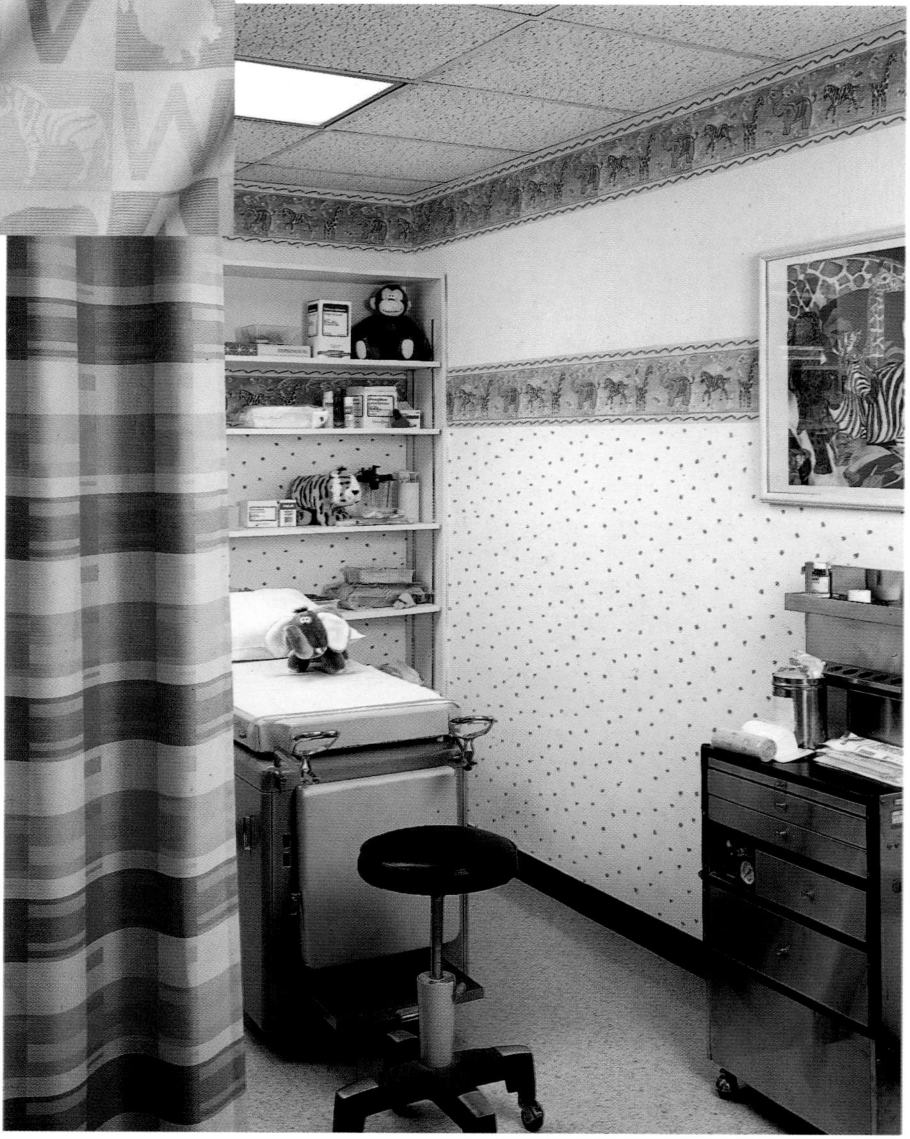

COLOR PLATE 8: Frequent changes of borders, accessories, and artwork can create variety in a space.

PROJECT: pediatric exam room.
WALLCOVERING: Guard® Harmony 54-inch contract wallcovering.
CUBICLE CURTAIN: Fantagraph.
PHOTO: Patricia Rodemann, Designed for Success, Lewis Center, Ohio.

COLOR PLATE 9: The harmony in nature needs to be present in healing art to remind people of the ebb and flow of the breath of life.

PAINTING: *Blue Heaven*, oil on canvas, by Laurie Zagon, Flagstaff, Arizona.

COLOR PLATE 10: Participants in color/paint workshops are encouraged to express their feelings in an abstract format, thus eliminating the fear of not being able to draw images appropriately.

PAINTING: Children's Hospital of Los Angeles, painted by a child with AIDS.
PHOTO: Laurie Zagon, Flagstaff, Arizona.

COLOR PLATE 11: Works of art created by professional artists or students of art who have been hospitalized due to a life-threatening illness can be an expressive narration of the healing process.

PAINTING: *Her Body Was No Longer Hers to Control*, oil pastel on paper, by Hollis Sigler, Prairie View, Illinois.
PHOTOGRAPHY: Michael Tropea, Chicago, Illinois.

COLOR PLATE 12: Environ consists of a combination of soybean flour resin blended with additives and processed waste paper to create a product that resembles granite.

PHOTO: Phenix BioComposites, Mankato, Minnesota.

COLOR PLATE 13: The hospital garden can take many shapes or forms. Materials that are warm and inviting include cut flagstone, gravel, wood, and plants that are seasonal in nature.

GARDEN: by Randy Thueme, for Scott Murray and Peter Corippo, San Francisco, California.
PHOTOGRAPHY: Christopher Yates, Piedmont, California.

Color Plate 14: The Shirley Burnett Cancer Garden in Texarkana, Texas, offers patients moving water, tropical fish, a variety of birds, and seasonal blooming plants.

Landscape Design: The Office of James Burnett.
Photography: James F. Wilson, Dallas.

progress and/or medical discoveries. It is thus mandatory that lighting systems strike the best possible balance between their *first cost* and the *operating cost*. The first cost includes fixtures, installation, wiring, and control systems. Operating cost includes replacement of lamps, cost of electricity, and miscellaneous repairs. Unfortunately, only too frequently, first cost and operating cost fall into separate budgets and sources of money that compete with each other. The best approach is to consider the total cost throughout the estimated life of the lighting system. Specialized lighting that is subject to periodic changes in medical technology (in surgical suites and laboratories, for example) should not be full of "bells and whistles" because it may be replaced well before its useful life runs out. On the other hand, architectural lighting equipment should be of high enough quality to assure long life of fixtures, ballasts, controls, and other parts.

One caveat about lamps—there are many marginal lamp manufacturers who cut their prices at the expense of quality and useful lamp life. Many purchasing people fall for the lure of the lower prices, only to incur higher total expense in the high percentage of early lamp failures and the accompanying cost of relamping labor.

Lighting design for a successful visual environment must go hand in hand with architectural forms, as well as with interior materials and finishes. Lighting designers should be involved from the outset of the project in the decision-making process concerning these issues. Light is a form giver in architecture, and a successful interior space is one where the interior designer knows, by previous experience or from mock-ups, how the surfaces and furnishings will appear in conjunction with the planned lighting systems. Once all decisions have been made, it is of utmost importance not only that the specified lighting fixtures, their locations, and the lamps they use be installed correctly and without substitution, but that the maintenance personnel of the healthcare facility follow—to the letter—the original design intent. It is also imperative that the facility keeps on hand a supply of specified lamps for future replacement.

It is a known scientific as well as empirical fact that people need exposure to daylight for their physiological and psychological well-being. This is particularly true for sick people, especially those whose conditions require a prolonged stay indoors.

It is thus essential that this fact is given a high priority at the outset of the design process for healthcare facilities. Of utmost importance is the orientation of the building(s) on the site, which—in conjunction with the floor plans—should give ample exposure to daylight for all patient rooms and for those spaces in which ambulatory patients congregate—lounges, library, dining rooms, for example. It is also important that bedridden patients have visual contact with the outdoor world.

Depending on the geographic location of the facility, time of the year, and weather, uncontrolled daylight (and sunlight) may result in excessive heat gain and disturbing glare. Both factors should be taken into consideration during the design process, again remembering that sick people are more sensitive to any discomfort than those who are preoccupied with their daily activities.

Daylight may be controlled in many ways, such as architectural exterior sun baffles, louvers, tinted glazing, interior adjustable sunshades, and blinds. First cost and ease of maintenance and cleaning are among the factors to be considered during the design process in selecting the most suitable control system(s) for each healthcare facility.

SPECIFIC AREAS

Although a major facility has a large number of spaces with varied types of activities (and thus visual requirements), lighting systems generally fall into two categories: lighting that is specific to the type of activity in the space and general lighting (see Tables 10.1 and 10.2). Whatever the needs of the former, general lighting in most spaces should flow naturally from space to space, avoiding harsh contrasts and deep shadows. Lighting should be of high color-rendering (affect of light on colors of objects) quality for two reasons. First, it should make the spaces as pleasant as possible for occupants and visitors alike, not only through the optimized appearance of the space, but also because of a well-known phenomenon that seeing other people's natural appearance will increase the beholder's sense of well-being. Second, and even more urgent, high color-rendering lighting enables medical personnel to spot any danger signals in the appearance of the patients. These signals may be missed under illumination that has a color spectrum too insensitive to subtle changes in patients' appearance.

This philosophy applies to all interior spaces. Having two classes of spaces— "high end" and "low end"—implies storing many more types of lamps than necessary and invites errors in relamping. More significant is the fact that cost differences between lamps with a high color rendering index (CRI) of 80+ and those with a lower CRI have been steadily shrinking so as to make the economic factor less and less significant.

Public Spaces

Spaces in this category include entrances, lobbies, atria, lounges, dining facilities, libraries, and the like. Patients, medical personnel, and visitors all may use these spaces. Whatever their architectural and interior design features, it is important to give these areas a cheerful, friendly, and restful, atmosphere. Good visibility is a high

TABLE 10.1 CURRENTLY RECOMMENDED ILLUMINANCE CATEGORIES AND RANGES FOR
GENERIC-TYPE ACTIVITIES IN HEALTHCARE FACILITIES

| Type of Activity | Illuminance Category | RANGE OF ILLUMINANCES | | Reference Work-Plane |
		Lux	Footcandles	
Public spaces with dark surroundings	A	20–30–50	2–3–5	General lighting throughout spaces
Simple orientation for short temporary visits	B	50–75–100	5–7.5–10	'' ''
Working spaces where visual tasks are only occasionally performed	C	100–150–200	10–15–20	'' ''
Performance of visual tasks of high contrast or large size	D	200–300–500	20–30–50	Illuminance on task
Performance of visual tasks of medium contrast or small size	E	500–750–1,000	50–75–100	'' ''
Performance of visual tasks of low contrast or very small size	F	1,000–1,500–2,000	100–150–200	'' ''
Performance of visual tasks of low contrast and very small size over a prolonged period	G	2,000–3,000–5,000	200–300–500	Illuminance on task, obtained by a combination of general and local (supplementary) lighting
Performance of very prolonged and exacting visual tasks	H	5,000–7,500–10,000	500–750–1,000	'' ''
Performance of very special visual tasks of extremely low contrast and small size	I	10,000–15,000–20,000	1,000–1,500–2,000	'' ''

Source: The Illuminating Engineering Society of North America, New York City.

TABLE 10.2 CURRENTLY RECOMMENDED ILLUMINANCE CATEGORIES FOR HEALTHCARE FACILITIES

Area Activity Illuminance	Category	Area Activity Illuminance	Category
Ambulance (local)	E	Emergency outpatient[a]	
Anesthetizing	E	General	E
Autopsy and morgue[a,b]		Local	F
Autopsy, general	E	Endoscopy rooms[a]	
Autopsy table	G	General	E
Morgue, general	D	Peritoneoscopy	D
Museum	E	Culdoscopy	D
Cardiac function lab	E	Examination and treatment rooms[a]	
Central sterile supply		General	D
Inspection, general	E	Local	E
Inspection	F	Eye surgery[a,b]	F
At sinks	E	Fracture room[a]	
Work areas, general	D	General	E
Processed storage	D	Local	F
Corridors[a]		Inhalation therapy	D
Nursing areas—day	C	Laboratories[a]	
Nursing areas—night	B	Specimen collecting	E
Operating areas—delivery, recovery, labs, suites, service	E	Tissue laboratories	F
		Microscopic reading room	D
Critical care areas[a]		Gross specimen review	F
General	C	Chemistry rooms	E
Examination	E	Bacteriology rooms	
Surgical task lighting	H	General	E
Handwashing	F	Reading culture plates	F
Cystoscopy room[a,b]	E	Hematology	E
Dental suite[a]		Linens	
General	D	Sorting soiled linen	D
Instrument tray	E	Central (clean) linen room	D
Oral cavity	H	Sewing room, general	D
Prosthetic lab, general	D	Sewing room, work area	E
Workbench	E	Linen closet	B
Local	F	Lobby	C
Recovery room, general	C	Locker rooms	C
Recovery room, emergency examination	E	Medical illustrative studio[a,b]	F
		Medical rooms	E
Dialysis unit, medical[a]	F	Nurseries[a]	
Elevators	C	General[a]	C
EKG and specimen room[a]		Observation, treatment	E
General	B		
On equipment	C		

(continued)

TABLE 10.2 *(Continued)*

Area Activity Illuminance	Category	Area Activity Illuminance	Category
Nursing stations[a]		Pulmonary function laboratories[a]	E
General	D	Radiological suite[a]	
Desk	E	Diagnostic section	
Corridors, day	C	General[b]	A
Corridors, night	A	Waiting area	A
Medication station	E	Radiography/	
Obstetric delivery suite[a]		fluoroscopy room	A
Labor rooms		Film sorting	F
General	C	Barium kitchen	E
Local	E	Radiation therapy section	
Birthing rooms[c]	F	General[b]	B
Delivery area		Waiting area	B
Scrub, general	F	Isotope kitchen, general	E
General	F	Benches	E
Delivery table (see Table 10.3)		Computerized radiotomography	
Resuscitation	G	section	
Postdelivery recovery area	E	Scanning room	B
Substerilization room	B	Equipment maintenance	
Occupational therapy[a]		room	E
Work area, general	D	Solarium	
Work tables or benches	E	General[b]	C
Patients' rooms[a]		Local for reading	D
General[b]	B	Stairways	C
Observation	A	Surgical suite[a]	
Critical examination	E	Operating room, general[b]	F
Reading	D	Operating table (see Table 10.3)	
Toilets	D	Scrub room[b]	F
Pharmacy[a]		Instruments and sterile	
General	E	supply room	D
Alcohol vault	D	Cleanup room, instruments	E
Laminar flow bench	F	Anesthesia storage	C
Night light	A	Substerilizing room	C
Parenteral solution room	D	Surgical induction room[a,b]	E
Physical therapy departments		Surgical holding area[a,b]	E
Gymnasiums	D	Toilets	C
Tank rooms	D	Utility room	D
Treatment cubicles	D	Waiting areas[a]	
Postanesthetic recovery room[a]		General	C
General[b]	E	Local for reading	D
Local	H		

[a]Good to high color-rendering capability should be considered in these areas. As lamps of higher luminous efficacy and higher color-rendering capability become available and economically feasible, they should be applied in all areas of healthcare facilities.
[b]Variable (dimming or switching).
[c]Supplemental illumination as in delivery room must be available.
Source: The Illuminating Engineering Society of North America, New York City.

priority, particularly at steps, escalators, ramps, and doors. Directional signs should be easily read.

All this implies that designers should combine good indirect illumination with accent lighting, such as wall-mounted sconces, pendants, and table lamps. Use floor lamps with caution because of the danger of them overturning or people tripping on floor cables. Wherever possible, use fluorescent lamps (linear and compact varieties). The old prejudice against those lamps was justly based on the inferior color rendering they offered (standard cool and warm white, as well as that oxymoron, the daylight lamp). Modern fluorescent lamps offer high CRI, making incandescent lamps labor-costly and energy-inefficient relics of the past.

Corridors and Elevator Cabs

High visibility and absence of glare are two imperatives in corridors and elevators. In addition to pedestrian and wheelchair traffic, there are patients on gurneys who should be spared looking at ceiling-mounted light fixtures unless they are of the indirect type. In corridors, indirect lighting is best, preferably by wall-mounted valences and coves. The goal should be to produce a luminous perimeter where a relatively low light level combines with ease of orientation good vertical illumination of people and objects, which could become obstacles. We must remember to facilitate visibility and orientation for the first-time visitors, elderly, and visually impaired.

Corridor guidelines apply to elevator cabs as well. Additionally, it is important that tall passengers be spared from bumping their heads against wall-mounted lighting fixtures. A good solution for elevators is a luminous ceiling, but keep in the mind that its surface brightness should be moderate for the benefit of the gurney occupants.

Patient Rooms (Adult)

Typically, patient rooms fall into private and semiprivate categories. Obviously, occupants have the most control over their environment in private rooms, where they can modify the amount of light they wish at a given time. It is important that the quality of light and appearance of lighting fixtures have a residential character. We must, however, remember these requirements:

- Good reading light for patients in bed.
- Good (and separately controlled) examination light, either ceiling mounted or portable. Ceiling-mounted light is more practical if more than one person is expected to participate in the examination, but it is obviously more expensive.

- Comfortable lighting at the lounging chair where the patient may wish to read.
- Night light—this must be shielded from the bed. It should provide a safe path from the door to the bed, but it is not intended as the source of general illumination. Insomnia is often caused by environmental factors in the hospital (noise, glare, and so on), while sound sleep is most desirable during illness.
- Comfortable lighting in the private bathroom is essential for patients who wish to apply makeup or to shave.

Lighting in semiprivate rooms should satisfy all of the requirements for private rooms. In addition, visual privacy should be respected. Dedicated lighting for one bed should not cause discomfort for other patients. Whenever possible, room mock-up is highly recommended to verify trouble-free interaction between all room components.

Examination Rooms

Technology in examination rooms, like elsewhere in healthcare facilities, has made giant steps forward in just a few years. Video monitors have become commonplace, and adjustable portable or overhead surgical-type light fixtures are gradually being replaced. Nevertheless, the latter are still being used many places alongside the video monitors.

General illumination plays an important role in both scenarios. Light should always be dimmable—in the first case, in order not to interfere with the self-illuminated monitors; in the second, to provide the important transition from the high brightness of the focal field (generally small) to the lower brightness of the surrounding area.

Nurses' Stations

Nurses' stations represent a high-energy hub of activity with specific lighting requirements. For first-time or occasional visitors, a nurses' station should be easy to locate visually. A few examples of visual means of signaling the presence of the nurses' station are lighting on walls, a floating lighting panel over the station, or a higher level of general illumination as compared with adjacent corridors.

Successful lighting systems for nurses' station should

- Be as shadowless and glareless as possible
- Clearly define faces of people standing in front of the station
- Light both the vertical and horizontal work surfaces

Pediatric Areas

The closer pediatric areas resemble a healthy child's world—be it a room in a family home, a playroom, a classroom, or a daycare facility—the more they help in relieving the stress of being a sick child separated from his or her family and playmates. Whimsical decorative lighting fixtures for general illumination can become a part of general decor. Examinations lights are preferably portable (on wheels) and are generally stored out of sight.

Surgical Suites

Design of lighting in operating suites is generally dictated by the preferences of senior surgeons in the facility, who are kept abreast of technological progress by the manufacturers of surgical lighting equipment. Flexibility is very important because of the great variety of surgery performed. One common element in all parts of the surgical suite is the general illumination system. Its two main tasks are lighting the perimeter walls and work surfaces and providing good lighting for setting up before the operation and cleaning up afterwards.

Dialysis Unit

Dialysis is a procedure that is lengthy and repetitive, and it often causes discomfort. Every attempt should be made to alleviate the anxiety of the patient. Lighting can be very helpful here: low-level, preferably indirect, general illumination should be augmented by accent lighting on plants and wall-mounted artwork. Higher-intensity cleanup lighting should be separately controlled. If individual reading lamps are deemed useful by the doctors in charge, they should be well shielded so as not to disturb other patients.

Dental Suite

A dental suite generally consists of four areas: waiting room, reception, laboratory, and surgery. The size of each area varies from one healthcare facility to another, but lighting requirements are pretty similar.

In the waiting room, people like to read or at least browse through periodicals or their own reading material, so the general level of illumination should be adequate for that task. Lighting should also be soft and soothing, given the typical anxiety accompanying a visit to the dentist. Illuminated artwork on some walls helps to create a relaxed mood.

The receptionist needs good lighting on horizontal work surfaces, on file cabinets, and, last but not least, on patients' faces.

Lighting requirements in the dental laboratory depend on the scope of work performed there.

In dental surgery, there are two lighting elements: the surgical light fixture and lighting for general illumination. The former is a fully adjustable, high-intensity, narrow light beam fixture that focuses on the oral cavity and must have sharp light cutoff to avoid disturbing glare. This type of fixture is color corrected and has a heat filter to protect the patient from burns.

Lighting for general illumination should be diffuse so as to minimize discomfort from glare for the patient. Typically, one 2×4-foot ceiling-mounted fluorescent fixture does the job quite well. If possible, indirect uplights mounted on side walls (or partitions) are preferable if they do not interfere with other needs in the typically small surgery.

Laboratories

Lighting in laboratories depends on the general layout of the equipment. The light source of choice is linear or compact fluorescent lamps. The important requirements are absence of glare, adequate lighting on horizontal surfaces and under the overhead cabinets, and avoidance of dark areas and corners. If the ceiling heights permit, pendant direct/indirect linear fixtures work very well in laboratories. Exercise caution to avoid body shadows on work surfaces.

Emergency Department

High levels of nonglare general illumination are required here. In addition, there should be surgical lamps over operating tables. Avoid shadows and high contrasts. Other requirements should follow those for surgical suites.

Critical Care Areas

General illumination in critical care areas must be flexible in keeping with their constantly changing medical requirements. The light should be dimmable and non-glary. It should facilitate observations of patients and the monitoring equipment. In addition, surgical procedure task lights should be available for emergency procedures. It is important to ensure that patients are clearly visible from the nurses' station. Conversely, lighting fixtures in nurses' station should be well shielded from the patients to avoid discomfort from glare.

Access to daylight has an important psychological role for critical care patients and should not be sacrificed for expediency of layout or economy.

Geriatric Facilities

In designing lighting for geriatric facilities, the designer should consider the following factors:

- Elderly patients are very sensitive to glare.
- Aging eyes need more light than those of young adults for ordinary seeing tasks.
- Eyes of patients whose cataracts have been surgically removed are very sensitive to ultraviolet light, even in the near range.
- Elderly patients may be easily disoriented in areas outside their rooms. It is important that corridor lighting accents the patient room doors so that room numbers can be clearly visible.
- Changes in floor elevation (steps, ramps) should be signaled by intensified illumination and changes in floor coloring.
- Basic illumination could be provided by fluorescent fixtures. Many elderly patients will see a moderately bright fixture as a very bright spot in a murky field of vision, making shielding of light sources very important. Indirect general illumination is preferable.
- In patient rooms, incandescent, dimmable, adjustable reading lamps should be provided for each bed and at each lounging chair.

Physical Therapy Suite

Good general visibility is the primary goal here. Remember that many patients will be prone or reclining, so the preferred lighting system is direct/indirect. Fluorescent lamps are most practical, but, if the ceiling height is generous (12 feet and more), consider high color-rendering metal halide lamps in well-shielded pendant fixtures.

Emergency Lighting

Design of emergency lighting systems is governed by the National Electrical Code and other federal and local codes and regulations (see Table 10.3). It is important, however, to review the basic goals of emergency lighting:

- To facilitate evacuation of patients, personnel, and visitors under adverse conditions.

TABLE 10.3 CURRENT RECOMMENDED ILLUMINANCES IN LUX (FOOTCANDLES) ON TASKS FOR EMERGENCY OR CONTINUITY SERVICE (FOR USE WHEN NORMAL SERVICE IS INTERRUPTED)[a]

Task Location	Lux	Footcandles
Exit ways		
Corridors leading to exits, at floor	30	3
Stairways leading to exits, at floor	30	3
Exit direction signs, on face luminaire	50	5
Exit doorway, at floor	30	3
Operating room, surgical table	27000	2700
Operating room, emergency table	2200	220
Delivery room, obstetrical table	27000	2700
Recovery rooms, for OR and obstetrical	100	10
Nurseries, infant, 760 millimeters (mm) (30 inches) above floor	100	10
Nurseries, premature, 760 mm (30 inches) above floor	100	10
Nurseries, pediatric, 760 mm (30 inches) above floor	20	2
Medication preparation area, local	300	30
Nurses' station	50	5
Pharmacy	50	5
Blood bank area	50	5
Central suction pump area	50	5
Telephone switchboard, face of board	50	5
Central sterile supply, issuing area	50	5
Psychiatric patient bed area	20	2
Main electrical control center	50	5
Hospital elevator—exit lighting/stairwells	50	5
Life safety areas (life-support areas)	50	5
Cardiac catheter laboratories	100	10
Coronary care units	300	30
Dialysis units	200	20
Emergency room treatment areas	500	50
Intensive care units	300	30

[a]These are the minimum lighting levels. It is particularly desirable that they may be increased to as near the levels normally provided in these areas the available capacity of the emergency electrical supply will permit.
Source: The Illuminating Engineering Society of North America, New York City.

- To provide life-support services to patients who cannot be evacuated, especially in surgical suites, delivery rooms, recovery rooms, nurseries, emergency suites, and critical care areas.

RECOMMENDED QUALITY AND QUANTITY

As stated earlier, it is recommended that the CRI of all light sources in a healthcare facility be not less than 80. In surgical suites, examination rooms, and critical care areas, a CRI of 90+ is recommended. The visible spectrum of all light sources should be continuous.

Preferable correlated color temperature of light sources in healthcare facilities has been a subject of lengthy discussions. There is an empirically proven relationship between the level of illumination in a given space and the preferable color temperature of light sources in that space. At illumination under 100 footcandles (fc), lower color temperature is preferable, and 3000K is recommended as a standard.

For the three critical areas of surgical suite, examination rooms, and critical care areas, a higher color temperature (3500K to 5000K) is recommended, but it is advantageous if one color temperature is selected for all those areas.

LIGHTING DESIGNER'S ROLE

Architectural lighting design evolved as a full-fledged profession quite recently—shortly after World War II—with the United States taking the lead globally. A bona fide lighting designer must be versed in architectural and interior design, psychology, construction process, and economics, among other disciplines. With lighting technology developing constantly, staying on top of new developments is a full-time job.

There are many advantages of having a lighting designer on the project team. The most important lies in his or her ability to integrate the visual requirements of the multitude of tasks performed in a healthcare facility with the challenges of the proposed architectural forms and interior materials and finishes. Next, the lighting designer will make sure that the emerging lighting schemes are user friendly, fit into the project budget, and make maintenance as simple as possible. Finally, he or she will guard against fads and unproven technologies.

A lighting designer will be most effective if included on the project team during the schematic design phase. At that time, it is relatively easy to accommodate the often contradictory requirements of various disciplines participating in the project. It is important to reach consensus before the client/user becomes enamored with an interesting scheme or detail only to find out later that the favored scheme has serious flaws.

After the initial input during the schematic design, a lighting designer should be required to select appropriate lighting fixtures, to perform necessary calculations, and to prepare lighting fixture layouts, fixture schedules and budget, and finally fixture and controls specifications. During this process, it is often beneficial to build mock-ups that demonstrate to all concerned the soundness (or weakness) of the proposed schemes and allow for changes in details, materials, and finishes before they become liabilities.

It is most essential, during the bidding phase, that the lighting designer review and make binding recommendations about proposed substitutions. After the contract has been awarded, he or she should review shop drawings, examine required fixture samples, participate in site demonstrations, and, finally, perform final inspection of the completed installation.

During design and construction of a complex project such as a healthcare facility, each of the players (the owner/user, architect, interior designer, contractor, and so on) comes to the table with his or her own set of goals and priorities. Lighting designers must be able to understand and to respond with their expertise to each of the players—support them when possible and challenge them where the good of the project is at stake. This is not an easy task, and it requires a lot of tact combined with firmness. Most important, lighting designers must do their homework thoroughly to be able to make their case convincingly.

In selecting a lighting designer for a healthcare facility, the most essential qualifications are previous experience on similar projects and general expertise in healthcare. Nowhere else in the field of built environment does the ever-changing complex technology challenge so much (and get challenged by) the various categories of people who come in contact with it. Lighting design can and should make that contact a success, whether the contact is with patients, medical and clerical personnel, maintenance workers, or visitors.

In the search for a good, qualified lighting designer, word of mouth can be helpful. Architectural firms specializing in healthcare facilities are generally well known, and they often use lighting designers on their projects. Another good source is the International Association of Lighting Designers (IALD). A professional resume of the firm under consideration should be required and reviewed, followed, if possible, by a personal interview with individuals who would form the design team if the firm is selected.

Jules G. Horton is founder of Horton + Lees Lighting Design, a 28-year old firm with offices in New York City, Los Angeles, and San Francisco.

EDITOR'S NOTE: *For a glossary of lighting terms, see Appendix D.*

11

TEXTILES

Marty Gurian, Affiliate IIDA, Affiliate IFMA, ASTM

U pholstery, wallcovering, panel cloth, cubicle curtains, and drapery are important textiles in healthcare environments today. They provide a more residential-like, attractive quality and serve many functional needs. More and more studies are concluding that the environment can play a vital role in relieving stress and promoting healing. Through knowledgeable selection, textiles are a source of color, design, texture, and soft and warm tactile qualities. They are significant specifications in today's rapidly evolving healthcare environments. Because healthcare products demand high performance and safety, many new types of textiles have been developed that address infection control, stain resistance and cleanability, fluid control, flammability, and durability.

Because people are living longer, healthcare services and senior living needs are receiving greater attention. Healthcare textiles will continue to be specialized and upgraded, but under careful budget constraints. Expect long product life cycles with proper care and maintenance guidance.

Many of the textiles discussed in this chapter did not exist a few years ago. Furniture fabric assembly systems with fluid barriers for moisture control, special fire barriers to meet stringent new flammability regulations, more effective antimicrobial agents, easy-to-clean protective coatings, and high-performance vinyls are just a few of the new features. Standard textile fabrics, as well as new, improved fabrics with attractive healthcare features, can be further enhanced by using new technology and technology from other industries, interfacing the industrial textile world materials and know-how with traditional and interior materials. New high-performance vinyls, polyurethanes, and even new categories of man-made textiles continue to be developed to serve demanding end uses such as healthcare. Environmental concerns also play a major concern in healthcare facilities, particularly those related to air quality, recycling, and such.

Healthcare spaces have a wide range of special needs, from the traditional administrative areas with corporate-like requirements to the most severe, heavy-duty, stain-prone applications, such as emergency areas, ambulatory outpatient clinics, and surgical facilities, not to mention the most infectious wards. The format of this chapter first classifies, defines, and explains healthcare textiles in a generic and simplified manner, but in an analytical framework. I have provided more detailed information and illustrations devoted to new specialized healthcare textiles than traditional interior types, but it is important to understand the features and limitations of both. Finally, and most significant for proper closure, I have provided a case study of a healthcare installation as a comparative analysis of the features and constraints of four potential upholstery types for a high-performance seating project. This important summary exercise illustrates the analysis and problem solving that should be undertaken by healthcare specifiers (with help from their suppliers) if the optimum selection is to be accomplished with the myriad of choices and information available.

Healthcare textiles are truly a new creative, innovative, and challenging opportunity for suppliers and users where constant education will become increasingly more valuable for progressive and successful organizations.

UPHOLSTERY

In addition to traditional upholstery and enhanced types (e.g., vinylized fabrics) that have been used for many years, several new types of materials have been developed in the last five years that offer high performance. I have identified and organized all related available types into appropriate categories and then provided a brief description of each type.

Upholstery types are sometimes characterized as either fabriclike or plasticlike, in particular with respect to their surface character (such as the tactile quality, warmth, appearance, and so on). Thus, for purposes of categorization, upholstery types have been placed in either the fabric or plastic quadrants of Figure 11.1. The closer to the middle of the diagram an upholstery type is, the more the type is of a mixed fabric/plastic character. Next, the upholstery types are further characterized as either being a fluid barrier within themselves or not, even though it is recognized that all may be further enhanced with fluid barriers. Therefore, an upholstery type is initially characterized by two important criteria that are vital to healthcare specifiers—the surface character of the upholstery and whether a fluid barrier is easily achieved.

- *Regular fabric types* encompasses the majority of typical commercial upholstery fabrics that are not differentiated by any of the other categories. These fabrics achieve their color by stock dyeing the fiber, yarn dyeing, or piece (fabric) dyeing, but do not involve 100-percent solution-dyed fibers. They may include printed fabrics, but that is not likely without a protective finish or coating, which would

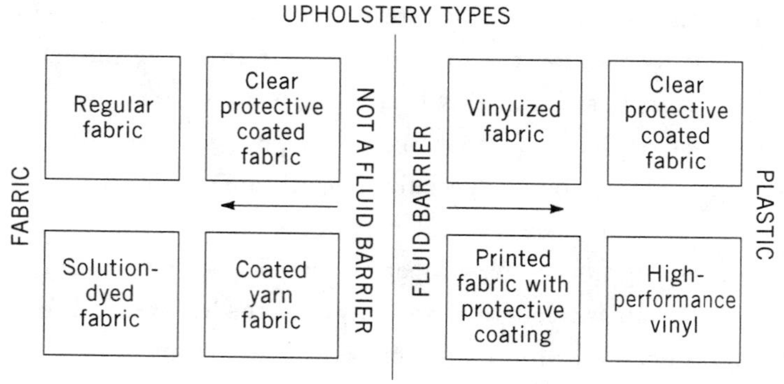

UPHOLSTERY TYPES

Figure 11.1 Upholstery types are characterized as either fabriclike or plasticlike. Source: Marty Gurian, New York City.

suggest another category. Fabric construction is mostly woven, but does include some knitted fabric. Heavy-duty regular fabric may suit the requirements of many healthcare applications.

- *Solution-dyed fabrics* are composed of 100-percent solution-dyed fibers whose pigments were included in the polymer in fiber extrusion (see Figure 11.2). A 100-percent solution-dyed fiber content requirement is required if these fabrics are to be safely cleaned with diluted bleach without color loss. The ability to clean with bleach is a highly desirable feature to many healthcare specifiers for infection-control purposes. The Center for Disease Control's (CDC's) Housekeeping Guidelines recommend the use of bleach when needed, especially for blood spills. One-hundred-percent solution-dyed fabrics are available for healthcare upholstery in nylon (e.g., BASF Zeftron T200 Nylon), olefin, and, to a limited extent, polyester.

- *Regular vinyl, polyurethane, or matrix materials* have many desirable healthcare attributes, such as being easy to clean with soap and water (since they are themselves a fluid barrier) and usually possessing heavy-duty durability levels. Vinyl has served the healthcare industry well for a long time and certainly has made housekeeping and maintenance staffs generally happy, as opposed to many types of fabric in demanding applications. Standard vinyl is not manufactured specifically to endure the ultimate demands of healthcare, such as the repeated use of strong cleaning agents like bleach and ammonia. It is not antimicrobial, it is not manufactured for maximum abrasion resistance, and it does not necessarily have protective coatings to resist many healthcare stains. Further, typical vinyl upholstery does not contain special flame-retardant additives that help meet new stringent furniture flammability codes (such as California Technical Bulletin 133 and NFPA 701) also needed in other demanding commercial applications, such as those regulated by the U.S. Coast Guard (e.g., cruise lines registered in the United States and riverboat casinos).

Figure 11.2 Solution-dyed fibers have pigments that are included in the polymer during fiber extrusion. Photo: Marty Gurian, New York City.

- *High-performance vinyl* has been specifically developed for specialized applications such as healthcare. As a result of special formulations and several top coatings, this type of vinyl is usually resistant to prolonged exposures to even concentrated bleach, and it is usually highly stain-resistant and easy to clean. High-performance vinyls can reach levels of durability not previously possible, such as 60,000 double rubs on a Wyzenbeek abrasion machine with a wire screen abradant. Further, special antimicrobial additives have been included in the formulation to achieve resistance to microorganisms considered the most problematic in healthcare (bacteria, fungi, and mildew). In addition, special flame-retardant additives are usually added to the coating formula so that demanding flammability standards can be passed (such as the stringent California Technical Bulletin 133) for an average furniture assembly using an appropriate fire barrier and standard California 117 foam. Some high-performance vinyl upholsteries can pass NFPA 701. High-performance vinyls usually have good sulfide stain resistance, scuff resistance, and cold crack resistance.

- *Modified polyurethanes and urethane types* include a range of materials made primarily from urethane and provide an easy-to-clean surface as well as a fluid barrier. There is even a special category of modified polyurethanes that are faux leather types. The properties of these faux leather types vary as their processes and formulas are different. Some, for example, are bleach cleanable. They appear to have different stain resistance qualities as well as different effectiveness in California Technical Bulletin 133 assembly tests. For example, DesignTex's modified polyurethane faux leather material, Watershed, can usually meet this standard in an average assembly with an active fire barrier and standard California 117 foam.

- *Vinylized fabric* is characterized by fabric laminated on the fabric face with a clear or matte vinyl film (commonly 6 mm) to provide a highly stain-resistant, easy-to-clean, very durable, fluid barrier. Although it is possible to formulate a special film with flame-retardant and antimicrobial additives, this is usually not done. So, typical vinyl lamination is a readily available enhancement that can preserve the actual texture of a textured weave for easy-care properties, but it changes the surface quality of a fabric to a plasticlike character. Yet, it preserves the pattern and largely the color of the fabric selection. The vinylized fabric may lose most or all of its elongation (stretch) in the processing, so ease of upholstering should be confirmed with the furniture manufacturer when using laminated fabric. Delamination and yellowing are possible constraints.

- *Clear protective-coated fabrics* are a relatively new development that attempts to achieve most of the positive attributes of a plasticlike surface, yet maintains the fabriclike surface and elastic qualities of a fabric. As exemplified by C-1 (DesignTex) enhancement coating, this coated fabric has superior stain resistance and easy cleaning properties for most water- and oil-based stains, including a host of healthcare stains. Further, C-1 has an antimicrobial additive that provides durable protection from many bacteria, fungi, and mildew. The original elastic character of the fabric is maintained to provide easy upholstering. The coating is very durable, and many fabrics can be effectively treated. It is not a fluid barrier, although the coating repels moisture, but a fluid barrier can be added to the fabric back.

- *Coated yarn fabrics* containing fabrics made from synthetic filament yarns—commonly polyester or nylon—which have been coated with vinyl provide another upholstery type that combines the attributes of a plastic and a fabric. The stain resistance, safe bleach cleanability, and durability of vinyl can be achieved, yet the design range of wovens (including jacquard weaves and the stretch of a woven) is incorporated. The fabrics are commonly breathable, and consequently they are not woven tightly enough to provide a fluid barrier. One version uses a typical outdoor furniture fabric for sling type lounge chairs. Another type involves a combination of coated yarns and conventional textile types, notably solution-dyed yarn, such as DesignTex's Hardwear-type fabrics.

- *Printed fabrics with clear protective coating* have been recently developed by using a clear coating over a printed polyester substrate that results in a highly stain resistant, easy-to-clean fluid barrier. The fabric type pioneered under the name *Crypton* is now available from a number of fabric and furniture suppliers. It has considerably less plasticlike character (as opposed to the vinylized fabric), but it is still somewhat rigid. Crypton has some breathability, which is an advantage over vinyl or urethane unless perforated. Crypton also contains an antimicrobial additive for protection against bacteria, fungi, and mildew.

FLUID OR MOISTURE BARRIERS

The function of a fluid or moisture barrier is to prevent body fluids or other fluids from penetrating into the furniture assembly (see Figure 11.3). Such fluid penetration could result in the spread of disease, deterioration of the interior components of the assembly, and possibly the development of odor. Certain upholstery types, such as vinyl and urethane coatings and films, are, by their inherent structure, a membrane. Fluid barriers can be successfully laminated to the face or back of many fabrics. Vinylization—the lamination of a clear or matte film, usually to the fabric face—is the most common approach. The film provides good stain resistance and an effective barrier, but results in a vinyl characteristic and a rigid substrate that may be problematic for some types of upholstering. To preserve the fabric character, the film can be laminated to the fabric back. While rigid films are common, new state-of-the-art laminations involve stretchable films that can preserve most of the original stretch of the upholstery so that there will be fewer constraints on upholstering. An example of such a stretchable fluid barrier system is S-1 Plus (DesignTex), which involves a 2-mil polyethylene film that also includes antimicrobial additives in the adhesive system. The adhesive system of this fabric has been developed so that it can withstand common water and solvent (WS) based cleaning methods, including hot-water extraction (steam cleaning).

Sometimes furniture manufacturers may choose to upholster a fluid barrier into the assembly. Perhaps the most established fluid barrier used in this manner is StaphCheck (Herculite Corporation), which is a knitted fabric that is laminated to a vinyl film. StaphCheck is antimicrobial and flame retardant and has been used for some time in a variety of healthcare applications, such as mattress pads.

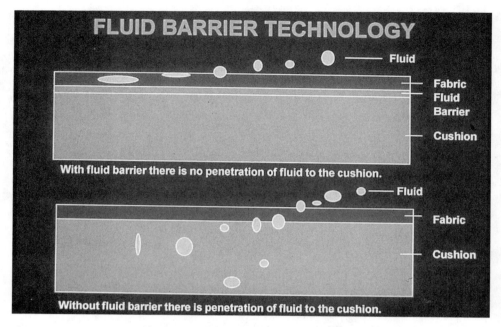

Figure 11.3 Fluid barriers can be successfully laminated to the face or back of many fabrics. Photo: Marty Gurian, New York City.

WALLCOVERING

There are different requirements for wallcovering products in healthcare environments, and a range of wallcovering types are available. From a performance perspective, in the very heavy use applications (such as a major corridor in a busy hospital), a durable vinyl is usually required to provide resistance to the abrading, crushing, tearing, and scuffing of gurneys, wheelchairs, and equipment (Type II as shown in Table 11.1).

In most heavy traffic areas and in areas that require rigorous cleaning (e.g., infectious areas), scrubbing is essential, and flat minimal-textured surfaces are desirable so that dirt and microorganisms can be readily accessed. There are different viewpoints on which standard should be used to classify vinyl wallcovering into Types I or II. The most recent government standard, CCC-W-408C (7/11/89), which is based on performance factors, not weight or backing, is probably the most useful and appropriate (see Table 11.1).

Type III is not on Table 11.1 as it essentially doesn't exist commercially and therefore is not relevant.

It should be noted that certain vinyl wallcovering suppliers have products that are provided with a special protective coating to further upgrade the stain resistance and cleanability. Likewise there are vinyl wallcovering products with special protective

TABLE 11.1   VINYL-COATED WALLCOVERING FEDERAL
SPECIFICATION CCC-W-408C

Requirements	Type I	Type II
Colorfastness to light	200	200
Washability (cycles, minimum)	100	100
Scrubbability (cycles, minimum)	200	200
Abrasion resistance (cycles, minimum)	200	200
Breaking strength (pounds, minimum)	40	50
Machine direction	30	55
Crocking	Good	Good
Stain resistance (reactants)	1–9	1–12
Tear resistance (both directions) (scale rating, minimum)	12 w/o weight	25 w/weight
Blocking resistance (scale rating, maximum)	2	2
Coating adhesion (pounds/inch, minimum)	2	2
Cold crack resistance @ 20°F	No change	No change
Heat aging resistance (7 days at 158°F)	Sample shall not become stiff, brittle, soft, tacky, discolored, or show loss of grain.	Sample shall not become stiff, brittle, soft, tacky, discolored, or show loss of grain.
Flame spread	25	25

[a]See Federal specification CCC-W-408 C for test methods and notes on testing procedures.

high-performance films, such as DuPont's Tedlar polyvinyl fluoride film, which provides a very high level of abrasion and stain resistance, especially suitable for a busy hospital corridor.

Other new high-performance wallcoverings that may also be considered for use in most healthcare areas are those composite fabric constructions composed largely of vinyl-coated polyester yarns. These provide the durability and easy cleanability of vinyl, yet have the textile and aesthetic qualities of a woven jacquard. An example of such a product is DesignTex's Hardwear collection. This is a coated vinyl composite fabric, and, if it contains a solution-dyed warp, it can be cleaned with diluted bleach, which is desirable as a disinfectant.

Another category of durable wallcoverings are acrylic-backed olefins. Composed all or largely of abrasion-resistant air-textured olefin filament yarns, these popularly priced wallcoverings are probably some of the more durable, easy-to-clean textile types available. As a result of the solution-dyed yarns involved, diluted bleach, a strong high-level disinfectant, can be used for cleaning. Fabric suppliers sometimes provide such olefin wallcoverings with antimicrobial additives in the backcoating.

Beyond the especially durable wallcovering types just described, there is a wide range of decorative textile wallcoverings that could be used satisfactorily in noncritical healthcare applications, such as administrative areas. Some of these may be washable or scrubbable—which would obviously be desirable—by housekeeping for infection control.

WRAPPED PANELS

In healthcare environments, there may be workstations, conference rooms, auditoriums, and other spaces that involve wrapped panels. These commonly provide acoustical absorption, tackable surfaces, and decoration. These fabrics are commonly all polyester or a polyester blend. They can be variously upgraded or may contain soil and stain repellant and antimicrobial and/or antistatic finishes, which may be desirable in a healthcare environment.

WINDOW TREATMENTS

There is a wide range of fabric types used for window treatments. Most window treatments must meet commercial building code requirements, typically NFPA 701 Small Scale. Because of this stringent flammability code, it is not surprising that many of the curtains and draperies are inherently flame-retardant polyester or Visa with intrinsic flame resistance, as washing and dry cleaning are commonly involved. Trevira FR or Trevira for Flame Retardant Polyester incorporates a flame-retardant additive in the polymer solution before fiber extrusion. Visa with intrinsic flame resistance is based on a fabric treatment where flame retardants are incorporated in the fabric like a dyestuff and exhausted into the fabric. As neither method involves solution-dyed colors, color is achieved by traditional methods of yarn dyeing, piece dyeing, or printing. Selection of dyestuffs and subsequent colorfastness testing must be carefully done, as fabrics must be repeatedly commercially laundered or dry-cleaned. Furthermore, lightfastness, crocking, dimensional stability, and pilling must be within tolerances and industry standards. Fabrics should ideally release stains in laundering. The common industry voluntary performance standard for lightfastness is a Class 4 minimum at 60 hours (AATCC 16A or E). Soil and stain repellants and antimicrobial treatments are sometimes used to upgrade performance, but flame retardancy must not be significantly affected and finishes may lose their effectiveness with cleaning. Topically treated flame retardants are usually water-based systems, and, if that is the case, then solvent-based systems must be used for cleaning. All types of fabrics are used for window treatments, including wovens, knitted casements, and nonwovens in a wide range of weights.

CUBICLE CLOTH

The curtains used in patient rooms, emergency rooms, clinics, and the like for privacy where more than one patient or person shares an area makes up a major portion of textile use in healthcare. In a modern healthcare environment, cubicle cloth can be a multicolored dobby, jacquard, or warp print—sometimes specially designed and selected for an area such as maternity, pediatrics, surgery, or geriatrics (see color plate 7). Cubicle cloth must meet a number of stringent performance requirements. It must be flame retardant and pass NFPA 701 Small Scale after repeated commercial launderings that involve water temperatures of 160 degrees Fahrenheit. That is why permanent flame-retardant approaches, specifically inherently flame-retardant polyester (Trevira FR) have become the most popular product types used. Soil and stain repellants and antimicrobial treatments are sometimes used on cubicle curtains, but the supplier should be mindful that flame retardancy must be maintained, as it may be reduced in effectiveness with each laundering.

Cubicle cloth is often combined with some type of mesh in the creation of the curtain. Certain suppliers of warp-knitted cubicle curtains have developed proprietary knitted constructions that have interknitted the mesh into the construction so that mesh does not have to be sewn. The most common width for cubicle cloth for woven fabrics is 72 inches wide, 100 inches for knitted integrated mesh curtains.

A new, permanently antimicrobial cubicle fabric has been developed by De-signTex. It is based on the incorporation in the fabric construction of a small content of Microsafe acetate, a new fiber by Hoechst-Celanese Corporation, which contains a Microban B antimicrobial additive. This important innovation is achieved by incorporating yarns in the fabric construction that have been cotextured containing Micro-safe acetate and Trevira FR polyester. The final content by weight involves 7–9 percent Microsafe and 91–93 percent Trevira FR polyester. After repeated commercial launderings, the fabrics continue to meet NFPA 701 Small Scale requirements, as well as providing continual active resistance to bacteria, fungi, and odor, based on laboratory tests and several years of research. It has been observed that topically applied antimicrobial finishes will wash off after repeated commercial launderings. Standard cubicle cloth contains no active means to kill microorganisms. Such active antimicrobial characteristics are very important during the product's use, especially when laundering is infrequent.

ANTIMICROBIAL PRODUCTS

Antimicrobial finishes and additives are used in interior fabrics to inhibit the growth of bacteria, mildew, fungi, and odor. Although healthcare professionals as well as the CDC still consider proper housekeeping the appropriate protocol of an infection control program for environmental surfaces, antimicrobial products are gaining greater popularity as extra insurance in infection control.

Antimicrobial finishes can be effectively applied topically to most interior fabrics in the finishing stage. They can be included as an additive in coatings, laminations, and adhesive systems. There are now permanent antimicrobial fibers available, such as Microsafe Acetate (Hoechst-Celanese) that can be blended with other fibers or combined in fabric mixtures to provide the same antimicrobial features, with a potential advantage of maintaining greater effectiveness despite cleaning and wear. Some of the examples of typical antimicrobial products, along with how the antimicrobial additive is included, are described in Table 11.2.

When the effectiveness of an antimicrobial is evaluated, it is usually tested with regard to gram-positive bacteria, gram-negative bacteria, and fungi. The specific microorganisms that are selected are usually *Staphylococcus Aureus, Klebsiella Pneumoniae,* and *Aspergillus Niger,* as these microorganisms represent these three key types and are related to diseases or conditions of major concerns to healthcare facilities and infection control professionals (see Table 11.3).

There are a number of popular laboratory tests to evaluate the effectiveness of an antimicrobial product. When an antimicrobial is soluble in water, AATCC Test Method 147-1988, the Parallel Streak Method, is often used. Effectiveness is then measured by the size (diameter) of the zone of inhibition around the treated specimen that was incubated in the specific culture (see Figure 11.4). Another popular test is the Shake Flask test developed by the Dow Corporation. When an antimicrobial is incorporated in the product, such as in a coating, NYS 63 Test for Bacteriostatic Activity is the appropriate choice. For antifungal activity, AATCC Test Method 30-1989 is very commonly employed.

Results may vary by test method, and the user may need to analyze carefully different results from several tests before reaching a conclusion on effectiveness.

TABLE 11.2   TYPICAL USES OF ANTIMICROBIAL FINISHES AND ADDITIVES

End Use	Antimicrobial	Name of Product
Upholstery	Topical treatment	Available from most major contract fabric finishers
Protective face coating	Additive to coating	Hi-Tex's Crypton DesignTex's C-1
Fluid barrier	Additive to adhesive system	Herculite's StaphCheck DesignTex's S-1 Plus
Wallcovering	Additive to acrylic and/or latex backcoating	Available from most major contract fabric finishers
Upholstery	Additive to acrylic and/or latex backcoating	Available from most major contract fabric finishers
Vinyl upholstery	Additive to vinyl coating	DesignTex's high-performance vinyls (Galileo, Mendel, Newton)

TABLE 11.3   TYPE OF MICROORGANISMS AND RELATED DISORDERS

Microorganism	Microorganism Type	Disease or Condition
Staphylococcus Aureus	Gram-positive bacteria	Boils, impetigo, pneumoniae, osteomyelitis, meningitis, food poisoning, urogenital infections, toxic shock syndrome
Klebsiella Pneumoniae	Gram-negative bacteria	Severe pneumonia, respiratory, and urinary tract infections, and chronic pulmonary infections
Aspergillus Niger	Fungus	Aspergilloma (pulmonary lesion) and otomycosis

CARE AND MAINTENANCE OF TEXTILES

Proper care and maintenance of a textile is important to achieve satisfactory appearance retention, to encourage product performance for a longer life cycle, and—in the case of healthcare environments—to maintain proper infection control.

Cleaning codes have been established and are being used by progressive fabric

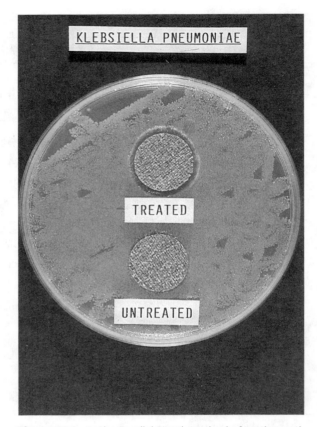

Figure 11.4 In the Parallel Streak Method of testing anti-microbial products, effectiveness is measured by the size of the zone of inhibition around the treated specimen that was incubated in a specific culture. Photo: Marty Gurian, New York City.

suppliers to provide appropriate maintenance and cleaning guidance as well as to reduce the risk of color change, bleeding, dimensional instability, effect of finish, and other related factors. The most widely used cleaning code system and definitions are as follows:

W—Clean only with water-based shampoo or foam upholstery cleaner. Do not overwet.

S—Clean only with mild detergent or shampoo, foam or dry-cleaning solvents, as desired. Do not saturate with liquid.

WS—Clean with mild detergent or shampoo, foam or dry-cleaning solvents, as desired. Do not saturate with liquid.

X—Do not clean with either water- or solvent-based cleaner. Use vacuuming or light brushing only.

A WS cleaning code is understandably very desirable (most 100-percent synthetic interior fabrics are coded WS) as minimal constraints and risks are involved. Even more versatile are fabrics coded WS on which diluted bleach can be used to allow an effective cleansing agent for colored stains and on which a strong disinfectant can be used for infection control.

Water-based procedures are especially effective in removing the following stains: benzoyl peroxide, blood, coffee, cola, urine, cough syrup, germicide (phenol), Maalox, and mayonnaise. Solvent-based agents, such as a volatile solvent, are applicable to the removal of oil-based and greasy stains, quaternary germicides, ice cream, and ketchup. Since removing blood and other body fluids can involve serious risks, all removal procedures and personnel training should be in compliance with the Occupational Safety and Health Administration (OSHA) Bloodborne Pathogen Standard.

In healthcare upholstery, when water-based cleaning is possible, a recommended wet extraction method involves applying an upholstery prespray. The prespray should sit for 10 minutes and then followed by wet extraction using liquid rinsing and an emulsifying agent. This popular professional cleaning method, often referred to as steam cleaning, is the first step in intensive upholstery stain removal. A hot-water extraction machine can be used for the extraction cleaning method in conjunction with an upholstery hand tool for injection and extraction.

When the use of diluted bleach is possible, such as in the case of 100-percent solution-dyed fabrics (certain nylon, olefin, and polyester fabrics), the following procedure is suggested for effective and safe use:

- Highly colored stains that are not removed by hot-water extraction or blood stains requiring bleach as a disinfectant as well as a cleaning agent should be treated with a diluted solution of four parts water to one part household bleach (e.g., Clorox) left on the fabric for 60 minutes and blotted. The fabric should be thoroughly rinsed with water or steam extracted.

- Cleaning in healthcare facilities may often involve disinfectants (such as various types of germicides), and there is an important distinction between the two major chemical types as to their recommendations with regard to nylon- or polyester-content fabrics. Quaternary-type germicides can be used safely if proper rinsing with water follows cleaning to eliminate any possible straining due to the germicide itself. Phenol type germicides are not recommended, as this type of chemical may result in fabric staining even after proper rinsing. It is important to note that disinfectants such as germicides should be used in the proper concentrations recommended by the manufacturer. Disinfectants applied at full concentrations or in highly concentrated solutions may cause problems and prove harmful to fabrics.

- Spotting treatments may be required when a stain is not removed by standard cleaning methods. For example, effective spotting treatments for olefin wallcoverings for healthcare stains include

Betadine—diluted bleach (1:4 bleach to water)
Blood—protein spotter, diluted bleach
Hot coffee—tannin spotter
Germicide (quaternary)—diluted bleach
Scuff marks—chlorinated solvent

It is important to take the following precaution in any cleaning method or spotting treatment:

- Pretest a cleaning method on an inconspicuous area of the fabric to determine if color bleeds, fabric shrinks, or fabric texture or character is altered. A professional cleaning service should be consulted if there is any doubt.
- While the U.S. Department of Health guidelines do not identify surfaces such as upholstery fabrics, cubicle cloth, or wallcovering as prime sources of disease transmission requiring extraordinary measures (such as sterilization), it does urge that good housekeeping practices be followed. Specifically, cleaning and removal of soil should be conducted routinely. Scrubbing is equally as important as the antimicrobial effect of the cleaning agent used.

With respect to cleaning of vinyl upholstery, the following procedures can be followed:

- Most stains can be easily cleaned using warm, soapy water, followed by a clear-water rinse. The use of moderate scrubbing with a medium-bristle may help to loosen soil from the depressions of textured surfaces. For more stubborn stains, certain commercially available mild detergents may be used in accordance with the manufacturers' instructions, and specific cleaning products are often suggested by vinyl upholstery suppliers. Indiscriminate use of strong solvents can severely damage vinyl. Certain vinyl upholsteries, especially high-performance types with special protective coatings, can be safely cleaned and disinfected with diluted bleach, following the manufacturers' directions. With respect to the types of disinfectants, sodium hypochlorite bleach is considered a high-level disinfectant to be used at the proper concentration. It is an optimum choice and involves the least complications. Glutaldehyde, while a high-level disinfectant, must be used carefully, as phenols can, in themselves, induce serious stains on fabrics and vinyls and extract plasticizers from vinyls. Iodophors (iodine) can badly stain fabrics and vinyls. Ammonia is considered an intermediate-level disinfectant, but can be used safely on vinyl.

- Cubicle curtains are ideally cleaned by commercial laundering, with temperatures that reach 160 degrees Fahrenheit for a minimum of 25 minutes to effectively inactivate microorganisms. For additional protection, the use of a small amount of chlorine bleach combined with a mild acid neutralizes the alkalinity to inactivate microorganisms. The microbicidal action and loosening action of soaps or detergents is also quite effective.

FLAMMABILITY TESTS

Some of the flammability standards in the United States are as follows:

- Upholstery is largely unregulated in the United States with the exception of a few states, such as California, Illinois, Massachusetts, and the Port Authority of New York and New Jersey where California Technical Bulletin 133 is enforced (this regulation was discussed earlier in this chapter). Many follow the Voluntary Performance Standards of the Association for Contract Textiles (see Appendix B), which uses California Technical Bulletin 117, Section E, as an upholstery standard.
- Most building code regulations require wallcovering to meet a Class A rating in accordance with the ASTM E-84 (adhered mounting), with Smoke Density sometimes limited further for certain areas. The typical Class A requirements are not to exceed a flame spread of 25 and a smoke density of 450.
- Most building code regulations require wrapped panel (including workstations) and stretched wall upholstery installations to meet an ASTM E-84 (unadhered or panel mounting) Class A rating with similar modifications in certain areas for smoke density. Some building codes allow one lower rating for sprinkled facilities and conversely may require a more severe standard for a nonsprinkled facility, such as the room or corner test (U.B.C. 42-2).
- Most building codes require all curtains, draperies, and window treatments in commercial installations to pass NFPA 701 Small Scale. If laundering is involved, such as in cubicle cloth, it must be included in the test procedure.
- California Technical Bulletin 133 is a stringent commercial furniture assembly test standard that has been enforced in a number of states in the 1990s, requiring furniture manufacturers, suppliers (e.g., fabric manufacturers), specifiers, and even end users to understand this demanding assembly test and the interrelationship of furniture components and furniture design. The test involves a full-scale test of actual furniture pieces or a mock-up of cushions following the test protocol, which are then exposed to an intense open flame from a gas burner for 80 seconds (see Figure 11.5). Various criteria cannot be exceeded, such as tempera-

Figure 11.5   California Technical Bulletin 133 is a full-scale test of actual furniture pieces or mock-up of cushions that are exposed to an intense open flame from a gas burner for 80 seconds. Photo: Marty Gurian, New York City.

ture increase, smoke opacity, carbon monoxide, weight loss, and heat release for a pass. As of the writing of this book, this regulation, in various forms and modifications, is mandated by three major states—California, Illinois, and Massachusetts—and the Port Authority of New York and New Jersey. Directed at first at high-risk commercial facilities (specifically healthcare institutions and public meeting places that did not have sprinkler systems), the regulations now include, in some states (Massachusetts, especially the City of Boston, and the Port Authority), a far wider range of commercial facilities. Some new or refurbished facilities choose this standard, although it is not mandated.

Full-scale California Technical Bulletin 133 testing has revealed that the various potential key components, such as fabric type, varies in fire performance primarily by fiber content and weight. The results of this test can be significantly improved by variously upgrading the foam, using special flame-retardant finishes and backcoatings and especially by the use of specially developed flame-resistant fire barriers that are usually composed of fiberglass or aramid. Furniture design is a major factor, particularly in healthcare projects involving fully upholstered arms and high backs.

Most healthcare furniture manufacturers have developed test databases for their product lines and often have preapproved fabric types or various categories or systems to rate Customer's Own Material (COM) fabrics. Often, joint tests by furniture manufacturers and fabric suppliers are required on larger projects when insufficient test information exists. The Association of Contract Textiles and the Decorative Fabrics Association spearheaded a joint industry flammability study with cooperation and support from the California Bureau of Home Furnishings and Insulation, as well as other major related trade organizations. The 26 most-used fabric types were studied in full-scale tests as well as by the Cone Calorimeter, a promising bench-scale test. The full-scale test results were made available to all related industries in June 1995.

COMPARATIVE ANALYSIS

In selecting the optimum textile or material for a specific healthcare application, develop a list of priorities or needs. Rank these priorities or needs in order of importance and note and address any essential criteria first. Table 11.4 lists some of the critical characteristics of four upholstery materials for clinical lounge seating.

The subsequent analysis and conclusions would differ depending on what is most essential to the user.

- If an essential need is to have a fabric-like quality, then the solution-dyed fabric and clear protective coated cotton/polyester fabrics are potential candidates.
- If an essential need is outstanding furniture workability (where stretch is required), then vinylized fabric is not a good alternative.
- If the use of diluted bleach is an essential need for infection control, then clear protective coated cotton/polyester fabric is eliminated, but a clear protective coated solution-dyed fabric could be considered.
- If a fluid barrier is required, but there is no budget to pay the cost of laminating an additional fluid barrier to either the solution-dyed fabric or the clear protective coated fabric, then the high-performance vinyl or vinylized fabrics that have built-in fluid barriers would be more optimum candidates.

By such comparative analysis and listing of needs, the appropriate alternative can be identified and possible constraints of various alternatives best understood. Healthcare textiles and materials will continually be improved, and totally new developments will evolve that may present fewer constraints. An analysis like Table 11.4 will need to be continually updated to incorporate any advances or changes.

It is clear that education on healthcare textiles and appropriate problem-solving exercises or case discussions are important needs that require proper attention. In this way, the healthcare textile or material specifier can be better served in an ever widening array of more complex alternatives.

TABLE 11.4 COMPARATIVE ANALYSIS OF FOUR HIGH-PERFORMANCE UPHOLSTERY MATERIAL TYPES FOR HEALTHCARE CLINICAL LOUNGE SEATING

			FABRIC DESCRIPTION		
Performance Factor	*Solution-dyed Nylon*	*Clear Protective Coating[a]*	*High-Performance Vinyl*	*Vinylized*	
Method of design	Jacquard	Jacquard	Print	Jacquard	
Content	100% nylon	65% cotton/35% polyester	100% vinyl face	65% cotton/35% polyester	
Weight—ounces/yard (oz./yd.) (54″)	17 oz.	19.4 oz.	32.0 oz.	26.4 oz.	
Finish/additives	Acrylic backcoating and soil- and stain-repellant finish	Thin coating with soil- and stain-repellant and antimicrobial additives	Protective face coating and vinyl with antimicrobial and fire-retardant additives	6-mil matte PVC film	
Surface characteristics/ texture/comfort	Fabric character unchanged	Much of the original fabric character maintained	Plastic surface	Plastic surface	
Breathability[b]	Excellent	Excellent	None	None	

Property				
Fluid barrier properties	Not a fluid barrier, but a fluid barrier can be laminated to the fabric back	Not a fluid barrier, but a fluid barrier can be laminated to the fabric back	Active fluid barrier	Active fluid barrier on the fabric face
Antimicrobial properties	None, but can be easily added through a topical finish enhancement	Excellent	Excellent	Usually none, but an additive could be added to film
Furniture workability (nonmolded)	Excellent	Excellent, but cannot use steam	Excellent	Fair, manufacturing that requires stretch will not be feasible
General stain resistance	Good	Excellent	Excellent	Excellent
Cleanability	Excellent, W/S cleaning code and can use diluted bleach; cannot use certain disinfectants that stain	Excellent, W cleaning code; cannot use bleach with this cotton-blend substrate[c]; cannot use certain disinfectants that stain	Excellent, W cleaning code; can use diluted bleach; cannot use certain disinfectants that stain	Excellent, W cleaning code; can use diluted bleach; cannot use certain disinfectants that stain

[a]Such as C-1 type on a cotton blend.

[b]Based on Moisture Vapor Transmission Test (ASTM E-96).

[c]Can use bleach on fabrics that are solution dyed and coated with clear protective coating.

Marty Gurian is manager, technical services, for DesignTex, Inc., in New York, New York.

EDITOR'S NOTE: *See Appendix B for a list of textile specification standards.*

References

ACT/DFA Joint Industry Flammability Study. California Technical Bulletin #133, Full Scale Test Results, June 1995.

Becker, C., ed. "Occupational HIV Infection, Risks and Risk Reduction." *Occupational Medicine.* Vol. 4, 1989.

DesignTex Contract Upholstery Cleaning Manual. New York: DesignTex, Inc., 1992.

DesignTex Contract Wallcovering, Panel, and Wall Upholstery Cleaning Manual. New York: DesignTex, Inc., 1992.

Williams, W. "Guideline for Infection Control in Hospital Personnel." Atlanta: U.S. Department of Health and Human Services, Centers for Disease Control. July 1983.

<table>
<tr><td></td><td>12</td></tr>
</table>

WALLCOVERING/ SURFACE DESIGN

Patricia A. Rodemann, IIDA, Affiliate Member ASID, CMG

Far from just a "pretty pictures" side of the business, surface design and the selection of wall treatments assume even greater importance in the healthcare setting. Choosing the appropriate treatment can be an integral component in setting the tone for a healing and stress-reducing environment, so necessary in a healthcare facility. When asked how important the surface material selection is in the design process, architects and interior designers responded as follows (Rodemann, 1991):

Very important	72%
Somewhat important	21%
No opinion	2%
Not that important	1%
Totally insignificant	3%

Furthermore, making the recommendation or writing the specification is only half of the story. Several aspects unique to the healthcare setting, including functional/performance, financial, and aesthetic considerations, place this type of specification apart.

In examining functional considerations, there are questions of flammability, toxicity/environmental regulations, indoor air quality (IAQ), specific maintenance needs, and replacement needs. The financial concern relates not only to the initial cost of a product, but also to surface preparation, renovation needs, and the bottom line of attracting customers by presenting a specific image or ambiance and long- versus short-term approaches. The appearance or aesthetic of the space has a behavioral and psychological impact on both the staff and patients and their families and friends. This aesthetic consideration is more pronounced in the healthcare setting because of its diagnostic and healing role.

Let's start with a few construction and facility fundamentals and the orientation of the site. It is important for the designer or space planner who is specifying wallcovering and surface materials to understand the availability of natural lighting, the synthetic lighting that will be installed, the direction of the light source, and the lighting controls that will be available. These factors will have an impact on the specific hue, saturation, color, and texture being selected. Incandescent fixtures will render warm tones better; fluorescent lights will render cool tones better. Downlights can accentuate texture, and flicker will accentuate a perception of pattern movement and afterimages.

From an HVAC standpoint, the designer always assumes the best, but needs to consider humidity and airflow/air registers. Areas with excess humidity or higher moisture content are prone to the growth of mold and mildew spores and bacterial contaminants. These factors, coupled with a need for frequent cleaning with biocides and other chemical cleaning agents, have direct bearing on the material selection and whether the final surface will be *hard*—tile, stone, laminate, paint, glass, metal, wood—or *soft*—wallcovering, fabric, panel, upholstery.

Other architectural and site factors relate more to the intangibles: the view, landscaping, ambiance, proximity to other landmarks, and the historic background and name/origination. Obviously, the size of a space and its particular subspecialty will have the greatest bearing on the interior material selections. A sole practitioner with a family practice in a small town will have far different needs than the emergency room in a hospital of a major city. Not all spaces within healthcare facilities are medical treatment areas—there are offices, halls, and cafeterias. Working in tandem, the design and build teams can create the best possible space for all needs, more effective than the designer working in isolation.

One final significant factor also has an influence on the selection of surface products. A recent professional practice survey of several thousand designer/specifiers in the architectural and design community revealed the following about client input in the selection process (Rodemann, *Survey,* 1991):

Makes the decision	12%
Quite a lot	40%
Some	32%
Not much	4%
None	2%

Design decisions are not always objective and do not always follow the best recommendations of professionals. The surgeon's wife's decorator may have ideas other than those of the chief facility manager; the inner city AIDS hospice may rely on donated products.

FUNCTIONAL AND PERFORMANCE CONSIDERATIONS

The most important single factor is the activity that will take place in the space. A heavy/high-use space will obviously be subject to more abuse, wear, and tear and will require more frequent cleaning and renovation.

Building codes and federal, state, and local regulations also need to be taken into account. New construction versus renovation also impacts the selection process. In a renovation, out-of-service time and minimal impact on surrounding activities and processes are very important. For example, the chief facility designer for a large metropolitan hospital made a decision to go with a latex water-based fleck paint coating because of low volatile organic compounds (VOC) emissions, which would not have the drying odors associated with oil or alkyd products. Because of the proximity of the space to patient areas, it simply was out of the question to use the more durable oil-based products. In addition, harder smoother surface finishes would tend to show nicks and other abrasions more quickly due to the action of carts and other equipment.

In another example, a clinic with many smaller offices and a high patient load opted for fabric-backed vinyl wallcoverings, but didn't need a heavier-weight Type II product in wide width (refer to Chapter 11 and Table 11.1 for a discussion of Type I and II products). The selection of 27-inch fabric-backed vinyls and borders suited its needs and gave greater surface interest and longevity than a flat paint surface. An ob/gyn clinic preferred using wallcovering because of the homelike ambiance and its ability to visually unify the many utilitarian tables, chairs, and furniture finishes by picking up many of their colors.

For an emergency room setting in a major city, wallcovering was clearly not the answer, even in a Type II weight for the patient waiting area. While Type II wallcoverings can be purchased with a stain-resistant top coatings, none resisted the effects of a particular waxlike hair-styling product for African Americans who were big users of the facility. Family members in the waiting area (often for hours on end) would sit back in the chairs and rest their heads against the wall, leaving a brownish-orangish stain. To solve the problem, the specifier used tile to a higher-than-chair-rail level with wallcovering above it.

The rigid wallcovering products (Acrovyn and others) also offer good performance, especially in below-chair-rail applications, although there may be seam treatments required with some products.

It is imperative that the designer/specifier check the manufacturer's product specifications for each product carefully and evaluate whether a particular product will stand up to the demands of the space. In many cases, closed specifications can serve the needs of a facility better than the open spec that allows substitution. Designers should require product test results or literature showing product performance regarding common staining agents and should review abrasion testing.

It is also a good idea to consider maintenance. Many products do not stand up well to scrubbing with bleach or other cleaning solutions. Replacement/refinishing of damaged areas may yield less than desirable results. It's important to consider whether the facility will need backup inventory of a particular wallcovering (especially a custom order) of a given lot number to avoid color variation from a new lot. Designers should find how easy/difficult it will be to replicate a multicolor fleck coating invisibly.

Most facilities today have a combination of products, from laminates to tile to paint coatings and fabric-backed wallcoverings. Table 12.1 shows performance and cost variables for different surface design products.

In new construction, drywall may have differing levels of porosity. This is why a good primer is critical. Uneven porosity can cause a painted surface to have different sheen levels. The face paper of the wallboard can vary too. Porous paper leaves little binder on the surface as it sucks up paint. This lessens adhesion of future paint coats and could also affect wallcovering adhesion, either causing a viselike grip or less stability if not primed.

With wallcoverings, there are other unique problems. For simple stripes and textures, a random match is often recommended. Yet, sometimes this recommendation isn't followed on the job site and the wallcovering *shades* resulting in an edge-to-edge variance instead of a seamless appearance. This can be particularly noticeable in long corridors or in sidelighting or downlighting conditions, or it can stand out at a specific time of day. Designers should always include hanging instructions in the product specification.

FINANCIAL CONSIDERATIONS

There are stories from installers about submitting a bid to "do the job right" with removal and disposal of an old wallcovering, mildewcide application, proper surface cleaning, and two-coat priming, and then installation of a new Type II wallcovering in "miles and miles" of corridors. In one case, the job went to the low bidder, selected by the purchasing agent who advised the facility manager and purchasing manager that it wasn't necessary to clean, prime, and apply mildewcide because the bidder's more aggressive adhesive would already contain mildewcide. The low bidder also made a product substitution on the stipple finish. What appeared on the product tip card and what arrived on site were slightly different colors, which threw the designer's palette out of whack. The designer arrived to meet with the facility manager and discovered the unpleasant surprise. Testing a corner of the product for removability, the two

TABLE 12.1 PERFORMANCE AND COST VARIABLES: SURFACE DESIGN PRODUCTS

Treatment	Performance Traits	Life-Cycle Costs	Product Considerations
Latex paint	Smooth coverage/minimal odor	Will require repainting in high-traffic areas; shows wear & tear	Priming, number of coats, surface prep & labor—investigate new formulations
Oil-based paint	Excellent coverage	More durable than latex	Greater drying time; VOC (odor) concern, plus above considerations
Multicolor fleck coating	Excellent coverage	Touch-ups may be obvious	Multistep process; both water-based and oil-based products
Stucco/plaster	Excellent coverage; additional coating required	High depth may harbor bacteria; good maintenance required	Locks in a look; not advisable for some spaces
Cellulose fiber coating	Excellent coverage	Touch-ups visible; new product	Different installation technique; trowel or spray; may not meet all healthcare specs
Paintable wallcoverings	Excellent coverage	Not typically for high-use areas	Requires multistep installation
Wallpaper	Good coverage	Not a high-use product	Usually Class A, but may not meet all commercial specs or scrubbability
Breathable wallcoverings	Good coverage	For problem areas: high humidity	May offer additional design options; not for ICU or patient rooms
Fabric-backed vinyl wallcoverings—Type I & II	Excellent coverage; Type II—corridors, heavier use	6–10-year life +/−; many textures	Durable, scrubbable, some environmental opposition
Fiberglass wallcoverings	Excellent coverage; can be painted	6–10-year life +/−	Rugged, not as many appearance options; depth may harbor bacteria
Textiles/polyolefin, etc.	Excellent coverage	4–6-year life +/−; specialized labor/maintenance	Requires specialized installation; not advised for ICU, patient room; difficult to clean

(continued)

TABLE 12.1 (*Continued*)

Treatment	Performance Traits	Life-Cycle Costs	Product Considerations
Semirigid wall sheeting or Type II wallcovering vinyl	Excellent coverage	10-year life +/−; removal may damage substrate	Specialized installation/removal; seams treated differently
Rigid/hard wall sheeting panels	Excellent coverage	10-year life +/−	For exceptionally demanding spaces; seams need cover strips; specialized installation; adhesives
Tile/laminates	Excellent coverage	10-year life +/−	Grout/seams need special cleaning treatment; healthcare specific

Note: Many new healthcare-specific products are being developed all the time. Many new finishes are being introduced, and many test results are improving. Ask for results from your supplier.

discovered that removal would also take off whatever was left on surface underneath and leave it lumpy and unsuitable for future coatings or wallcoverings without significant additional cost. Worse yet, the repaired section stood out for all to see.

Fully 85 percent of specifiers always or often spec surface design. But there are other inputs. In one case, a major hospital with a standards manual for all finishes had limited the selection to eight surface treatments across all areas of the facility. Some of the administrative staff and top surgeons wanted their own suites designed to their own tastes. This had not been budgeted. The nursing staff and a volunteer group selected children's borders for a playroom and another waiting room area. A similar thing happened in the obstetrics wing. Before long, there were other surprises to deal with.

In yet another project, the board of administrators enforced a specific look that necessitated spending considerably more in the public areas and skimping in the staff areas. In yet another project—a renovated office complex adjoining the healthcare facility—the designer (or perhaps the installer) went wild with the zolatone spray mix. The mix was custom designed to incorporate multiple colors of flecks—black, gray, red, aqua, and yellow—covering doorways, trim, and even the water fountains and pipes. Even with the furniture, vinyl-composition tile floor, and carpet installed, the space had an *Alice in Wonderland* sort of appearance. Over time, the nicks, abrasions, and discolorations accumulated. A new tenant moved in, and the space became a nightmare in a subsequent renovation, necessitating costly replacement of the finish.

In bidding a project for healthcare facilities, designers should consider how often replacement will be needed and whether maintenance practices will be adequate. In many cases, a short-term decision costs more. For example, perhaps the square-foot cost of a wallcovering is higher than paint, yet in the life-cycle time frame of wallcovering, the area will require two or three repaintings. Sometimes it simply isn't necessary to create the long-lived interior. In one office tower complex, the Type II printed wallcovering installed 20 years ago is in almost perfect condition; yet it clearly says "1970s." If the occupant will be changing uses of a space, renovating often, or keeping up with a more timely appearance, Type I wallcovering may work fine, or the latex paint may be just what the doctor ordered. Restaurants live and die on menu and format changes—the restaurant serving California cuisine of the early 1980s could be the late 1980s diner and then the Tex-Mex palace of today. Healthcare environments, while not quite in the same league, do cater to the same customers whose tastes are constantly being updated.

One designer whose practice caters to sole practitioners and small clinics uses a one-wall pattern treatment in the examining rooms—just enough to brighten and freshen the space, but not enough to add substantially to the cost. The same designer relies on more frequent changes of borders, accessories, and artwork—a delight to the staff who spend countless hours in the space. She periodically changes accent uphol-stery colors of lobby chairs and uses many similar design tricks as part of her business plan on a quarterly retainer fee (see color plate 8).

Another cost-effective technique is to use a different surface treatment on abut-ments and at transition points. In a senior living facility, this technique successfully mixed a soft-peach, silk-appearance, low-weight Type I wallcovering with a blueber-ry-color-embossed Type II texture on abutments. Cherry wood mouldings, artwork, and subtle patterned carpet added elegance. The main elevator areas were accented with decorative borders and a floral pattern on one wall only—the wall with a large window and traditional swagged window treatment. This saved money beautifully.

A particularly nice feature of the textural options of many commercial wallcover-ings is their ability to lend a richer appearance in lower lighting conditions. In the presence of spotlights, fan lights, or accent fixtures, the embossing is accentuated. In the passageway from a concrete block parking area, a durable hard-surface laminate or Acrovyn can serve as a more pleasing transition than the stained and spotted painted concrete block surface.

There are many positive examples where use of a new surface treatment or renovation can make a substantial difference in the perception and performance of a facility. Given a choice between the offices of two equally talented endodontists, one with a dated waiting area and the other with fresh new decor, most people would opt for the latter. Even the small-town hospital with 1950s-issue chest-high green tile can accomplish a facelift with a decorative border. With a competitive economic environment, it makes financial sense to put the best appearance forward in the community to attract customers and assure them that they count.

AESTHETIC CONSIDERATIONS

There are many written and unwritten rules about healthcare colors and patterns. Healthcare usage is heavily context dependent. Beyond the age and condition of the people who use the healthcare facility, one needs to consider the universal qualities and both physiological and behavioral responses to pattern and color. There are several conditions that are known to be affected by pattern exposure in sensitive individuals. They include the following (Rodemann 1991):

1. Migraines
2. Motion sickness
3. Epilepsy
4. Certain visual corrections
5. Conditions requiring medication that may predispose individual to sensitivity
6. Alcohol or drug use (anesthesia)
7. Advanced age
8. Dementia/mental instabilities

Of the respondents in a professional practice survey, 68 percent felt that surface design has the ability to affect an occupant's behavior (Rodemann 1991). This belief is well founded. Eighty-two percent of migraine sufferers were found to be stripe sensitive, while only 6.2 percent without migraines showed the same sensitivity. "Many subjects who found the striped patterns aversive reported, after testing, prior experience of stripe-induced discomfort involving looking at escalator treads, ironing striped shirts, or looking at miniblinds, striped wallpaper, or paneling" (Soso and Marcus 1989). The suitability of different patterns for healthcare settings is shown in Table 12.2.

People's likes and dislikes depend a lot on age. The same geometric patterns liked by 50 percent of the median age 27 group were disliked by 77 percent of the median age 77 group, and the positive ranking dropped to zero. This information comes from a four-year, five-part thesis research project on the behavioral response of individuals to pattern design. The studies involved focus groups, interviews, and hidden video-taping in addition to behavioral mapping at two locations. In every study, three common themes were evident: timeliness/dated quality of a pattern; the rendition (whether it appeared cheap/poorly drawn or expensive); complexity of the pattern (how busy the pattern was; few subjects were tolerant of too much "busy-ness").

TABLE 12.2   PATTERN CATEGORY SUITABILITY FOR HEALTHCARE SETTINGS

Usage	Floral	Geometric	Stripe	Graphic	Texture	Textile
Suitable for healthcare	47%	24%	24%	59%	53%	40%
Suitable for home	59%	47%	53%	70%	40%	40%
Suitable for all 4 walls	70%	(76% disagree)	47%	76%	76%	65%
Invites relaxation/restful	24%	(94% disagree)	12%	18%	53%	24%
Perception of movement	41%	65%	53%	65%	12%	24%
Perception of afterimages	18%	65%	65%	18%	12%	6%
Most preferred style of design category	53% contemporary brushed	70% diagonal-plaid; light rendition	41% freeform light squiggle	40% chevron, avoid dots; high contrast	47% faux effect	59% vertical silk

Source: Rodemann, 1991.

One of the most important factors in use of pattern in healthcare settings is whether the pattern has "movement." The lower the perception of afterimages and movement, the better. What are we referring to? The natural physiology of vision, the spacing of our eyes, and the eye-brain connection, along with our inherent tendencies to want to fill in the lines, connect the dots, or reach closure are all biologically, psychologically, and neurologically based.

Let's examine this usage in Table 12.2 further. Obviously, the perception of movement or afterimages is not a desirable attribute if the goal is relaxation and healing. High-contrast graphics, florals that appear to crawl, and hard-edge stripes that appear to vibrate aren't good selections.

Interviews with dozens of subjects led to the preference listing in Table 12.3. There was an unfortunate side effect of an acoustical dot pattern on some of the research subjects that was documented during a POE. The pattern appeared to move to 86 percent of those using the space; the same percentage found the space "uncomfortable"; 93 percent found the pattern disruptive; and 79 percent found it wearying. For many (79 percent), the pattern appeared to vibrate, and this perception of vibration became overbearing to 72 percent during the course of less than one hour. Similar dot patterns are frequently used for ceiling tiles. In situations where the patient must wait for long periods of time, avoid these pattern types.

Pictorial designs and historic or novelty themes such as renditions of shells, fish, fruit, horses and hunt scenes, cartoon and licensed characters, dishes, and dolls. In general, these looks are more faddish and can date themselves quickly in a commercial

TABLE 12.3   WHAT DOES WORK AND WHY

FLORAL DESIGNS	GEOMETRIC DESIGNS	STRIPE DESIGNS
the right scale	low contrast—light touch	neatness in rendition
simple	familiar	crisp
not overbearing	contemporary	orderly
not fussy	not too busy	keep subdued
doesn't crawl	simple	low contrast
not involved	least printed pattern	not busy or too close
orderly	keep it subtle	together
contemporary rendition	watch the scale	freeform, artistic
casual feel	diagonals best	make fun
brushy look, watercolor	watch spacing	watch the spacing
not too busy	not hard edged	comfortable, familiar
		good "bridge" pattern

GRAPHIC DESIGNS	NATURAL TEXTURE DESIGNS	FABRIC/MATERIAL LOOKS
light feeling	simplest rendition	like comfy clothing
refreshing	usable anywhere	variegated surface
like shapes like vacation—chevrons, boats	subtle surface interest	has depth to it
familiar	peaceful	airy, simple, quiet
homey	orderly feel	less busy
differing values	avoid poor imitations	gentle look
don't make regimented	keep it light; not heavy or dense	casual elegance
watch 'connectibility'	want to look more closely	avoid dense or fussy
keep soft and intriguing	stone looks could appear cold; wood dated	watch faded effects
soothing in open areas	avoid contrived renditions	avoid roughness/coarse

Source: Rodemann 1991.

setting. Many (in all three age groups) found the familiarity of these types of patterns almost irritating, suitable for only certain types of settings. Subjects were highly sensitive to the rendition of the pictorial design. A watercolor design of a seashell was deemed "cheap" and unimaginative.

As mentioned earlier, context is very important. What works in the public areas for the majority of the population might not be suitable for those with a high degree of visual correction or advanced age. One elderly person reported that a marble design appeared to be fuzzy textured. In a nursing home, the delicate sheen of a satin stripe might be lost on all but the family who may feel it is paying too much for a facility with such expensive decorative touches. The patient with dementia may find that the large cabbage roses look like terrifying faces that talk back. The heavily sedated patient in the hospice may find the soft watercolor stripe unsettling. A large children's hospital had to replace what was intended to be a "cute" floorcovering design with

TABLE 12.4   SELECTED PATTERN ATTRIBUTES/ATTITUDES FROM BIPOLAR
ADJECTIVE CHECKLIST[a]

	Florals[b]	Geometrics[c]	Stripes[d]	Graphics[e]	Naturals[f]	Textile/Texture Prints[g]
Appealing	53%	18%	24%	47%	59%	40%
Hospitable	59%	12%	18%	40%	35%	47%
Restful	24%	6%	12%	18%	53%	24%
Positive	29%	6%	12%	24%	35%	24%
Livable	41%	24%	12%	47%	53%	53%
Comfortable	47%	18%	29%	47%	59%	35%
Like	41%	0%	26%	65%	47%	41%

[a] Subjects shown four patterns per category; rated individually and in groups.
[b] Florals include: random small, traditional, contemporary, stylized.
[c] Geometrics include: gingham, plaid, check, diagonal.
[d] Stripes include: ticking, broad, narrow, freeform.
[e] Graphics include: chevron, flame, minidiamond, medallion.
[f] Naturals include: stucco, stone, wood, faux sponged.
[g] Textile/textures include: burlap, silk, damask, casement.
Source: Rodemann, Implications, 1991.

squares and ladybugs because children crawling over the surface perceived the pattern
as optical and undulating. On medication, and close to the surface, they tended to feel
a sense of motion sickness and vomited more often than they did after the offending
pattern was removed.

A sense of familiarity also varies from individual to individual based on upbring-
ing and cultural heritage. Stereotyping seems to be second nature to us, and pattern
selection is no different. The same checkerboard pattern appears on a flag at the
racetrack, on Italian restaurant tablecloths, and on Ralston-Purina signage, but has
quite different connotations. Connotative meanings do not always overtly extend
consciously to walls, floors, or sofas. Sometimes the designer is covert (as in the set
design of a TV sitcom) in setting the mood or triggering a memory. Table 12.4 shows
some selected pattern attributes.

As creatures with centuries of acclimation to the exterior environment, we are
used to designs from nature—the changing patterns of light and color during the day
and the season. Simulating or effecting such an interior can help the patient feel
connected and centered if it is not contrived or overly aggressive. Using a color palette
in sync with these patterns is perceived as pleasant and relaxing. Wherever possible,
allowing the patient a sense of comfort and control over his/her space is paramount.
Since this usually cannot be accomplished with wall treatments, adjustable lighting
and/or art selection (an integral part of surface design) is advised for patients with

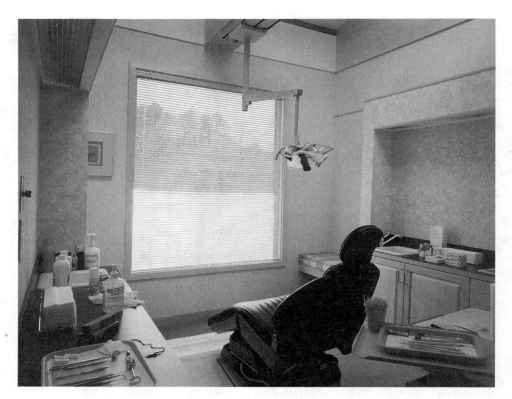

Figure 12.1 It is best to select a treatment and color palette that will not significantly date itself in the hard-surface finishes and avoid selecting noisy wallcovering patterns. Project: dental office. Wallcovering: Satinesque Designer Supplement 27" wallcoverings. Photo: Patricia Rodemann, Designed for Success, Lewis Center, Ohio.

longer-term stays. For the clinic, laboratory, or other institutional space, select a treatment and color palette that will not significantly date itself in the hard-surface finishes, and avoid selecting "noisy" patterns in the wallcoverings and soft goods treatments (see Figure 12.1).

Fully 39 percent of the architectural/design community is engaged in some type of healthcare design (Rodemann, *Survey*, 1991). This could be broken down further into design for laboratories (6 percent), government (16 percent), schools/universities (22 percent), senior living (12 percent), hospital/institutional (18 percent), and offices (70 percent).

Current practices suggest a high level of pattern awareness and specification. Table 12.5 shows what pattern types are specified for wallcoverings.

The research continues with two major national studies culminating in 1996. These will take color combinations into account among many other new variables.

Finally, it is important to consider the awareness and exposure level of the individual patient or staffer. In several months of behavioral mapping of two sites

TABLE 12.5   PATTERN TYPES SPECIFIED FOR WALLCOVERINGS

Pattern Type	Often/Sometimes	Seldom/Never	Patterns Deemed Suitable for Healthcare by Public
Floral	43%	57%	47%
Stripe	73%	21%	24%
Plaid/check	36%	64%	24%
Geometric/graphic	78%	21%	59%
Natural textures	86%	15%	53%
Solids	84%	14%	n/a
Historic prints	29%	71%	n/a
Novelty designs	20%	45%	0%
Borders	65%	34%	n/a

Source: Rodemann, 1991.

with geometric and stripe patterns installed, there was a dramatic difference in behavior. This was confirmed by hidden video camera. These patterns were not "pop art," and are commonly produced and specified. The "attention-getting ability" behavior in response to the pattern rose from 8 to 71 percent in the presence of the stripe pattern and from 0 to 51 percent in the presence of the geometric pattern. The behavior of engaging others in conversation dropped from 54 to 11 percent in the stripe pattern room, and more conversation took place in the other room. Subjects exhibited more nervous behaviors (i.e., glancing around) in the striped room, and their time spent in the space dropped; conversations declined from 29 to 8 percent.

In a follow up survey, the staff found both designs distracting and wearying (75 percent), and 100 percent felt both patterns appeared to move. Twelve percent of the customers claim to have spent less time as a result of the design, and 75 percent of the staff avoided looking at the wall.

Surface pattern design and selection is important. The right environment can create an uplifting, positive, calming, and healing effect. Often the effects can be subtle and subliminal, barely noticeable at all. Knowing that designers can make a difference in their specifications, impacting potentially thousands of people over the course of many years, adds value and validity to the profession and an intangible reward for practicing design.

Patricia A. Rodemann is the former vice president of business development and planning for Borden Inc. (Guard Contract Wallcovering). She is president of her own design research firm, Designed for Success, in Lewis Center, Ohio.

References

Rodemann, P. A. "The Implications of Surface Design: A Behavioral Response." Thesis research, Ohio State University, 1991.

Soso, M. J. and Marcus, D. "Migraine and Stripe Induced Visual Discomfort." *Arch. Neurology* 46 (October 1989).

III

HUMAN NEEDS

13

DESIGNING FOR THE SENSES

Wayne Ruga, AIA, IIDA, Allied Member ASID

ur training has led us to believe that we perceive the environment through information received by the five senses. This is true, but only to a limited degree.

THE EXPERIMENT

To provide the evidence that may cause you to consider other possibilities for receiving information about the environment, we might conduct the following experiment.

OBJECTIVE

To gather data about the human ability to perceive color over a limited distance with closed eyes.

SUPPLIES

- Six colored pieces of paper—each a minimum of 8½″ × 11″ and all the same size (red, orange, yellow, green, blue, purple)
- Index cards—one for each subject
- Writing instruments—one for each subject

EXPLANATION

This is best administered to a large group of subjects.

- Each subject is given an index card and a writing instrument.
- It is best if the test environment is neutral in color and has abundant natural light (not a requirement).
- It is best if the administrator wears clothing that is neutral in color (not a requirement).
- It is also best if, before beginning the exercise, the administrator explains to the group members what they are going to do.

PROCEDURE

- The administrator stands in the front of the group, in the center, clearly visible of all of the subjects.
- The administrator then holds up the six pieces of colored paper for the group to see. After doing this, he or she shuffles the papers.
- The administrator asks the subjects to get into a comfortable position, relax, take several deep breaths, and close their eyes.
- A volunteer sitting near the front center is then asked to select one of the six pieces of colored paper with eyes closed. The six pieces are fan spread. The administrator takes the volunteer's hand and passes it over all the sheets of paper several times before instructing the volunteer to select one. The administrator describes this process to the group as it is occurring. The group is told when a specific piece of paper has been chosen, but not which color.
- The administrator then stands in position and holds up the selected piece of paper to the group for two minutes. The task of the subjects is to "feel" the color being "transmitted" to them and to write the name of the color on the index card after they have felt it. (It is necessary for the subjects to have the index cards and writing instruments in hand and to write with closed eyes.) Once the color is written down, the subjects may open their eyes. The group must remain silent during the experiment.
- The administrator tells the group when 60, 90, and 120 seconds have elapsed.
- When two minutes have elapsed, the index cards are collected and the results tabulated.

DISCUSSION

Both objective and subjective data will be available as a result of the experiment.

OBJECTIVE DATA

- Does the evidence support the human ability to perceive color over a distance with closed eyes?

SUBJECTIVE DATA

- What was the experience like?
- Where was the data received?
- What did the data transmission feel like?
- What environmental conditions could have interfered with the transmission of the data? Ambient color, light, sound? Clothing of the group subjects?

REPLICABILITY

This experiment may be repeated with different groups in different settings. The results will vary from one setting to another as a function of a number of variables.

Practical Application

Both the objective and subjective data appear to provide compelling evidence that human beings have the inherent ability to discern color with closed eyes. This evidence may cause those who introduce color into the human environment (design professionals, in particular) to more seriously consider the impact of their decisions on the physiology of the human beings that inhabit these environments.

The impact of the physical environment on human physiology may go beyond the use of color. If one accepts the implications of this experiment as significant, all elements of the environment may affect the human physiology.

In the book, *Vibrational Medicine,* Richard Gerber discusses the concept that human beings are really "energy beings," as are all the elements of our universe (Gerber 1988). He uses the work of Albert Einstein to make the vital distinction that all matter is energy, and energy is matter. If you accept this distinction as truth (it is helpful to read Gerber's explanation), then you can easily see that humans are energy beings.

Following Gerber's logic, one possible way to explain why the experiment produces the data it does is to visualize the energy of the colored paper traveling out into the room and entering the energy field of each subject. As this happens, the frequency of each subject changes (perceptibly perhaps) to reflect the introduction of new environmental data. It may be that those who selected the correct color in the experiment are those whose bodies are sufficiently sensitive to decipher the new data.

So, if we do have five senses, how is it that the color data was so positively received by certain individuals? What was the sense that received this data? Could it be possible that we have more than five senses?

Consider this joke: "What did the bartender say to the mushroom who walked up to the bar and ordered a drink? He said, 'You must be a fun-guy.'" If you found this to be funny, you laughed. But where do laughs come from? Have you ever been told that you have a *sense of humor*? This "sense" is not included in the five common senses. What about riding a bicycle? Do we have a *sense of balance*? Have you ever gotten lost or disoriented and discovered your way with your *sense of direction*?

The point of this discussion is to offer the possibility that there are more than five senses. Look up *sense* in the dictionary. It may surprise many of us to learn that the dictionary does not limit the number of senses to five.

RELEVANCE TO HEALTHCARE DESIGN

When we design for healthcare facilities, we must take into account the specific environmental needs of the defined user groups—the patients, caregivers, employees, visitors, and community at large. Each of these groups has a particular set of needs that must be met (or exceeded) if healthcare delivery is to be provided effectively. Each group has its own requirements for the following needs:

- Functional needs (appropriate space, equipment, and proximities related to the effectiveness of their task performance).
- Perceptual needs (data from the environment enabling human beings to create the sensation of an experience).

If both categories of needs are not satisfied, individuals will not have an optimal interaction with the process of healthcare delivery. In any case, it is the responsibility of the design professional to assure that both categories of environmental needs are met. Assuming that the functional needs will all be met, how can we design for the perceptual needs to create increased health and well-being?

The human senses are like antennae. We are all constantly scanning our environment to receive signals about the world around us. Our physical environment is a rich source of information that enables us to manage our experience. We move toward the environmental information that resonates with our needs and move away from those environments that are offensive to us. Unfortunately, sometimes we can't move away from the offensive information.

Have you ever tried to concentrate on a task with a baby crying nearby? If we cannot move away or stop the baby from crying, we can become anxious and irritable. And so it is for all of our senses. As our senses are offended, we become stressed and lose effectiveness in accomplishing our tasks. Whether we are working on a crossword puzzle or recovering from a life-threatening illness, the result is the same. Our energies focus on reacting to the stress rather than working on the task at hand.

In healthcare facilities, more often than not, people do not have the choice of moving toward positive information or away from what is offensive. Patients are confined to their rooms, staff must remain on their units, and visitors have little choice in selecting the environment. The challenge to healthcare design professionals is to design environments that maximize opportunities for positive environmental experiences, offer the widest range of personal choice, and minimize the exposure to offensive conditions.

The colored paper experiment demonstrated the very subtle nature of environmental information and gave us a glimpse of the exquisite, dynamic relationship between a human being and the environment.

The human experience is composed of multiple "channels" receiving and processing continuous, diverse environmental information simultaneously. Frequently, the information can be conflicting. For example, imagine the delight of watching a beautiful sunset coupled with the irritation of listening to a crying baby.

In her presentation at the Sixth Symposium on Healthcare Design, healthcare designer Jain Malkin described the work of Austrian physician and scientist Hans Selye. In 1936, Selye's "research demonstrated that hormones released during stress participate in the development of many degenerative diseases, including brain hemorrhage, hardening of the arteries, coronary thrombosis, certain types of high blood pressure, kidney failure, arthritis, peptic ulcers, and cancer."

Malkin further stated that Selye's "definition of stress refers to wear and tear on the body resulting from attempts to cope with environmental stressors." From the work of Selye and others, it has become apparent that the physical environment is an essential element of healthcare delivery—good design has the ability to support desired outcomes, whereas poor design is capable of encouraging illness and disease (Malkin 1994).

THE FIVE COMMON SENSES

Let's consider the five common human senses and develop strategies for the design of positive environmental conditions that could have a beneficial influence on desired health outcomes.

The description by Roger Ulrich, Ph.D., of his landmark study is an ideal example of what might be achieved in healthcare by sensitive design for the visual sense. Ulrich writes that "a study of hospital patients recovering from gall bladder surgery found that individuals had more favorable postoperative courses if windows in their rooms overlooked a small stand of trees rather than a brick building wall. Patients with the natural window view had shorter postoperative hospital stays, had far fewer negative evaluative comments in nurses' notes (e.g., 'patient is upset,' 'needs much encouragement'), and tended to have lower scores for minor post-surgical complications such as persistent headache or nausea. Further, the wall-view patients needed more doses of strong narcotic pain drugs, whereas the nature view patients more frequently received weak analgesics such as acetaminophen" (Ulrich 1991).

In their presentation at the Fifth Symposium on Healthcare Design, musicians Susan Mazer and Dallas Smith discussed the therapeutic benefits of intentionally designing the aural environment. They said, "A study done by Dr. Standley was conducted in a neonatal intensive care unit. The music therapist measured the decibel level of the respirators and the incubators in the intensive care unit. It was about 75 decibels, which is louder than a freight train and not quite as loud as a boiler room. A lullaby tape with a woman's voice, ethnically matched to each child, was recorded and played at 80 decibels, so as to mask the sound of the respirator. Researchers found that the experimental group that had the tapes and lullabies left intensive care seven to 10 days earlier than the control group of infants who had not received the music therapy" (Mazer and Smith 1993).

Also at the Fifth Symposium, aromatic consultant John Steele outlined the therapeutic benefits of environmental fragrancing. In doing so, he distinguished between "aromachology (the psychological impact of fragrance) and aromatherapy (the diffusion of therapeutic aromatic oils)."

As an example of the benefits of aromachology, Steele said, "Perhaps the most notable example of stress reduction using fragrance in a medical setting is at the Sloan Kettering Memorial Hospital, the world's largest private institution devoted to cancer research. Funded by the Olfactory Research Fund (a sister organization to the Fragrance Foundation), Dr. William Redd and Dr. Sharon Manne have been using heliotropin, a vanilla-like scent, to reduce patient anxiety during magnetic resonance imaging (MRI). This aromachology study 'opens up a broad range of possibilities for the clinical application of aroma during stressful medical procedures.' Medical specialists use MRI, a sophisticated diagnostic procedure, to take detailed pictures of internal organs in the diagnosis of cancer and other serious diseases. Many patients experience anxiety at having to lie motionless for one hour in the claustrophobic space of the scanner's cylindrical core. Patient anxiety can cause up to 10 percent of these expensive scans to be prematurely terminated. Dr. Redd and Dr. Manne concluded that a control group who were exposed to the fragrance experienced 63 percent less anxiety."

To discuss the benefits of aromatherapy, Steele said, "In one cubic meter of forest air, Valnet calculated that on the average, five pathogenic organisms are found. Whereas in a sample of one cubic meter of hospital air there are 10,000 germs. Many years ago, [Valnet] writes, a doctor put some of this hospital air into a flask and then added a few drops of aromatic oils; 40 percent of the microbes were destroyed in 20 minutes, 80 percent in an hour and 100 percent in nine hours. Valnet concludes that 'the administration of diffused aerosol aromatic oils should be common practice in sick rooms, operating theaters and clinics.' He does note that a few of the essences can cause allergic reactions. However, Dr. Valnet has diffused a blend of thyme, lavender, pine, and eucalyptus for his patients on a daily basis for 15 years with no ill effects" (Steele 1993).

Researcher Alice Ware Davidson, R.N., discussed the role of therapeutic massage: "To investigate the tactile sense, we studied massage and the therapeutic effects of this modality on both patients and employees. In a series of three studies from 1990 to 1993, we found patients perceived improved appetite, improved well-being and mood, and diminished pain after massage and for several hours thereafter. In another study, employees felt massage reduced their stress, and decreased sick days were noted on their work records when they received weekly massages" (Davidson 1995).

At the Second Symposium on Healthcare Design, Gerber also provided a scientific basis for better understanding the contribution that touch can make to the desired outcomes. He said, "Dr. Kreiger, who coined the term therapeutic touch to get away from the esoteric idea of psychic healing, found that plants treated by healers contained more chlorophyll. Since chlorophyll is structurally similar to hemoglobin, she measured amounts of hemoglobin in patients after healing. She found that healers using therapeutic touch therapy on patients caused a statistically significant increase in patients' hemoglobin levels, even if they were on bone-marrow-suppressive drugs that induced anemia."

Gerber continued, "Kreiger eventually teamed up with Dora Kunz, who believed that everyone has the gift of healing. Together, they created a graduate-level course in therapeutic touch called 'Frontiers of Nursing: Therapeutic Human Field Interactions' at the New York University College of Nursing. Sixty nurses who graduated from the course were asked to participate in an in-hospital study replicating experiments with healers. The study indicated that nurse-healers could actually increase hemoglobin levels in patients regardless of the patients' medical condition. This provides strong evidence that we all have the ability to be natural healers of others, in addition to having the ability to heal ourselves."

Gerber concluded that "since Dr. Kreiger's study, thousands of U.S. and European health care practitioners, doctors, nurses, and allied health care workers have been trained in therapeutic touch. The National Institutes of Health has actually funded studies in therapeutic touch that proved this form of therapy helps decrease patient anxiety in coronary care units and other systems" (Gerber 1990).

As an example of how the fifth common sense—taste—can influence design of the healthcare environment in such a way that desired clinical outcomes can be enhanced, consider the presentation by former Planetree executive director Robin Orr at the First Symposium on Healthcare Design. "We had to have a kitchen in the Planetree unit of the hospital. I'm not talking about a hot plate. I'm not talking about a place that only the nursing staff and other hospital staff can use, but a place patients and family members can also use. If we were really going to provide good nutrition—which we all know is a very important part of the healing process—and we were going to create a healing environment, we had to have a kitchen. We had to have a place where a nutritionist could do cooking demonstrations, a place to prepare whole-grain breads and fresh salads and wonderful foods for the patients on the unit. We had to have a place where somebody could prepare a cup of tea in the middle of the night. What better way to encourage patients to get out of bed and ambulate, as we in the health profession say, than to provide them with a wonderful kitchen in which to fix a special treat? All of a sudden you're sick and you're in the hospital. If you're used to getting up in the middle of the night at home when you're hungry or if you're a hospital patient who missed lunch or dinner because of a test or because you didn't feel good, access to food is very, very important. This is just common sense" (Orr 1989).

DESIGN STRATEGIES

Given the experiences that have just been described, which lend support to the notion that designing for the perceptual needs of healthcare users is a critical element in the effective delivery of healthcare, what strategies can be generalized for application to other projects?

According to healthcare architect Don McKahan, "In studies by Frankenhaeser and Kennedy, environmental stress was shown to increase blood pressure levels and muscle tension. Chemicals—stress hormones—start working at immunosuppressants in the body, which reduces one's ability to fend off disease.

"Three major hospital stressors are loss of control, loss of privacy, and loss of contact."

McKahan elaborated on these stressors:

Loss of control. According to Ulrich, many studies have found that a lack of control is associated with such negative consequences as depression, passivity, elevated blood pressure levels, and reduced immune system functioning.

Loss of privacy. A recent survey of patients' 50 greatest fears about hospitalization revealed that their greatest concern was "sleeping in a room with a stranger." This, McKahan concluded, "is just one of the reasons most new hospitals are being designed with all single-bed rooms."

There are also privacy problems for hospital patients who are left on gurneys and exposed in hallways. "More and better-designed patient holding areas are needed, as well as improved privacy for toileting functions," McKahan stated.

Loss of contact. Studies in 1985 by Sarason and Sarason, Cohen, and Syme show that "individuals who have high levels of social support experience less stress and have higher levels of wellness." To achieve those higher levels of wellness for patients, design professionals must provide improved physical accommodations for families. McKahan stressed, "We must understand that when we hospitalize a patient, we have hospitalized a family as well" (McKahan 1993).

The strategies that Ulrich suggested are as follows:

- To promote wellness, healthcare facilities should be designed to support patients in coping with stress.
- As general compass points for designers, scientific research suggests that healthcare environments will support coping with stress and promote wellness if they are designed to foster a sense of control, access to social support, and access to positive distractions and lack of exposure to negative distractions.
- A growing amount of scientific evidence suggests that nature elements or views can be effective as stress-reducing, positive distractions that promote wellness in healthcare environments (Ulrich 1991).

What if there really are more than five senses? What would the impact be on the design of the healthcare environment? At the Sixth Symposium on Healthcare Design, Jain Malkin said, "Many researchers think the immune system has a level of sophistication that we are just beginning to understand. It may operate as a sixth sense, detecting elements of the environment that elude the other senses: an extension of the brain in the form of a peripheral receptor organ altering it to new bodily threats. It is a sensory organ. The distinction is that the phenomena it senses are not in the realm of sight, sound, touch, taste, or smell. The immune system is a sensory system for molecular touch" (Malkin 1994).

In conclusion, designing for the senses—particularly in healthcare settings—is far more serious than just embellishing the environment with aesthetic enhancements. In the healthcare setting, design of the physical environment truly takes on the significance of a component of the prescribed therapy. Sufficient evidence exists to support an argument that design of the healthcare environment can positively influence the desired outcomes, all as a result of perceiving the environment through our senses. It can

- Enhance desired therapeutic outcomes
- Improve staff satisfaction and performance
- Increase visitor and family participation
- Encourage additional community support

Design, used in this manner, can be seen as a form of technology. In the same way that medical equipment technology can be applied to respond to patient's needs, design of the environment as a technology is equally capable of doing so. Design in this regard is an *intellectual* technology, rather than an *industrial* technology like medical equipment.

The degree of science in this field of healthcare environmental design technology, an essential element of healthcare delivery, is limited. Much clinically based outcomes research must be completed with sufficiently large data universes, with uncompromised experiment design, to elevate this work to where it will be accepted within the traditional halls of science. It is encouraging to see this work occurring and the awareness expanding that design of the physical healthcare environment can make a valuable contribution to increased effectiveness of healthcare delivery.

Wayne Ruga is an architect and interior designer who is the president, founder, and CEO of The Center for Health Design, a nonprofit organization in Martinez, California, whose mission is to facilitate, integrate, and accelerate the creation of health and life-enhancing environments. His organization produces the annual Symposium on Healthcare Design.

References

Davidson, A. W. "Using the Environment to Promote Human Well-Being." *Journal of Healthcare Design* 7 (1995).

Gerber, R. "Future Trends in Healing." *Journal of Health Care Interior Design* 2 (1990).

Gerber, R. *Vibrational Medicine.* Santa Fe, NM: Bear, 1988.

Malkin, J. "The Design of Healing and Prosthetic Environments." *Journal of Healthcare Design* 6 (1994).

Mazer, S. and Smith, D. "Beyond Silence—Music as Environmental Design." *Journal of Healthcare Design* 5 (1993).

McKahan, D. "Healing by Design—Therapeutic Environments for Healthcare." *Journal of Healthcare Design* 5 (1993).

Orr, R. "Health Care Environments for Healing." *Journal of Health Care Interior Design* 1 (1989).

Steele, J. "Environmental Fragrancing." *Journal of Healthcare Design* 5 (1993).

Ulrich, R. "Effects of Interior Design on Wellness: Theory and Recent Scientific Research." *Journal of Health Care Interior Design* 3 (1991).

WHAT IS HEALING ART?

In the past five years, the term *healing art* has become a popular phrase, especially among consultants attempting to sell works of art to those responsible for healthcare facilities. Many believe that, because art is subjective, and because everyone has different taste in art, it is difficult to define what constitutes healing art. Others feel that, in order to be appropriate, the content of the art must be representationally serene and pastoral, which excludes all forms of abstract work.

These types of generalizations tend to pigeonhole art as a healing force and do nothing to proliferate the serious need for art in healing environments. The real criteria for healing art should be its universal content and mass appeal due to its spiritual intention (see color plate 9). Elements the general public has been known to appreciate in art include a luminous palette of many colors based on their familiarity to nature (perhaps a multicolored flower garden) and the organic and asymmetrical movement also found in nature, such as the flow and movement of water. For example, there is no hidden agenda in a lovely floral garden. Its beauty is its essence. Healing art needs its true nature and purpose to be clean and free of human microcosmic conflicts that interfere with the greater macrocosm, which is the path of least resistance in nature. Energy flows in a natural path until it is obstructed or detoured. Disease in humans is similar—the body's natural flow and movement of energy is interrupted by something that is causing blockage or disturbing its ebb and flow. The harmony in nature needs to be present in healing art to remind us of the ebb and flow of the breath of life.

There have been many different methods of using healing art. One popular method is to use New Age paintings, which feature images of personalized healing angels or mythological gods and goddesses. This is not appropriate for healthcare settings because these works have their own spiritual agenda and may be offensive to patients of various religions and belief systems.

Another method in children's environments is to use images of popular cartoon characters. However, using these types of images creates a dated look and does not induce new and imaginative thoughts. Children are the most innovative artists until they are taught other people's visions to imitate. The child that spends his or her time copying other artists' work will be less able to be inventive in his or her own works later on in life.

CATEGORIES OF HEALING ART

There are three categories of healing art. The first is a body of work created by a group of nonprofessional artists who are convalescing in a healthcare facility or receiving treatment as outpatients. These "artists" may also be staff members of the facility. Over the past ten years, I have facilitated several group art programs in alcoholic and drug addiction rehabilitation treatment centers and in an AIDS treatment facility for children (see Figure 13.1). The color/paint exercises I have developed are designed to get participants to express their innermost feelings about their disease and their lives. Participants are also encouraged to create images of integration and wholeness to express health. They are encouraged to express their feelings in an abstract format, thus eliminating the fear of not being able to draw images very well (see color plate 10). This method helps to

Figure 13.1 Color/paint exercises help children with AIDS express their innermost feelings. Photo: Laurie Zagon, Los Angeles, California.

inspire the innate creativity that we all possess, regardless of talent. It also works well to use collage techniques—pasting colors and shapes cut out from magazines.

The second category of healing art is art that reflects a visual narrative, perhaps on canvas or through drawing, printmaking, and sculpture. These works are created by professional artists or students of art who have been hospitalized due to a life-threatening illness, perhaps for an extended period of time. For this type of individual, expressing his or her emotions through art can be an incredible catharsis. Exhibitions of works such as this can also be an expressive narration of the healing process for others to see who are going through similar experiences. This type of healing art should be viewed in an exhibition space rather than in permanent healing environments. Art such as this, with a personal motivation and agenda, requires permission from its viewer because the reflectance of human suffering in art can induce a powerful psychological conflict of emotions. The conflict induced by viewing this type of art may require a professional social worker, psychologist, or psychiatrist to help get it resolved.

An outstanding example of this type of art is the work of renowned artist Hollis Sigler (see color plate 11). Sigler's work is a visual narrative of her experiences with breast cancer. In 1994, a major exhibition of her healing work (in part sponsored by the National Institutes of Health) was mounted at the prestigious National Museum of Women in the Arts in Washington, D.C.

The third category of healing art is art that is

motivated by the natural laws of nature. This type of healing art offers a visual spirit of goodness and righteousness that transmits positive energy to the viewer. An interactive force of energy takes place as a personal interchange between the art and viewer. It is an invisible magnetic force that calls to its audience with power and authority and seems to have a life of its own. This life force can be measured by the sublime affect that art has had on human beings throughout history. The power and the glory of art as a civilizing force has given the word a sense of uniqueness expressed only in the fine arts of painting, sculpture, drama, poetry, and music.

CHARACTERISTICS

Art chosen for healing purposes in environments such as hospitals, clinics, nursing homes, and hospices should be free of a political agenda. It should possess a natural harmony that is reflective of the natural structural progressions in nature. The movement should flow organically to imitate the life force in humans. The subject matter can be representational or abstract, as long as the spiritual content is pure and the coloration is a flowing, integral part of the innate structure. The elements of design within the art should be asymmetrical in content, as human life force flows best in an organic structural path.

Some art critics believe that all art heals because of its soul essence reflected by man. Yet negative images, such as darkness and death, have often been expressed by renowned artists throughout history. Francisco Goya's black paintings, for example, reflect the enormous suffering in Spain and would definitely not be considered as healing art. On the other hand, the extraordinary iris paintings by Vincent Van Gogh pulsate with the life force of energy and therefore would be very appropriate for healthcare environments.

Color should always be a primary consideration when choosing healing art. Studies have demonstrated the psychological influence of specific colors and associations to nature that occur when viewing the spectrum. Color can be the most noticeable element in healing art due to its powerful visual impact and its welcomed familiarity. Many experts believe that, because color and light are synonymous (as Sir Isaac Newton showed in 1666 by scientifically breaking a beam of light into seven spectrum colors), when organized in this same natural progression, color—just like light—may positively affect health and well-being. The idea is that each color has a specific electromagnetic wavelength and an energy that can heal. The most common associations and physiological reactions to specific colors are as follows:

Red. Its nature symbol is the earth, defined often by its qualities of high energy and passion. Studies have shown that red has the ability to excite and raise blood pressure.

Orange. Its nature symbol is the sunset, defined often by its qualities of emotion, expression, and warmth. Orange is noted for its ability to encourage verbal expression of emotions.

Yellow. Its nature symbol is the sun, defined often by its qualities of optimism, clarity, and intellect. Bright yellow is often noted for its mood-enhancing properties. Yellow must be carefully applied in certain settings, as it causes thought associations of aging and yellow skin tones associated with jaundice.

Green. Its nature symbol is growth—grass and trees—defined often by its qualities of nurturing, healing, and unconditional love. Because it is the opposite on the visual spectrum to red, it is often thought of as a healer of blood.

Blue. Its nature symbol is the sky and the ocean, defined often by its qualities of relaxation, serenity, and loyalty. It is known to lower blood pressure and is excellent as a healing color for nervous disorders. Due to its temperature being cool, it is also good for relieving headaches, bleeding, open wounds, and so on.

Violet. Its nature symbol is the violet flower, defined by its qualities of spirituality. Violet is also a stress reducer and will create feelings of inner calm.

The level of contrast and potency of colors in art will also have an effect on the viewer. If white is added to lavender, it is a softer and more diffused dosage of violet. Pink is a tint of red and would have a softer and more delicate impact than red upon the viewer.

The softer colors that are closer in contrast are more difficult to discern by people who have vision impairments. The elderly, for example, have difficulty seeing soft muted colors. When waking from an operation, some patients may have blurred vision. Also, anyone who needs visual aids, such as glasses or contact lenses, is probably not wearing them in the recovery area. Therefore, the postoperative setting requires art that has bolder and higher-contrast colors. A patient undergoing various tests or convalescing might require a softer, less contrasted works of art.

For the average person, art may not only be healing, but may also be culturally enhancing. Those choosing art for healthcare facilities should be careful when selecting individual permanent works of art. Art for decoration is not necessarily appropriate for healthcare environments. Only art that has a true integrity and purpose and possesses a healing spirit related to the natural order of nature will enhance the healing process.

The best types of healing art are original works designed to be installed on the walls or ceilings of healthcare facilities. Original work has a life force that exudes power and energy from its intention because the hand of the artist always remains present. A poster or print can also be attractive and decorative in a healing environment, but often has a flat, duplicated look.

ESTABLISHING A COLLECTION

Many art schools and departments throughout the United States have students who are willing to donate their works to healthcare facilities. Artists always want to contribute their work to a worthy humanitarian cause and to have their art exposed to a large audience. This is an excellent way to create a healing art collection. Advertisements in major art periodicals can encourage artists to submit healing art that will become part of the healthcare facility's permanent collection. (This method of soliciting art from artists is common in the art world.) A panel of experienced healthcare experts can be assembled to jury the works. To encourage excellence, small cash awards can be presented.

Another economical method of creating an immediate healing art collection is to hire a healing art facilitator to work with staff and patients to create paintings on canvas. This is a fun way to bring people together and tap their innermost resources to paint healing art. They know better than anyone what can help lift another person's spirit when he or she is ill. The paints, canvasses, and brushes needed to produce this art are low in cost in comparison to purchasing an art collection for the facility.

If using reproductions of works of art is the only possibility, then it is imperative that the color printing quality be excellent and the overall imagery be clear and not out of focus. Prints will have an effect on the healing process, not as profound as original art, but, indeed, more than blank walls. Prints will induce a psychological response from the design content, whereas original art will produce a psychological and physiological response. The energy from the original will reflect electromagnetic energy from its surface and therefore produce a more physical result. A reproduction does not have a surface that will reflect color wavelengths.

When true healing art is appropriately installed in a healthcare facility, it will become a gift to the environment and will be noticed and appreciated by the many people who will spend hours enjoying it. Healing art is capable of calming the spirit, creating an interchange of energies between itself and its viewer, and, most important, remind us that it is worth living.

Laurie Zagon, MFA, is a color instructor and fine artist known for her use of full-spectrum color in abstract paintings and sculpture who lives in Los Angeles, California.

14

CREATING NONTOXIC, HEALTH-ENHANCING ENVIRONMENTS

Andrew Fuston, IIDA and Kim Plaskon Nadel, IIDA

As an architect and designer, I have come to realize that often the very stuff with which we make things and the systems we mobilize for their delivery cause us to destroy more than we create. Our pattern of designing, taking, making, and wasting is clearly beginning to cause terminal stresses in humanity and nature. I wonder if it must always be so.

William McDonough

Most people spend over 80 percent of their time indoors. Of all the interiors that we occupy, interiors of healthcare facilities may be the most critical because employees and patients spend an extended duration of time in these buildings. Therefore, the importance of environmentally safe and nontoxic interior design in healthcare facilities cannot be overstated. Healthcare today is about healing ourselves and the planet. Designers must explore ways to mitigate the harmful effects of particular materials on the health of the building's users.

Today, the activities of humans have affected nearly every element in the biosphere. The most profound negative impacts from peoples' activities are the spoiling of large areas of the biosphere's land, water, and air with poisonous waste and the deaths of millions of other species of trees, birds, large sea and land mammals, and coral. Most of this negative impact is due to human ignorance and greed. It is our professional responsibility to reduce that impact as much as possible, to slow down this destructive trend. A disproportionate amount of energy and resources are used in the United States at the expense of other species of plants and animals in our biosphere, decreasing vital biodiversity. Our industry's impact is substantial. There is a reason why you are reading this chapter at this time. We all need to be, and have the capacity to become, revolutionaries in our time.

GLOBAL ENVIRONMENT OVERVIEW

The Industrial Revolution brought an elevation of coal and wood combustion, a by-product of which is carbon dioxide. The burning of fossil fuels and the artificial cooling of buildings are creating the greenhouse effect—a process in which heat is trapped in the earth's atmosphere. This accelerated warming could lead to devastating changes in our geology and our cities and homes.

Before the Industrial Revolution, the earth and its atmosphere maintained a balance with the rainforests and oceans. Recently, many countries have cut down their rainforests to raise cattle, which can provide a more immediate economic benefit. Other chemicals further threaten the balance with global warming, acid, rain, and ozone depletion:

- Methane, which results from the production of cattle and rice.
- Nitrous oxide, produced by car emissions and chemical fertilizers.
- Chlorofluorocarbons (CFCs), a serious chemical found in refrigeration processes.

Although CFCs have been phased out, hydrochlorofluorocarbons (HCFCs) also damage the ozone layer. With further damage to the ozone layer, reduced blocking of ultraviolet (UV) radiation will affect the entire world food chain. Furthermore, there will be more infectious disease because of reduced immune systems, more skin cancer, and other problems that we did not foresee. The immediate solution is to reduce emissions and the burning of fossil fuels. Electricity consumption continues to deplete the planet's reserves of these nonrenewable fuel resources.

Illness is just as attributable to environmental pollution as it is to organic or infectious diseases. Toxic air pollutants are considered to be the fourth-ranking cause of increased cancer risk in our population.

The overall approach for the design industry must be to balance a building's complex chemical, physical, and biological processes that affect building occupants' health and well-being. The correct selection of safe building materials is one aspect of this approach to create a healthy indoor environment with minimal exposure to toxic materials.

ENVIRONMENTAL METHODOLOGIES

There are several concerns when it comes to interior design and the environment, including the following:

1. *Sustainability.* Sustainability means that we are able to meet the needs of the present without compromising the ability of future generations to meet their needs. Sustainable materials can be replenished by properly managed forestries, farms, and plantations. A renewable resource is an example of sustainability.
2. *Embodied energy.* Expanding on the concept that energy must be used to convert materials and elements into usable products, the embodied energy concept holds

that materials actually contain or embody the amount of energy required to make them. When this energy is measured in British thermal units (BTUs), it becomes clear that certain materials like aluminum require enormous amounts of resources to acquire, purify, process, and transport to each step in the process.

3. *Baubiologie.* This is a methodology that seeks to simplify the built environment, creating healthy, less energy-intensive, natural spaces. This holistic viewpoint incorporates the relationship between people and their buildings. It conceptualizes the home as our "third skin" and the importance of buildings for our health and comfort. This system uses materials that are as close to their natural state as possible. *Baubiologie,* taken from *bau—building* and *biologie—life* developed in Germany over 25 years ago, is the study of the building environment upon the health of people and its application to the construction of healthy spaces.

4. *Recycled content.* The use of recycled-content building materials and products does us double service by reusing a material that might have gone to a landfill or become pollution from an incinerator. In addition, this methodology saves the energy needed to acquire virgin material. Maximum effectiveness is achieved by using as much postconsumer material as possible, and by allowing the material to be recycled yet again by maintaining purity, especially with plastics. Postconsumer recycled content applies to something that has already been used in the marketplace, like a newspaper discarded after reading that can then be recycled into another product. Preconsumer recycled content is industrial manufacturing waste and scraps. It is an important clarification to be aware of, since true recycling means postconsumer usage. Although specifying recycled-content material is positive, recycling should not be confused with reuse, a far superior method of energy and resource conservation.

5. *Chemical sensitivities.* Multiple chemical sensitivities (MCS) or environmental illness (EI) is recognized as a disability by the Social Security Administration. MCS can be caused by chemicals used in construction. Problematic factors could be pollen, mold, dust mites, dander, bacteria, and other biological contaminants; electromagnetic fields, formaldehyde, other volatile organic compounds; or other common components of interior air. Designing for chemically sensitive individuals is a very analytical and trial-based methodology. Designing generally for improved human health through superior interior air quality rescues people from the chemical stew created by particulates and gasses. By carefully examining the composition of offensive materials and finishes and finding out what components leave those materials over time, we can then exclude those identified materials from the immediate environment. Common approaches include using air and water filters, central vacuuming systems, and clean, smooth surfaces that are easily maintained.

Recognizing that all materials have a useful life, designers must consider how those materials can go back into the earth and decompose naturally without placing toxics into the soil, water, or air. In ecosystems, waste from one process becomes input into another within the cycle of that system. Looking at the urban environment or the life cycle of a material as an ecosystem is a good practice. Each of these methodologies is usually used together. Some techniques actually contradict others, and designers need to decide which concerns are most important to their clients, their particular ecosystems, and their own environmental ethics. It is important that we practice interior design to the best of our abilities, which, among many other things, includes minimizing our collective environmental impact.

LIFE-CYCLE ASSESSMENT

Life-cycle assessment gives a broad perspective on the environmental impact of developing and using a building and its components and can illustrate the phases in which an architect or designer can become an influence. The best way to evaluate products and materials is complete life-cycle analysis. One evaluates every step of the life of a product at each step—from its raw resource form to plant operations through construction installation.

STEP 1: ACQUISITION OF RAW MATERIALS. Examples: Removal of raw materials from the earth, harvesting of trees, extraction of crude oil.

STEP 2: PRIMARY DISTRIBUTION PROCESS. Examples: metal—mine to refinery; wood—forest to mill; plastic—oil field to refinery.

STEP 3: REFINING/PURIFYING/PROCESSING. In this step the material is refined and made into standard materials; for example, stock sizes or polymers.

STEP 4: MANUFACTURING/PRODUCT FABRICATION/TRANSPORTATION. These refined elements are made into products. They are then transported to showrooms and architectural and design libraries whereby they are distributed to specifiers.

STEP 5: DESIGNER SPECIFICATION. This is where the specifier has the control to exercise his/her choices and ultimately influence the product selection process.

STEP 6: CONSTRUCTION/INSTALLATION PHASE.

STEP 7: USEFUL LIFE OF THE PRODUCT. This step illustrates the useful life of an architectural product, from daily operation and maintenance through the renovation phase. LCA considers the maintenance of the material in its life in a building.

STEP 8: REUSE/REMOVAL/SALVAGE/LANDFILL/RECYCLE. This is the final stage and tells what happens to the material after its term. The idea is to extend a product's life as long as possible and get a lot of use from it. This step refers to a cradle-to-cradle approach, with the intention of open-loop recycling. The philosophy is that each of these steps takes energy, which ties into the embodied energy concept. Any of the options in this step requires energy.

Materials with short life cycles could be nylon carpeting, fabrics, or lightbulbs, whereas a material that has a long life cycle could be a marble-slab counter or a well-made desk.

One could incorporate other concepts into life-cycle analyses. For instance, a material (such as glass) could have a high embodied energy and have a long life cycle.

When we discuss materials later, we will evaluate a material's embodied energy, its impact on the planet, and the life-cycle possibilities that enable us to have a wide perspective and ultimately make intelligent "green" decisions about what we place into these healthcare facilities.

CONTROL OF INDOOR HAZARDS

The chemical revolution, like last century's industrialization, increased production of synthetic products, mainly from petrochemical sources. Our society has been dependent on synthetic chemicals and plastics since World War II. VOCs are usually associated with substances synthesized or extracted from petrochemicals. When most VOCs are at discernible levels, they have an impact on health. The symptoms are lung and throat irritation, headaches, dizziness, lightheadedness, disorientation, and blurry vision. Repeated exposure may lead to lung, liver, and kidney damage as well as damage to the immune system. With technology, there is a price: a significant reduction in the quality of indoor air. There are 20 to 150 hazardous chemicals indoors in concentrations 10 to 40 times those outdoors.

More than 6 billion pounds of formaldehyde are used each year. Formaldehyde is listed as a hazardous air pollutant in the 1990 Clean Air Act, requiring the EPA to set emission standards (Harte et al. 1991). A human carcinogen, it is typically found in pressed wood products, which are used for countertops, cabinets, subflooring, and furniture. It is also used in oil-based paints and stains and fabric treatments. Formaldehyde occurs naturally at 0.05 parts per million (ppm). Some testing for toxicity has a stringent threshold of 0.1 ppm. Formaldehyde gas releases slowly, or, in other words, it offgasses or outgasses, which causes headaches, respiratory difficulties, and other problems.

The Massachusetts Commission on Indoor Air Pollution has stated that 50 percent of illnesses in the United States are due to indoor air problems.

The environmental movement is growing steadily, and it is most evident in safer materials and products. As we redefine what good-quality design is, new thoughts of building methods will be the next step. Based on a new ideology and these new criteria, we believe that a new status quo will emerge. From new technologies and modified materials with improved environmental performance to new ways of reusing raw resources, new building methods are coming into the marketplace at a steady pace. Products are being made with formulations that are reducing the levels of VOCs due to government intervention, public concern, and our own awareness, but the process is quite slow and needs to speed up.

Indoor Air Quality

The EPA has called IAQ the most significant environmental issue we have to face now and into the next decade. EPA estimates that indoor air pollutants cause as many as 6,000 cancer deaths a year. Two modern phenomena have created the easily identifiable air quality problem of sick building syndrome:

1. The volume of chemicals used in materials and their manufacturing processes
2. Energy-efficient, sealed buildings with fixed windows and little fresh air introduced

People at risk in poor indoor air are people with chemical sensitivities or immune disorders, young children, the elderly, and anyone with a preexisting illness such as asthma or vascular disease. Factors that should be considered are operable windows, southern exposures, air intake locations, an increase of fresh air exchanges brought into the building, exhaust locations, air-cleaning options, space air distribution, heat recovery, microbial control and standards development, individual thermal control, and cross ventilation.

Biological pollutants that can cause problems include dust, mold, mildew, bacteria, and viruses. Bacteria can be found in many heating, cooling, and dehumidifying systems—those that control water and moisture accumulation.

Controlling VOC emissions during the construction process and initial occupancy can mitigate any indoor pollution caused by those remaining VOC-emitting materials. Extra ventilation during installation and before or during initial occupancy (when VOCs are at their highest levels) can reduce the absorption of VOCs.

Research by Dr. Bill Wolverton, senior research scientist at NASA, has shown that the leaves of certain plants absorb particular indoor air pollutants. It is said that one plant will purify the air of these chemical pollutants for every 100 square feet.

Testing for Indoor Pollution

VOC emission testing is being done more and more, although it is a very expensive method. There are independent testing labs, such as Anderson Labs and Air Quality Sciences that can conduct a Toxicity Chamber Test, which tests VOC emissions by placing the material in a chamber and carefully measuring its offgasing over time. Qualified engineers and consultants can help create strategies for mitigating and reducing the impact of air problems. If a problem is suspected, contact a professional for investigation who will offer environmental site assessments and IAQ assessments.

MATERIALS AND FINISHES

Every building material that design professionals choose affects the environment. Production and transport deplete resources and consume energy. More and more building materials are becoming scarce because it takes raw materials and nonrenewable energy sources (oil and gas) to produce them. There is controversy over how long the known supply of oil and gas will last. Some say it will be exhausted within the next 30 years.

Low energy, natural, renewable, sustainable, nonsynthetic, chemically stable products are the materials of choice, but they usually lose out to the cheaper and more available mainstream materials. Design professionals need to be aware of new and "green" materials.

How can you be sure that a product that is less toxic during use is not more toxic during the manufacturing process or in its disposal? This process is a difficult and confusing one. The industry is just now realizing how critical this information may be. The EPA and Green Building Council are in research development to provide national environmental standards. Certification groups and advocacy groups provide a lot of useful information

Material Safety Data Sheets (MSDS) can be used to evaluate materials. MSDSs are information sheets obtained from the manufacturers of products. They are invaluable in learning more about a product and obtaining irrefutable, factual data on its toxicity and potential health hazards. MSDSs are OSHA-mandated documents listing all hazardous substances contained in the product they cover. They were originally designed to help industrial workers understand the materials that they were working with and the associated hazards. They have been instrumental in informing designers, architects, and all parties involved in a product's downstream processing and use.

It is important to use MSDSs to compare similar products from manufacturer to manufacturer. It is not uncommon to find a wide variation in health effects between two seemingly similar materials. The goal is, of course, to select the least toxic of the products available. Most designers are not fully aware that the decisions they make in specification have a very real effect on new products in development and that they are, in a way, guiding major manufacturing industries. Designers must stay informed and guide manufacturers and their clients away from the products with chemical toxins frequently found in some MSDSs.

Certification Groups

Most building materials have to be tested and comply with approved standards, such as those for flammability, strength, density, and durability. Can one believe the environmental claims of manufacturers? Unfortunately, some manufacturers and suppliers usually fail to give information or don't know the answers. Specific standards have not yet been established for environmental and health impacts and ecological information. There is a movement to verify and evaluate materials and products. Scientific Certification Systems (SCS) is the first third-party certifier in the United States. SCS, formerly Green Cross, is a business that verifies environmental claims made by the manufacturer about a product or material rather than attempting to develop broad environmental standards. The information product that SCS produces is called the Eco-Profile (see Figure 14.1). Manufacturers provide information about major environmental burdens associated with the product, such as resources and energy consumed or water, air, and solid waste emissions. These are then compared to burdens of some conventional products. The Eco-Profile is important to designers because they can draw their own conclusion from the data reported. It is also important because it reflects improvement of industry and creates a universal means of comparing products on a factual, scientific basis. It will help manufacturers understand their industrial processes better and help them to plan, develop, and design products better. Hopefully, it will end confusion about "green" claims and increase the level of "environmental literacy" in all aspects of our society. Similar certification groups are operated by Canada, the European Economic Community, and Germany.

MATERIALS AND FURNISHINGS

In this section, we will introduce the building materials that are available to the designer and discuss the environmental costs associated with each of them. We will do the same with interior materials and furnishings. Designers should be aware of all of these factors when designing a facility so that they can make choices that will have a more positive impact on the world in which we live.

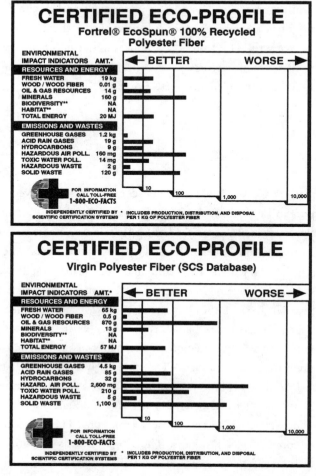

Figure 14.1 An Eco-Profile produced by Scientific Certification Systems, Oakland, California.

Gypsum Board

Although gypsum board is made from a natural sedimentary rock (which is a non-renewable source), gypsum production is very energy intensive, sending toxic emissions of nitrogen oxide and carbon monoxide into the air. Also the mining runoff is associated with killing aquatic life and contaminating waterways. Paper-faced gypsum board causes serious environmental problems with air and water pollution and has a high energy use. Bleaching paper bleeds toxic dioxins into our fresh waters. Fiber gypsum, such as Louisiana Pacific's Fiberbond is a better alternative since it has no paper facings. It is also denser and more impact resistant.

The other problem with this material is that only the construction waste of gypsum board—the material that is unpainted or unfinished—can be recycled. This is a problem because gypsum board needs to be finished for fire and building code reasons. An alternative would be to use prefinished panels or modular partitions. Prefinished panels are faced with paint, veneer, or wallcovering but are adhered to the substrate offsite, with the argument that most or all of the offgassing has already transpired, thus not contributing to indoor air pollution of healthcare environments. Of course, the substrate should be a nontoxic material. Modular partitions, made of environmentally benign materials of metal with nontoxic finishes and/or glass inserts, are movable, reusable, and resalvagable and therefore have a long life cycle.

Wood and Wood Composite Products

Composite wood and reconstituted boards are made from sawmill waste or low-grade wood. They contain natural or synthetic resins. In plywood, thin layers of wood veneer are bonded together with a high content of glue. The glues contain urea or phenol formaldehyde. Urea formaldehyde resins are less stable and offgas more than phenol formaldehyde resins, particularly under humid conditions. Its production creates demand for high-quality logs, meaning it puts pressure on old-growth timber that remains. Antifungal agents are added to exterior plywood, which, when landfilled, creates dioxin, polluting the soil and water. Interior-grade plywood is usually used for door skins, veneered wood paneling, and the core of birch plywood. It is made from lauan, which is Philippine mahogany. Quality lauan is threatened in the tropics due to unregulated cutting. Interior-grade plywood also uses resins that contain urea formaldehyde. Exterior-grade (or marine) plywood uses phenol formaldehyde resins with less formaldehyde offgassing than interior-grade plywood. It is more moisture resistant due to added antifungal agents that will cause water and soil problems if landfilled.

Manufacturers that use faster-growing hardwoods, such as birch and elder, are a better alternative. Specification of lesser known species (LKS) is an alternative because these tropical woods are being destroyed in the process of logging prized tropical woods. Gridcore was developed by the USDA as an alternative to lightweight composite wood core material. It is made from a variety of materials, such as newspapers, wood scrap, magazines, and possibly even some recycled plastic. Formed into straight or curved panels with a honeycomb pattern, Gridcore can be layered to create different thicknesses. Only white glue, which does not contain formaldehyde, binds it together, and there are no additives that would otherwise offgas. Gridcore has the advantage of being recycled in an open-loop cycle.

Particleboard is made from waste softwood chips or sawdust pressed into sheets using resins that may contain formaldehyde. It is manufactured with waste wood that otherwise would have been burned or landfilled several years ago. Technological development of medium-density fiberboard (MDF) has broadened its applications. Since fiberboard glues are over 15 percent of material's weight, there is a considerable problem with offgassing. Look for certification standards such as the E1 Standard (Exposure 1 or "European Standard"). Completely sealing the material on all sides with several layers of a sealant or laminating the material with melamine or plastic laminate will seal in up to 80 percent of VOC emissions. Recently, some manufacturers have developed a new line of MDFs that are formaldehyde free. Medite II is made using a polyurea resin matrix whereby the formaldehyde is neutralized; therefore, there are no formaldehyde emissions.

Other innovative composite products using natural resins made from soybean flour are readily available on the market. Soybean adhesives were developed in the 1920s and are now making a comeback. Soybeans and wastepaper are the main ingredients of a new building material called Environ from Phenix BioComposites (see color plate 12). It consists of a combination of soybean flour resin (a renewable resource) blended with additives and processed wastepaper, including newspapers, to create a product that resembles granite. Since it has the construction properties of wood, Environ can be milled, glued, sanded, or shaped with conventional woodworking tools. Environ can be used to make wall paneling, flooring, furniture, cabinets, mouldings, doors, and structural and decorative components.

Homasote is another useful material made from compressed postconsumer recycled newsprint and bonded together with a low-toxic adhesive that does not contain formaldehyde. It has a low environmental cost and processes waste material.

Wood and Lumber

A study commissioned by the International Tropical Timber Organization (ITTO), the body charged with overseeing the global traffic in tropical wood products, bleakly concluded that less than one-eighth of one percent of tropical logging is conducted on a sustainable basis (see Figure 14.2) (Poore 1989). Intensive, large-scale logging operations rank among the primary causes of rainforest destruction, accounting for about 25 percent of deforestation worldwide. Most softwoods and hardwoods are being clear-cut in North America.

There is a new breed of companies whose goals are to promote tropical and domestic harvesting of woods. Rainforest Alliance runs the SmartWood certification program for domestic or tropical sustainably grown woods. Smart Wood has certified operations in Belize, Honduras, and the Yucatan region of Mexico. Good Wood is the

Figure 14.2 Less than one-eighth of one percent of tropical logging is conducted on a sustainable basis, as shown in this photo. Photography: Scott Landis, York Harbor, Maine.

Friends of the Earth labeling certification program in England. SCS recently developed a Forest Conservation Program solely for wood products.

EcoTimber International is also one of these companies whose goal is to work for the preservation of the world's rainforests by establishing import markets for tropical woods that come from sustainable forestry. Timber traders like EcoTimber International support community-based harvesting operations, working with forest dwellers to develop harvesting systems that are ecologically sound and socially responsible, an effort that is referred to as *ecoforestry.* Ecoforestry stands as a viable alternative to the destructive mass logging that prevails across the forested regions of Southeast Asia, Africa, and Latin America (Poore 1989). One reason for global deforestation: forests are cleared because they are perceived as having greater value felled than left standing.

EcoTimber International will buy timber only from operations that comply with a number of social as well as environmental criteria, such as:

- Commitment to a forest management plan
- Recognition and promotion of land-use rights and land ownership for local communities
- Felling and extraction of timber in a manner that minimizes damage to the soil and surrounding forest
- Distribution of profits to forest workers in an equitable manner
- Acceptance of monitoring agencies to assure all of these criteria have been met

The company also promotes many exotic lesser-known species of wood not available before in the United States. By creating markets for these woods, EcoTimber diverts demand away from the overexploited species, increasing the value of forests, and thus helps maintain the natural forest ecosystem. There are several tropical forestry operations now in existence that are making a sincere effort to harvest timber on a sustainable basis. Each supplier should be able to provide its customers with documentation describing the exact sources and harvesting methods of the timber it purchases.

Domestic wood that is harvested from sustainable forestry operations is also available through an expanding number of companies, like Buchner Panel Manufacturing and EcoTimber.

To a significant degree, the fate of the rainforests lies in the hands of the educated designer and architect.

Glass

Glass is an inert, durable material with high embodied energy. Its extraction and manufacturing processes require a lot of energy and produce some air and water pollution. Glass has a lower embodied energy than metals. It is made of natural, abundant resources such as sand (silica), sodium oxide (soda), and calcium oxide (limestone) with mineral oxides and colorants.

Melted at extremely high temperatures and then cooled, tempered glass is more energy intensive because it needs to be fired higher temperatures than regular glass.

Making glass from recycled material takes nearly as much energy and produces as much or more pollution as making it from new material; therefore, the environmental benefit is marginal. But, although glass is technically recyclable, only recycling facilities for container glass (postconsumer) are widely available. Sheet glass does not contain recycled materials because it has more critical formulation requirements and cannot be allowed to contain certain impurities.

Some manufacturers are making products, such as glass block and floor tiles, with waste glass. Converting glass waste into another material instead of back into original form has more environmental merit. An example of waste glass products includes Terra-Green Technologies commercial ceramic floor Traffic Tiles made from 17-percent preconsumer windshield glass industrial waste and 55-percent postconsumer recycled glass content.

Metals

All metals are precious, since the mineral ores from which they come from are nonrenewable. Seventy-five percent of metals are still abundant, although 20 metals—including lead, tin, tungsten, and zinc—are becoming rare. The process of strip-mining these metals results in loss of environmental integrity plus a high environmental cost associated with air and water pollution.

Steel is comprised of five different metals and is very energy intensive. Recycled steel saves over 70 percent of energy used in manufacturing new steel from primary ore. Almost one-half the iron for steelmaking now comes from scrap-salvaged steel, which is even cheaper than recycled steel.

Aluminum has one of the highest embodied energies of all metals (one-fourth the embodied energy of steel). Mining bauxite (from which aluminum is made) is very damaging to the environment. Secondary aluminum (recycled) consumes only 5 percent of the energy used to extract and process primary ore. Gage ceiling tiles or wall panels are made of recycled aluminum and can be used for high-end applications. They are easily cleanable and long lasting. Adversely, typical acoustical ceiling tiles today, which are economical, do not have a long life cycle, are not really cleanable, and may continually emit airborne particles.

Alloyed metals such as chromium and nickel have the highest environmental cost.

Avoid any metals with chrome plating which uses cadmium, zinc, or chromium, as well as chemicals that produce toxic waste. Major advancements in protective metal coatings are powder coating and electrostatic coating, which don't require solvents and produce no hazardous waste. Less than 2 percent of finish material is wasted. Ultimately, bare unfinished aluminum or powder coating on metals is the best choice. Chemically sensitive and allergic people consider metal and glass as materials of choice because these materials are inert, antimicrobial, easy to clean and maintain, and have a very long life cycle.

Stone, Concrete, Brick, and Ceramic

Building with brick, concrete, and stone are good uses of natural materials from the earth. Brick and adobe can reduce the need for timber and are naturally fire rated. Concrete uses high embodied energy—it has high energy costs in production and transportation and can add recycled content aggregates. Fungicides and curing agents added to concrete may be toxic. Ceramics, porcelains, and bricks are fired at great heat, which results in high combustion and fuel consumption, but these materials are readily abundant. Stones are durable and easily maintained and, depending on how they are used, could have a long life cycle. But they are a nonrenewable raw resource and should be designed for reuse. Some stones are readily abundant, but some are already depleted and no longer available. There are high energy costs in quarrying, handling, and transportation of stone. Most stones are very fragile in the transportation stage. Also, quarries disfigure the land, producing erosion and altering drainage patterns. Some areas are required to restore the quarry by filling, planting, and altering drainage patterns. Other nonpolluting, natural, abundant resources include: stucco, portland cement, and plaster. Syndecrete by Syndesis Studio is a 100-percent cement-based cast material that contains flyash, natural minerals, waste polyfiber for reinforcing, and aggregates. Syndecrete is lighter than standard concrete and has twice the compressive strength. It can be specified as floor tiles or countertops. It needs a water-based sealant or acrylic wax. Up to 41-percent recycled waste can be added to its composition. Because it is a custom product, one can choose particular aggregates, from recycled glass chips to broken pencil parts.

Plastics

Plastics are made from nonrenewable petroleum. Petroleum production has caused some of the worst man-made environmental disasters of our time, including the Exxon Valdez oil spill. Plastic products, like vinyl sheet flooring, electrical wire, resilient wall bases, wall guards, and vinyl wallcovering are made from polyvinyl chloride or PVC. Offgassing in many facilities is attributed to PVCs. Consider alternatives to these materials; for instance, sustainably grown hardwood or ceramic tile could replace resilient vinyl wall base.

In general, the softer the plastic, the less stable it is and the more offgassing will occur. Conversely, the more rigid, the more stable the plastic. Approximately 2 percent of products are being made from recycled plastics, including plastic lumber, park benches, carpet, and seating. Plastic laminates are used throughout healthcare facilities. In producing plastic laminate, the production of resins, the manufacture of pigments and inks, and the manufacture of virgin kraft paper generate waste air emissions and wastewater that can adversely impact human health and the environment (American Institute of Architects 1994). As a result of the relatively inert nature of the resins used, no indoor air emissions are attributed to plastic laminates. Often, plastic laminates are used to seal in formaldehyde vapors from particleboard if applied on all surfaces. Plastic laminate systems such as counters or cabinets should be designed and installed for reuse since there is no way to recycle plastic laminates. All plastic laminates should be adhered using lowtoxic adhesives. There is a problem with smoke produced from burning plastics in a fire.

Hard and Resilient Floorcoverings

For health concerns, the best floorcoverings are smooth and hard, do not release chemicals into the air, are easy to clean, and do not collect dust or support mold growth.

Solid wood flooring is a good option when wood comes from suppliers with responsible practices. It has a long life cycle and can easily be refinished. Big City

Forest sells flooring made from reclaimed used wood pallets. Typically, domestic and tropical hardwood trees are cut down in order to make freight pallets; after their use, pallets are landfilled.

Ceramic and porcelain tiles are made from abundant natural earth resources. Floor tiles made by Terra-Green Technologies are recycled glass-bonded vitreous ceramic tiles that do not need sealer and whose color is inherent throughout the thickness of the tile.

Typically, vinyl sheet flooring is made from 100-percent PVC and can slowly offgas throughout its lifetime, so it would have to be sealed to mitigate its emissions. Conventional vinyl composition tile is actually made from mostly crushed limestone with some vinyl fillers and binders, so it is a more chemically stable material than a vinyl tile or sheet flooring. The following resilient flooring materials are sound alternatives to vinyl floorings:

- Linoleum is the most perfect man-made material. It is comprised of all-natural ingredients: pine tree resins, linseed oil, mineral pigments, and jute backing (except tiles that have a synthetic backing for stability). The sheet goods are 6 × 7 feet wide, and the material expands in width so there is no shrinkage of seams. It is resistant to cigarette burns, and its high linseed oil content makes it naturally antimicrobial. Linoleum can be heat welded and flash coved. Forbo and Gilbert/DLW are the largest linoleum manufacturers and have a wide variety of patterns and colors (see Figure 14.3).

Figure 14.3 Linoleum is the most perfect man-made material because it is comprised of all natural ingredients. Photo: Forbo Industries, Hazelton, Pennsylvania.

Figure 14.4   Cork is a renewable resource because it is harvested from a cork oak tree without damaging the tree. Photo: Ipocork, Riveridge, New Jersey.

• Cork is made from the cork oak tree, which is grown on plantations in Portugal and Spain. Every five to seven years, the bark is harvested without damaging the tree, which renews itself. Actually, bark harvesting strengthens the tree many times over during its lifetime of a few centuries. Cork, therefore, is a renewable resource (see Figure 14.4). Cork floor tiles have some recycled content because they use the industrial waste from the wine bottle cork industry. Ipocork veneer tiles come with a 26-mil top layer of PVC. Both Dodge-Regopul and Ipocork carry tiles that are available unfinished without the PVC top layer or with a waxed top layer. It is imperative to properly seal this floor type. It has great sound- and shock-absorption qualities and temperature insulation properties. Resilient flooring materials are secured with a specially formulated, water-based, low-VOC-emission adhesive.

Carpet

There are applications for carpet in the healthcare arena, but there is always the problem of cleanability. The ideal situation would be if the carpet could be laid in such a way that it could be lifted up and sent out for period cleaning offsite.

Under pressure from EPA, the Carpet and Rug Institute (CRI) recently began a voluntary certification and labeling program that indicates a carpet's compliance with CRI's own recommended emission thresholds. CRI only tests for total VOCs, formaldehyde, and a gas called 4pc. Over two years of testing, carpet emission levels have dropped 30–50 percent. The CRI identified 4pc and formaldehyde as dangerous components in the carpet backing, and manufacturers have developed lower-toxic backings.

Milliken's Earth Ennovations program revamps already installed carpet tiles with cleaning and overprint screening to make carpet tile look new and ultimately extend its life cycle.

The carpet industry is known for its excessive water consumption, especially in its dyeing processes. Using solution-dyed carpeting avoids the need for dyeing, since solution dyeing involves adding color pigment chips prior to the extrusion of the nylon. If wool can be a consideration, New Zealand wool carpeting is available undyed in several of the sheep's natural fleece colors, as a woven product with a cotton or jute backing. Woven carpeting as a rule uses less adhesives than tufted goods which have a primary and secondary backing glued to the fibers.

Generally, carpeting can be an aesthetic or acoustical improvement to the space. However, its application should be chosen wisely in that it is questionable that carpet can be cleaned thoroughly.

Carpeting is also available made from postconsumer recycled polyethylene terepthalate (PET) plastic bottles. Images Carpet is one company that takes PET chips and extrudes them to form fibers, which are then tufted and dyed and have a conventional backing system (see Figure 14.5). Note that the fiber is not as strong or resilient as nylon. BASF claims, in its 6ix Again program, that any carpet made from Zeftron 2000 nylon can be recycled into new carpet after its useful life is over, which eliminates the question of waste disposal. Usually, after the useful life of the carpeting, it either goes to landfills or is made into a type of plastic lumber.

The least amount of components making up the produce (i.e., carpet over tackless padding, which are separate and unattached components) the easier it is to recycle the carpeting.

Avoid carpet padding or cushioning made with CFC water-blowing agents. If adhesive is the only installation method applicable, use low-toxic-based adhesives and avoid double-glue installation. Alternate installation methods improve the quality of the carpeting and will not add to indoor air pollution. For instance, Takfast, available

Figure 14.5 Image Carpets takes PET chips and extrudes them to form fibers, which are then tufted and dyed using a conventional backing system. Photo: Image Industries, Inc., Armuchee, Georgia.

through most manufacturers, is a velcro-type fastener that allows the carpet to be lifted and replaced or reused multiple times. There are tack strips made from recycled carpet (United Recycling) instead of traditionally used wood for an installation avoiding any adhesives. Another invention is the dry releasable adhesive system used successfully in healthcare facilities that have no downtime in their daily operations, in which 6-foot-wide carpeting with attached padding can be laid down quickly and easily.

Floorcoverings are cited as the major perpetrator of irresponsible environmental practices. They can affect both the interior and the exterior environment negatively. One must look at materials and their manufacturing processes, as well as adhesives, finishes, and maintenance requirements when making choices.

Textiles

Textiles used in this industry may be made from natural or synthetic fibers. There are some new innovations. Typically, vinyl upholstery is a PVC petroleum-based product, typically made using solvent-based inks. Look for water-based rather than solvent-based technologies. DesignTex's line called Watershed is a polyurethane face with cotton/polyester backing made with water-based technology.

There are recycled content alternatives: Guilford of Maine's Ecodeme is a new panel fabric made from 45-percent postconsumer PET plastic. Each yard utilizes approximately four 2-liter soda bottles. This company was the first to start a recycling program whereby designers can return their used fabrics to a recycling center where it is remanufactured into appliance padding.

The William McDonough Collection of fabrics by DesignTex is produced by revisiting all stages of the manufacturing process with a result that creates no pollutants. The fabrics are woven from ramie, grown in the Philippines without pesticides, and wool from free-range sheep from New Zealand. There are no finishing processes which are usually added to the surface. After its life cycle, the product will decompose; in fact it can be composted without the release of toxic substances into the soil.

Cotton production depends heavily on the use of chemical pesticides and fertilizers for high yields (Leclair 1992). Look for organically grown cotton. FoxFibre, developed by scientist Sally Fox, is a naturally colored, organically grown cotton where the color is inherent in the plant, and it therefore utilizes no dyes. Fabrics produced with FoxFibre, like Coyuchi, would be excellent for people with chemical sensitivities or high immune deficiencies. The negative side to cotton is that it needs to be fire treated to pass certain codes.

Wallcoverings

Typically, vinyl wallcoverings are made from PVC, a petroleum product, and, due to its chemical instability, it slowly offgasses throughout its lifetime. Also, hazardous heavy metals, like cadmium, are used. Printing is usually done with solvent-based inks which produces an indoor air pollutant. A few manufacturers are beginning to use safer water-based inks. Look for alternatives that do not use heavy metals and employ water-based inks, like Blumenthal Wallcoverings.

Plaster-covered wallcovering covers cracked or uneven surfaces. Plaster-in-a-Roll by Flexiwall Systems is a gypsum-impregnated jute wallcovering that can then be painted. Traditional embossed wallpapers are still available, known as Lincrusta and Anaglypta, which when painted become hard and extremely durable. Recycled-paper wallcovering is becoming more available. Blumenthal Wallcoverings has recycled-content paper with water-based inks and also have a process of adding pattern embossing with sand to make it more durable. PallasWalls makes wallcovering from crushed porcelain beads glued to a paper backing for a durable product.

Paints

Fumes from solvents used in paints are harmful. Where does paint come from? The ingredients, like the binders, pigments, and solvents, may be purchased from a number of chemical companies. Paints are either water-based or solvent-based; water-based (or latex) paints have 7- to 10-percent solvent content, whereas solvent-based (or alkyd or oil) paints are 50-percent solvents. Solvent-based paints, which contain large amounts of toxic chemicals and dangerous hydrocarbons, may take months or years to fully offgas and cure completely. Water-based paints contain additives—for instance, preservatives to keep them fungus and mildew free.

Today, hazardous preservatives, such as mercury and lead, are banned from use. In some cases, chemically sensitive persons react negatively to fungicides and mildewcides.

Water-based paints are easier for cleanup than solvent types. Glidden Paints has a reformulated water-based line called Spred2000 that has a low odor when drying in which the petroleum-based solvents are reduced to almost zero. This brand is SCS certified. Benjamin Moore Paints has a similar reformulated water-based line called Pristine. Both companies use low-toxic pigments. These pigments are available light to medium colors only, so this is a reason to keep walls on the light side. In addition, there are natural organic paints based on plant chemistry. These paints, like Livos and Auro, are imported from Germany and are comprised of plant-derived natural materials, like pine-tree resins, linseed oils, and earth mineral pigments. These solvent-based types have a high odor, but it can be said that these are nonpetroleum-based products. They can be used for metals instead of conventional petroleum-based oil paints. Spray-on coatings have become more popular since they have been reformulated to include a water-based line. Also, stencilling and faux finishing using paints is an alternative to wall coatings or wallcoverings. Some communities have paint that is postconsumer recycled (collected and remixed) and sold in limited colors, which eliminates the problem of hazardous waste and disposal. And finally, if work is being done in a building that has been painted before 1979, first determine if there is lead in the existing paint before doing any sanding or preparation work.

Stains and Finishes

Stains have similar qualities to paint—fumes from solvents used in them are harmful. Water-based stains and finishes are acceptable for interior applications, especially if they are sealed with a clear, water-based coating. There are many reformulated water-based polyurethanes that have high performance. Plant-chemistry-based companies make all-natural wood stains, dyes, and glazes that are nontoxic and easy to handle.

Adhesives

This category relates to many products, such as those used for floors and walls. Avoid using large amounts of any solvent-based adhesive, such as for carpet or base trim.

They have highly volatile organic compound contents, including toluene—a hazardous air pollutant under the Clean Air Act of 1990 (OSHA restricts workplace levels of this substance) (Harte 1991). The general alternative is water-based adhesives. Another alternative is to design to minimize the amount of glue used, be it furniture or cabinetwork. Common white glues, such as polyvinyl acetate (PVA), are the safest and the lowest in environmental cost. Envirotect, by WF Taylor, and AFM produce extensive lines of low-toxic adhesives and building materials such as caulking compounds. These companies also make sealants. Specially formulated sealants (as mentioned earlier) can block out toxic fumes, like formaldehyde emissions, from materials. Pace Chem Industries makes several general nontoxic and hypoallergenic sealers. Livos and Auro have shellacs that are finishes but act as sealants as well.

Furniture

Furniture is a complex topic and encompasses other categories in this chapter. However, some furniture and casework guidelines include:

- Functionality, designed for disassembly
- Minimization or elimination of the joining of incompatible materials in manufacture (i.e., adhesives and fasteners)
- Clear identification of materials
- Cleanability and maintenance
- Circulation of air
- No negative impact on the environment during use and after use
- Elimination or reduction of foam padding, a low-emission product.

CONCLUSION

Sitting Bull once said that "we borrow the earth from our children and grandchildren." Design professionals have to accept a deep commitment to protect our troubled forests and reservoirs. Only then can they advise their clients and take a stand on the best of all principles. The answer is beyond selections of materials and finishes; we need to make a shift in all of our thoughts to take care of the biosphere in which we live. The shift has already begun. We are striving for a healthy and sustainable ecosystem for our communities.

We also need to examine our healthcare facilities and react to healing on a holistic level, from treating patients with alternative therapies to designing safe, nurturing spaces. We also have to accept a different measurement for these new materials in the healthcare environment. We cannot compare the conventional, toxic materials with alternate green materials. If our foremost criterion is to enforce a healing, nontoxic environment, then a new measurement of evaluation needs to be established. If using a recycled-content composite material with organic glues is substituted for the conventional PVC, clients cannot expect the "greener" material to be maintained in the same exact way.

So, design professionals have a new set of challenges in front of them. New products will be designed for the industry through experimentation. Green products being known as too costly will no longer be as costly as the demand for them increases hundredfold. We are entering a new era of changes and of new values. The expense of doing things the conventional way is too costly in the long run—for our health, our living spaces, our cities, our land, and our biosphere.

Andrew Fuston and Kim Plaskon Nadel are professionally certified interior designers working in New York City. They have been doing research on environmentally responsible design since 1991 and are coauthors of The Green Pages: The Contract Interior Designers' Guide to Environmentally Responsible Products and Materials.

References

Environmental Resource Guide. Washington DC: American Institute of Architects, 1992–1994.

Harte, J. et al. *Toxics from A to Z: A Guide to Everyday Pollution Hazards.* Berkeley and Los Angeles, CA: University of California Press, 1991.

Leclair, K. and Rousseau, D. *Environmental by Design: A Sourcebook of Environmentally Conscious Choices for Homeowners, Builders, and Designers.* Point Roberts, WA: Hartley & Marks, 1992.

Poore, D. *No Timber Without Trees: Sustainability in the Tropical Forest.* London: Earthscan Publications, Ed., 1989.

EDITOR'S NOTE: *See Appendix C for names and addresses of the product manufacturers mentioned in this chapter.*

THERAPEUTIC EFFECTS OF LANDSCAPE ARCHITECTURE

15

James D. Burnett, ASLA

Nature plays a vital role in speeding the healing process. This recognition is gathering momentum and is leading to the integration of the garden into the healthcare setting. While this information may seem obvious to some, it is still questioned by others. Hospitals of the past have centered their work on technology and efficiency, since it has been commonly believed in western medicine that body and mind are separate and that the environment is secondary. We are now hearing from researchers that these assumptions are not true.

The environment can contribute to the patients' ability to activate the body's inner healing process. Roger Ulrich, Ph.D., tells us that views of nature as opposed to a building shorten the length of stay and improve the experience of a hospital stay (Ulrich 1984). In her workshops, "Spaces Can Heal," Anita Olds, Ph.D., director of the Child Care Design Institute in Boston, Massachusetts, has discovered that, when led through a meditation exercise and asked to draw their optimum "healing setting," 75 percent of the participants draw outdoor spaces. The remaining 25 percent draw interior settings that always contain elements related to the outdoors—a prominent window through which are visible sky, trees, sun, a garden or yard, and indoor potted plants, flowers, and growing things. She says, "These images of healing spaces always involve nature as the healing agent" (Olds 1985) (see color plate 13).

The hospital of the future will have to address these important findings. For a hospital to be truly a "health center," then it must be an educational experience, promoting an environment that is nurturing and supportive. Dr. Leland Kaiser, futurist and educator, says, "Curing is scientific, technological, and focused on patients as bodies. Healing is spiritual, experiential, and focused on patients as people. Curing is high tech. Healing is high touch. A healing healthcare institution integrates both dimensions in an overall patient experience" (Kaiser 1994). This experience can be enhanced dramatically by strongly emphasizing the therapeutic garden.

THE ANCIENTS

The early pioneers of medicine inhabited the fertile valley of Mesopotamia from about 4000 to 1500 B.C. Religious and supernatural beliefs determined attitudes about ailments and cures. From about 2000 B.C., talismans and plant-based drugs assumed greater importance.

1. *Greece.*   To the Greeks, the universe was composed of four elements: earth, air, fire, and water. Aristotle (384–322 B.C.) taught that these elements paralleled the four bodily humors—blood, phlegm, black bile, and yellow bile—on which temperaments and fundamental qualities were based. The human body was considered a microcosm of the world, so it was essential for the bodily liquids to be in balance, since they ultimately affected the universe, or macrocosm. Thus, health was maintained through the balance of the humors, and most diseases would cure themselves.

    Hippocrates (468–377 B.C.), acknowledged as the father of medicine, was the first healer to record medical experience for future reference, thus establishing the scientific basis of medical practice.

2. *Rome.*   The Romans drew their medical knowledge from the Greeks. In A.D. 60, Dioscorides (A.D. 40–90) authored *De Materia Medica,* the cornerstone of medical texts in Europe through the Middle Ages. This illustrative book addressed and categorized some 600 plants and their medicinal uses. As the Romans developed their philosophy of the human body, viewing it as a machine that needed repairs, medicinal herbs were used as cures, and medicine became a highly profitable business.

    Galen (A.D. 131–199) was an incessant critic of the contemporary medical sects then flourishing in Rome. He opposed all who steered away from the Hippocratic teaching on the unity of living organisms and the force behind nature. Galen streamlined and enhanced his predecessors' ideologies and theorems. His efforts led to the development of a system for physiology and anatomy, and, in time, his books came to be the standard texts in western medical schools and societies.

3. *China.*   The Chinese have relied upon nature as a healing mechanism since 2500 B.C. Their philosophy stresses harmony and is based upon the premise that the universe is made up of five elements: wood, fire, metal, earth, and water. Each element and its related emotion and temperament is essential, since the key to harmony is balance.

    The associated theory of *yin and yang* complemented the balance theorem. The yin was associated to the female and the yang to the male. They were polar opposites, and thus their existence in equal parts created balance. Herbs, acupuncture, and natural treatments were prescribed to create and maintain this balance.

4. *India.* India acknowledged the relationship between health and nature as early as 2500 B.C. with what they termed *Ayurveda.* The term literally translates as science of life, however, in actuality it was an accumulation of herbal tradition with influences from the Persians, the Greeks, and even the Moghuls.

HERBALISM

As early as the second century in Europe, Galen taught the merits of herbalism. His theories on the body's four humors along with the classification of herbal qualities—hot, cold, dry, or damp—were later adopted by the Arabs in the seventh century. To this day, his theories are used in India and the Muslim world.

Throughout the Middle Ages, herbalism was in the control of the Church. The cultivation and standardization of herbal gardens in monasteries paved the way to introducing new herbs and remedies.

The concept of physic gardens came about during the Renaissance period, when universities first emerged. As well as providing physicians with the raw materials for their healing processes, these gardens were used as a teaching tool for medical students. The gardens were often walled and designed in a formal pattern.

In North America, early European settlers melded their own herbal traditions with those of the Native Americans. Samuel Thomson adopted the use of herbs and native rituals, such as sweat houses, and founded physiomedicalism. The concept was based upon keeping the nervous system and the tissues in balance through the use of natural elements such as herbs, which were classified as stimulants or sedatives, relaxants, or astringents. Thomson's theories as well as his book, *Thomson's Improved System of Botanic Practice in Medicine,* were widely popular in the early nineteenth century.

The tradition of combining herbs was at the heart of herbalism. The emphasis was on the whole instead of the individual parts of the herb, (i.e., leaves, roots, flowers). This holistic approach, however, dissipated when the effective ingredients were isolated. The extracted chemicals eventually became pills and later were produced synthetically. Although a remarkable medical advancement, there were negative repercussions. In the transition from the use of crude plants to clinical pills, modern medicine lost the art of combining herbs to modify toxicity and of using whole plants, which contain chemical ingredients that can reduce the risk of side effects.

HISTORY OF GARDENS AND STYLES

Throughout history, the garden has served humankind in many capacities and has undergone various transformations. The earliest written references to gardens were to the *paradise* gardens of the Persian culture. In the harsh environment of the Middle East, gardens came to symbolize paradise and the hope of a better life in the after-world. Some western civilizations used gardens to grow medicinal plants as early as 1000 B.C. Eastern societies, such as the Japanese, revered their gardens for their spiritual qualities and continue to do so to this day. It was during the Middle Ages, however, that gardens were first devoted solely to medicinal herbs. A space was designated within the compounds of monasteries for herbal gardens, located near the infirmary and the kitchen (see Figure 15.1).

In the eighteenth century, the English Landscape Gardening School developed from several influences, including the romanticized image of nature seen in the then-popular Italian Landscape Painting School and increased contact with the Orient and the North American wilderness. The Landscape Gardening style was of nature perfected. It consisted of wide, rolling expanses of lawn with irregular groupings of trees and shrubs and naturalistic—though often completely engineered—water features such as lakes and streams. The English landscape style became the model for many of the early psychiatric institutions in North America.

Gardening in North America went through a similar evolution, first borrowing from the classical formalism of the Renaissance garden in what became known as the *colonial* style. While yearning for the grace and beauty of Europe, Americans were practical, and the plants within this formal design structure were frequently herbal and/or edible.

Due to the close cultural relationship with Britain, the style of the English Landscape Gardening School was the next source of influence on North American gardening, first in the form of the *wilderness garden* and later in the rural *romantic* style. In the late eighteenth century, the wilderness garden was an attempt to blend the formal colonial style with the more naturalistic Landscape Gardening style through the use of transitional terraces. In the early to mid-eighteenth century, the rural romantic style was more directly influenced by the English Landscape Gardening style and developed in conjunction with a growing social consciousness and city planning movement. Typical characteristics of this style were curvilinear roads and paths that followed the topography, no foundation planting (a traditional approach to landscape wherein plants are positioned at the base of the building to "ground" or "anchor" it), large expanses of lawn, and trees and shrubs in clustered random groups. In the mid- to late nineteenth century, the rural romantic style was used and further refined for the grounds of institutions and for public parks.

The nineteenth century was a period of growth in the number and types of public

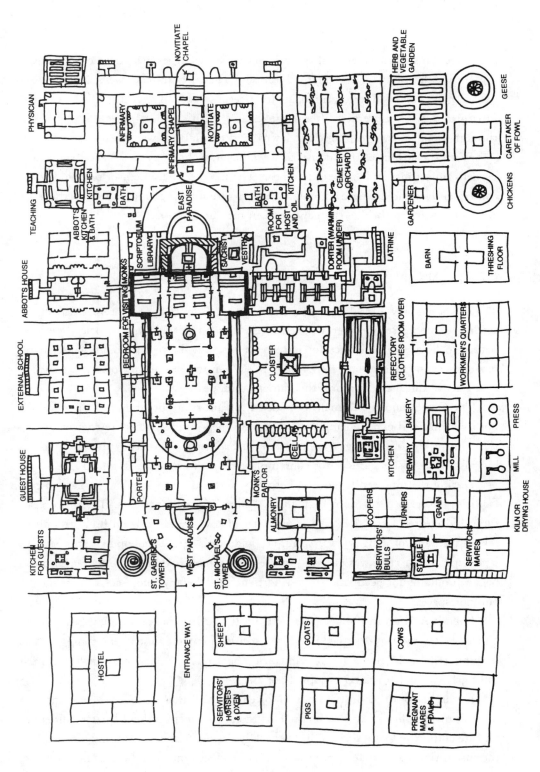

Figure 15.1 A drawing of about 830 A.D. preserved at St. Gall, Switzerland. Elements that would become standard in the monasteries of the Middle Ages are evident, including a cloister garden in the center for perambulation and contemplation. The physic garden was the prototype of specialized flower growing, with separate beds for each kind of plant. Drawing: Michael Chad Davis, The Office of James Burnett, Houston.

PHYSICIAN

NOVITIATE CHAPEL

INFIRMARY

INFIRMARY CHAPEL

NOVITIATE

HERB AND VEGETABLE GARDEN

CEMETERY ORCHARD

KITCHEN

BATH

TEACHING

ABBOT'S KITCHEN & BATH

KITCHEN

EAST PARADISE

SCRIPTORIUM LIBRARY

SACRIST

VESTRY

ROOM FOR HOST AND OIL

BATH

GARDENER

GEESE

CARETAKER OF FOWL

CHICKENS

ABBOT'S HOUSE

BEDROOM FOR VISITING MONKS

DORTER (WARMING ROOM UNDER)

LATRINE

BARN

THRESHING FLOOR

EXTERNAL SCHOOL

CLOISTER

REFECTORY (CLOTHES ROOM OVER)

WORKMEN'S QUARTERS

GUEST HOUSE

PORTER

MONK'S PARLOR

CELLAR

BAKERY

KITCHEN

BREWERY

COOPERS

TURNERS

GRAIN

PRESS

MILL

KILN OR DRYING HOUSE

ALMONRY

SERVITORS' BULLS

STABLE

SERVITORS' MARES

KITCHEN FOR GUESTS

ST. GABRIEL'S TOWER

WEST PARADISE

ST. MICHAEL'S TOWER

ENTRANCE WAY

HOSTEL

SERVITORS' HORSES & OXEN

SHEEP

GOATS

COWS

PIGS

PREGNANT MARES & FOALS

259

and private institutions. Several types of healthcare facilities were developed, including mental hospitals and veterans' hospitals. These "hospitals" were actually residential homes and had to accommodate long-term social and recreational needs. These institutions were patterned after large estates with curving drives, scenic vistas through woodlands, sweeping front lawns, and naturalistic water features.

With the advent of the Industrial Revolution, technology took center stage, and gardens unfortunately began to disappear. The rapid advancement of technology has consequently created a need to look back to nature for simpler solutions. Perhaps we are now seeking to bridge the gap between man and nature.

GARDENS IN HEALTHCARE SETTINGS

The use of gardens in healthcare settings has gone from being an integral part of the setting to nonexistence over the centuries. During periods when society believes nature to be a powerful force for human well-being, it provides more gardens and open spaces in the restorative environment. When the prevailing societal attitude is that science can master nature, the gardens disappear.

The Greeks and the Romans provided fresh air, sunlight, and outdoor spaces for both viewing and experiencing nature because they understood its restorative qualities. During the Middle Ages, the monasteries had herbal gardens to provide curatives but also had cloister gardens for contemplation and restoration (Figure 15.1).

During the nineteenth century, hospitals, veterans' hospitals, and long-term care facilities subscribed to more humane or "moral" care of patients. These hospitals typically selected large sites on the outskirts of towns and built on high ground to take advantage of long views, sunlight, and fresh air. The popular approach to landscape at that time was pastoral, in the rural romantic tradition. Mental hospitals began programs for occupational and horticultural therapy, more actively using the outdoor spaces.

Friends Asylum in Philadelphia (1817) was the first mental hospital built in the United States and was designed to create a secure, homelike, restful environment. The hospital still maintains its rural romantic character, surrounded by a forest with rolling lawns and scattered groupings of trees.

A number of other institutions followed Friends' lead in the development of a more humane approach to treatment. This moral treatment followed strict guidelines for care and proved very successful. Eventually, large numbers of immigrants came to the institutions, and state appropriations had to focus on more buildings; therefore, the grounds lost their importance.

A notable innovation in hospital design occurred in the mid-1800s, when Johns

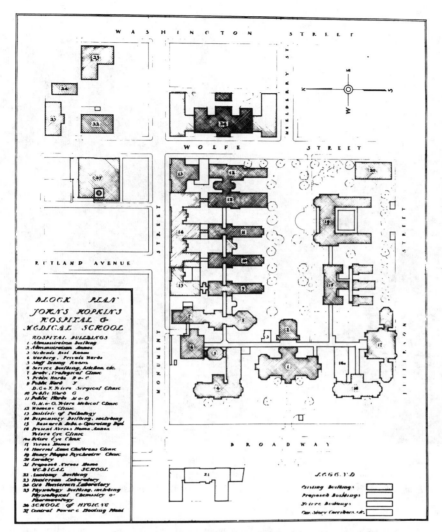

Figure 15.2 Site plan depicts the campuslike setting at Johns Hopkins Hospital in Baltimore, Maryland. Photo: The Alan Mason Chesney Medical Archives of The Johns Hopkins Medical Institutions, Baltimore.

Hopkins was designed in a campus pattern with breathing room around each of the low-scale pavilions. This design was a response to the problems incurred by the spread of infectious diseases in the previous hospital model. The spaces between pavilions became gardens. This provided good ventilation, views for the patients, and access to outdoor terraces for sunlight (see Figures 15.2 and 15.3).

The therapeutic use of gardens in hospitals in the twentieth century has been sporadic. Again, the mental hospitals, in most cases, have held that nature offers great relief for the distressed patient. The major medical centers based their growth on adjacencies and efficiencies and, for the most part, neglected the open spaces and

Figure 15.3   The bridges at Johns Hopkins Hospital in Baltimore, Maryland, linked the buildings together, allowing ample room for patients to get fresh air and sunshine. Photo: The Alan Mason Chesney Medical Archives of The Johns Hopkins Medical Institutions (circa 1910–1915), Baltimore.

views. Menninger Clinic in Topeka, Kansas, was an exception, integrating the hospital into the environment to create a healing setting, with activities that encouraged outdoor participation. This clinic was directed by Dr. Charles Menninger, who felt strongly that patients should be exposed to the restorative qualities of nature.

There has been emphasis of nature in the health centers that care for extended-stay patients, such as nursing care, hospice, and rehabilitation facilities, while the large medical centers focus on providing the technology to fight major illnesses. The lessons learned from the few good examples using nature are starting to change the design of all healthcare facilities.

THERAPEUTIC EFFECTS OF GARDENS

"People from a planet without flowers would think we must be mad with joy the whole time to have such things about us," wrote novelist Iris Murdoch (Murdoch

1970). Most people would agree. We have always known inherently that nature restores and heals. That is why we bring a plant or flowers to people in the hospital. This gift represents life. It gladdens the heart and lifts the spirit.

Environmental psychologists tell us that plants, daylight, and the sounds and smells of the garden are beneficial to the healing process. Ulrich did a ten-year study of patients who had undergone gall bladder surgery. In all respects, including nursing care, the groups were treated similarly. He discovered that, when patients were given a view of a grove of trees rather than a view of an adjacent brick building, they had shorter hospital stays, fewer negative comments, and less analgesic use (Ulrich 1984).

As a follow-up to Ulrich's research, architect Derek Parker used a 300-bed hospital with a 66-percent occupancy (198 beds) and 1991 industry figures to calculate the savings from this approach of giving all rooms a view of trees. He estimated that a design sensitive to views from patient rooms would save the hospital $118 per patient per day, or approximately $8.5 million per year ($118 multiplied by 198 occupied beds over 365 days) (Parker 1991).

The new Rehabilitation Hospital at St. Michael Health Center in Texarkana, Texas, provides every patient with a view of either a natural wooded area or a garden courtyard. "I've seen a drastic improvement in patients here," said Sister Damian Murphy, the director of pastoral care at St. Michael. "The average rehab patient is home now in two to three weeks, compared to about six weeks or more in the old facility."

The connection to nature is critical to our survival, said Dr. Eduard O. Wilson, an evolutionary biologist who is an editor of *The Biophilia Hypothesis*. The living world, wrote Dr. Wilson, is "the matrix in which the human mind originated and is permanently rooted" (Wilson 1984). Dr. Stephen Kellert, a professor of social ecology at Yale, believes that interaction with nature has had an important effect on a wide range of human characteristics, including intellect, emotions, and esthetics, or what we loosely refer to as fulfillment (Kellert 1993).

Rachel and Stephen Kaplan are professors of psychology and natural resources, respectively, at the University of Michigan. They have done extensive research with people who garden. They have determined that, through the close contact and commitment of tending a garden, one receives substantial psychological benefits. Stephen Kaplan said, "The concept of the restorative experience is based on the idea that mental effort, coping with hassles, and the everyday demands of living in the modern world all tend to fatigue one's capacity to direct one's attention. Since such fatigue makes one less competent, less pleasant, and less happy, recovering from it is a matter of some importance. A restorative environment is an environment that fosters this recover."

The Kaplans believe that gardening and exposure to nature are important to the restorative experience. They have discovered that gardeners receive great satisfaction from this activity. They have defined the primary garden experiences to be: desire to work in soil, wanting to see things grow, liking to be outside, and learning about gardening (Kaplan and Kaplan 1990).

Although gardens at healthcare facilities are becoming more widespread, they are still not the norm. Many of today's health centers grew very quickly during the boom days of the 1950s, 1960s, and 1970s. Dr. Sam Bass Warner, urban historian at Brandeis University, said, "Today's hospitals look more like office buildings or factories than places of healing" (Warner 1995). This is due to the emphasis on technology and efficiency. Medicine and machines were given top priority over views and one's connection to the healing qualities of nature. The regulations that control healthcare institutions are stringent with regard to health safety issues and the requirement for windows in patient rooms. However, outside the building there are no specific guidelines or requirements. While requirements are not always the best answer, having a dedicated amount of open/garden space would be a positive change. This has worked well in urban developments where an open-space formula is included in the building approval process. As positive research and good examples continue to grow, decision makers are becoming more aware of the substantial benefits of having gardens in the hospital setting.

The importance of gardens in the healthcare setting extends beyond the patient's perspective. Hospital administrators want healthy working environments for their staff. In the highly stressful world of healthcare, they need places for staff to relax and recharge. Gardens support their mission of recruiting and keeping the best people. Providing outdoor spaces for the caregivers to reflect and relax is important to a successful health center (see Figure 15.4).

Stimulating the Senses

The garden works in many ways to enhance the hospital setting. It provides a setting for a multitude of nature's gifts, all of which stimulate our senses in a positive way and help our bodies to heal.

SIGHT

One of the most important senses is that of sight. Often, a patient can experience the garden from his or her room. To provide visual interest, views must be carefully orchestrated. This can be achieved by seasonal blooming plants, color, and the richness of textures that engage the eye. The view to gathering areas within a garden is sometimes helpful in providing positive distractions. This active and changing environment provides relief for the long-term stay.

Figure 15.4 The recovery from the pressures of the hospital is also important for caregivers who need garden spaces for stress reduction. Landscape design: The Office of James Burnett. Photography: James F. Wilson, Dallas.

Shade is critical in the garden, as patients recovering from procedures or undergoing treatment are often sensitive to harsh light. It can be achieved by overhead structures, shade trees, and canopy umbrellas.

Awareness of the patients' viewpoint is important in the design of patient-focused gardens. Understanding that frequently they are in wheelchairs means providing views from that perspective. The use of raised planters can help to bring the plants closer to the patients and provide additional seating. Colors can alarm, excite, calm, and uplift. Just as color therapy is practiced in the interior spaces, it should also extend into the garden.

Charles Lewis, a leading horticultural therapist at the Morton Arboretum in Chicago, said, "Plants exhibit life-enhancing qualities that encourage people to respond to them. In a world of constant judgment, plants are nonthreatening and nondiscriminating. They respond to the care that is given to them, not to race, intellect, or physical capacities of the garden. The garden is a benevolent setting in which a person can take the first steps toward self-confidence" (Lewis 1990).

Plants should be chosen for their ever-changing qualities. The marking of the seasons is extremely important to understanding the passing of time and the life force by which we are all connected. The richness of blooming plantings can calm and comfort the viewer. This supports the idea of the garden offering relief from the clinical atmosphere of the hospital and further assists in the recovery process.

SOUND

The sounds of songbirds, rustling leaves, and falling water help to reduce stress and give the patient a feeling of comfort. The sound of water is probably one of the most significant, as it can screen out conversations and other unwanted noises. Water possesses tremendous healing qualities. It symbolizes the source of life and the washing away of disease. The sounds of waterfalls, rivers, and the ocean soothe and refresh, as is evidenced by their popularity on recorded relaxation tapes and sound machines (see color plate 14).

TEXTURE

Touch is a key consideration in the hospital garden setting. Research has proven that premature babies show a 49-percent faster growth rate when stroked for five minutes every four hours. We know that touch heals and that it promotes the growth of hormones in our bodies. Massage therapy and pet therapy have become important complementary treatments that focus on the healing powers of touch. The sense of touch in the landscape is critical to the successful patient garden. Plants and garden elements need to be soft and interesting enough to touch. Fountains should be designed to provide accessibility for those who wish to feel the moving water. Dr. Depak Chopra, an endocrinologist, said, "Our skin is a very active organ biologically. It is alive and it self-repairs. Our skin is the richest source of both hormones and immune cells. So when we stimulate the skin, we can cause a shower of growth hormones to be released into our bloodstream" (Chopra 1989). The therapeutic garden should adequately address the need for touch, both with our hands and feet.

SMELL

The fragrance of a garden is critical to creating a restorative experience. Aromatherapy is becoming popular as a complementary treatment for a variety of conditions. According to Vincent Healy, who teaches landscape architecture at the University of Southern California at Los Angeles, "Fragrance can work to recall fondly remembered or traumatic past experiences and thus be an important tool towards the clearing up of unfinished business. The scent of orange blossoms might bring back distant memories of landscapes permeated with the scent from hundreds of square miles of flowering citrus groves. Different fragrances evoke powerful emotions" (Healy 1986).

There are many opportunities to present an ongoing display of fragrances in the hospital garden. A richly scented rose can awaken the senses and provide the garden with a sweet scent. Many herbs such as lavender, rosemary, sage, and thyme also provide rich fragrance.

Fragrant plants should be incorporated in a design to provide interest, but should not overwhelm.

TASTE

Closely associated with the sense of smell is the sense of taste. Healthcare facilities that provide edible gardens offer visitors the fascination of seeing a landscape that gives back both aesthetically and nutritionally. Herbal gardens add interest by allowing the passerby the opportunity to pick a sample and experience the taste of a favorite herb. The garden offers fruits, vegetables, and herbs to beguile the palate. The sense of taste also has a connection to the past. In a nursing home setting, a resident-attended herb and vegetable garden would not only be a labor of love, but could also conjure up fond memories of family and friends. The taste of a ripe tomato used in a special sauce or a sprig of fresh mint floating on the top of a tall glass of iced tea may provoke healing memories.

Horticultural Therapy

The garden that produces food through patient horticulture therapy is a sacred place. This garden has a much stronger value to the long-term patients than the viewing gardens. Through participation in a garden, the character and personality of each gardener comes alive. In extended-stay facilities, horticulture therapy has produced remarkable results. Charles Lewis, in his work with horticulture therapy, defines the benefits as higher self esteem; understanding and fascination with the life process; contemplative benefits of working and observing; and increased social interaction among patients (Lewis 1990).

Horticulture therapy is widely practiced in rehabilitation and nursing facilities, where patients have exhibited startling results when participating with plants in the growth process. Horticultural therapy programs are growing in number, and many universities are now offering degrees in this important therapy (see Figure 15.5). Patients who traditionally underwent occupational and physical therapy are now being offered horticultural therapy as well. Lewis said, "Horticulture may be seen from many different perspectives. . . .We are now asking for another viewpoint on flowers and plants: to see them as reflections of life-force, the 'smile of God,' expressions of the presence of beauty and harmony in the world, prehistoric partners with man in his evolutionary journey, guideposts to the harmonious existence of man and this planet" (Lewis 1979).

ACTIVITY AREAS

The benefits of a hospital garden can be increased by extending the waiting and meeting areas to become part of the garden. Whenever possible, a hospital should use

Figure 15.5 The Chicago Botanical Gardens provides a variety of gardening classes with a focus on horticultural therapy. Photography: Paul Schlismann, Deerfield, Illinois.

nearby garden terraces and courts for gatherings and outdoor dining opportunities, providing noninstitutional settings for relaxation and conversation.

The garden can offer places for quiet contemplation, an important asset for family, patients, and caregivers. It provides a setting where they can reflect on sometimes overwhelming health challenges or where they can simply quiet the mind and focus.

THE LANDSCAPE ARCHITECT'S ROLE

It is important (whether redeveloping an older facility or constructing a new one) to include a landscape architect as a part of the design team from the outset. The design team typically consists of the architect, the interior designer, and the landscape architect. It is critical to the unity and cohesiveness of the project to have all of the areas of design represented, even in the earliest conceptual discussions. A landscape architect has a great deal to offer in the early phases of programming, site selection, and master planning that helps set the armature for future development. Probably the most critical is helping the team to understand the size and scale of the open spaces or spaces between the buildings and the parking areas.

During the conceptual phase, the design team and owner will formulate the goals of the healthcare facility. These goals will determine the image of the center. The landscape architect will offer concepts for the exterior spaces that reinforce these goals. The healthcare facility is an integral part of the community in which it is located, and, since the exterior spaces are most visible to the community and convey the first impression, the landscape should project the image determined in the goal-setting sessions. It should have meaning to its users.

The setting for the hospital is critical on two levels. On one level, it involves how the *community* perceives the hospital in a physical sense: caring, compassionate, and welcoming; or cold, bleak, and frightening. Another level is how the patient and visitors perceive the hospital from the patient room, cafeteria, and procedure and waiting areas. The hospital image can be greatly enhanced by the presence of gardens. Open space is one of the most obvious ways in which a hospital can change its appearance, in which it can demonstrate a commitment to a healing environment that begins at the property line.

In the programming stages, a landscape architect can help the client and the team determine a realistic budget for landscape. This should run between 3 and 5 percent of the total construction costs, depending on the scope and character of the landscape work. A landscape architect will assist the team in deciding which types and what scope of outdoor activities and spaces are needed. The landscape should be responsive to what is going on inside the building so that outdoor areas correspond to the interior layout and are easily accessible to the users they are intended for. Prioritizing these spaces is the key to a successful master plan, since the landscape and architecture must work as a dialogue, each reinforcing the other in both form and activity (see Figure 15.6).

We are reexamining healthcare delivery systems, and new facilities are expected to be flexible for the future. A landscape architect can help to assure that the exterior spaces are also adaptable. Because large healthcare facilities serve a variety of patient needs, potential conflicts in the use of space can be avoided through careful coordination in the development of the garden areas. Maintenance concerns and requirements should be a part of the programming discussion because these requirements will determine the types of materials to be used. They will also help to set the parameters for the design of special features such as fountains and lakes.

Will the project be constructed in phases? The landscape architect can help to coordinate the phasing in such a way as to minimize the potential disruption caused by future growth. Once the programming needs are determined, in the case of new construction, the design team will be able to decide how large the site needs to be and what sort of configuration is most desirable. The landscape architect's knowledge of environmental issues will prove invaluable to the site development process.

Certain site issues are critical for healthcare facilities and need to be addressed by a landscape architect in the master planning phase of the project. Landscape architects

Figure 15.6   A site plan of a nursing care facility in Northern California shows an arboretum, bird watching area, horticultural therapy, active recreation areas, and a children's play area for visitors. Photo: The Office of James Burnett, Houston.

can provide a comprehensive analysis of site legibility or wayfinding, environmental concerns, contextual issues, circulation patterns, building orientation, safety issues, and image. All of these are essential to the master planning process.

A landscape architect is able to analyze the existing site's environmental issues and help the client and design team to locate the facilities in a manner that will maximize the potential of the site. This includes analyzing the topography for maximum views and minimal disruption, examining the soils, determining the typical wind-flow patterns to capture the best breezes, studying the movement of the sun across the site, determining the most effective orientation for the building to allow sun into the courtyards, and analyzing the existing vegetation for possible preservation. Why spend $40,000 on small new nursery trees when a wonderful grove of irreplaceable 80-year-old walnut trees could be preserved?

A landscape architect should also analyze the potential views. Are there any distant views that are worth preserving, or are there any distant views that should be eliminated? Are there incompatible neighbors that should be screened or buffered from the hospital, such as an industrial or commercial area or a major thoroughfare? The purpose of a healing environment is defeated if all the views to the landscape for patients, staff, and visitors are through windows that are so heavily tinted that it looks like a thunderstorm is brewing. The architect may want the tinted glass to be the same throughout the building, but for energy efficiency the windows on the north face could have a much lighter tint than those on the southwest face. This is the type of issue that should be resolved early in the design process, and it illustrates the importance of having a landscape architect's point of view.

The landscape architect will also look at the context of the site—regionally, locally, and neighbor by neighbor. A quiet rural area will require a different approach than a busy metropolitan location. Seldom is the context simple or straightforward.

In the design process, it is crucial to determine who the users are and what their needs will be: patients, caregivers, and visitors. The therapeutic garden should be designed specifically for the facility type in the same way that the architecture and interiors are treated. An ambulatory care center does not look like or feel like an assisted living center or a hospice; therefore, the gardens should also respond to the use.

The variety of facility type calls for sensitivity in designing the landscape, and a landscape architect who specializes in healthcare facilities should be familiar with all the various patient needs. Children's hospitals and clinics should have outdoor play areas that are easily accessible and stimulating and should offer alternatives to active, highly physical play. In the case of cancer treatment centers, the ideal situation is one in which the patient can relax while undergoing chemotherapy and radiation treatment and view a landscape that offers positive interest and is calming. The landscape should also be responsive to what is going on inside the building, so that outdoor areas correspond to the interior layout and are easily accessible to the users they are intended for. Specific patient groups, such as cancer patients or maternity patients, may be best served by providing privacy and a certain amount of segregation. Alzheimer patients get disoriented easily and need outdoor spaces designed so that they cannot get lost.

Because hearing and smell are the two senses least affected by AIDS, the sound of water and fragrance of herbs is therapeutic. AIDS patients are often on medication that causes sensitivity to light and need shaded outdoor areas and nonglare surfaces.

Many rehabilitation facilities are beginning to adopt horticultural therapy programs to complement their physical and occupational therapy programs (see Figure 15.7), but they are often designed long before the horticultural therapist is hired. It is best when establishing this type of program to have a landscape architect who

Figure 15.7 Horticultural therapy gives patients an opportunity to experience the wonders of nature directly. The fascination of tending to a plant has proven to be a great success in speeding recovery and keeping the patients interested in therapy. Landscape design: The Office of James Burnett. Photography: James F. Wilson, Dallas.

understands the complexities and is able to design a space that provides for the many aspects of a horticultural therapy program in order to ensure its success.

CONCLUSION

The importance of nature in the healthcare setting is critical to the success of the center. Anita Olds said, "Current architectural practices and models of therapy require that one spend time almost exclusively inside buildings . . . all of which maintain predictable year round conditions defying the vicissitudes of nature and our relationship to her.

"In addition, primary determinants for the location of a therapeutic site involve proximity to target populations, public transportation, and energy sources; thus, hospitals, clinics, and therapeutic centres are generally located with little regard for site conditions and rarely in areas where natural features are present. In fact, the simplest and most cost-effective construction method is to raze the land, build regularly shaped buildings, and then put in a few young trees to make the structure less of an eyesore" (Olds 1985).

However, some very exciting examples of hospitals that support the healing, restorative experience are being planned at this time. Hopefully, as we experience this new wave of awareness, we will not digress again as we have so many times before.

In the not-too-distant future, we will be able to quantify quite accurately the therapeutic effects of the landscape so that medical technology will be combined with sensory stimulation in the natural garden environment to help the patient heal both body and mind. It is exhilarating to see the healthcare community come full circle after some 2,000 years and rediscover what is important in the healing process. It is quite simple. It is encoded in our DNA. For centuries, the *sound* of water, leaves, and animals; the *sight* of the landscape and the colors; the *smell* and fragrance of all the wonderful plants have been within us. Getting back to the long, enduring patterns of nature will heal us. These are our cues for design and the key to understanding ourselves.

James D. Burnett is an award-winning landscape architect who specializes in healthcare. His firm, The Office of James Burnett, is located in Houston, Texas.

References

Chopra, D. *Quantum Healing: Exploring the Frontiers of Mind/Body.* New York: Bantam Books, 1989.

Chopra, D. *Return of the Rishi.* Boston: Houghton Mifflin, 1988.

Healy, V. "The Hospice Garden: Addressing the Patient's Needs Through Landscape." *The American Journal of Hospice Care* 3 (1986): 5–6.

Kaiser, L. R. "Keynote Address: Transforming Healthcare—Designing for Quality." *Journal of Healthcare Design* 6 (September 1994).

Kaplan, R. and Kaplan, S. "The Restorative Experience." In *The Meaning of Gardens,* edited by M. Francis and R. T. Hester, Jr. Cambridge: The MIT Press, 1990.

Kellert, S. "The Biological Basis for Human Values of Nature." In *The Biophilia Hypothesis,* edited by S. Kellert and E. Wilson. Covelo, CA: Shearwater Books, 1993.

Lewis, C. A. "Gardening as Healing Process." In *The Meaning of Gardens,* edited by M. Francis and R. T. Hester, Jr. Cambridge: The MIT Press, 1990.

Lewis, C. A. "Healing in the Urban Environment: A Person/Plant Viewpoint." *Journal of the American Planning Association* 45 (1979).

Lewis, C. A. "Public Housing Gardens: Landscapes for the Soul." In *Landscape for Living.* Washington, DC: U.S. Department of Agriculture, 1972.

Murdock, I. *A Fairly Honorable Defeat.* London: Chattow & Windus and Viking Press, 1970.

Olds, A. "Nature as Healer." In *Reading in Psychosynthesis: Theory, Process & Practice,* edited by J. Weiser and T. Yeomans. Ontario, Canada: Ontario Institute for Studies in Education, 1985.

Parker, D. "A Better Building's Benefits." *Modern Healthcare* (December 9, 1991).

Ulrich, R. S. "How Design Impacts Wellness." *Healthcare Forum Journal* (September/October 1992).

Ulrich, R. S. "View Through a Window May Influence Recovery from Surgery." *Science* 224 (1984).

Warner, S. B., Jr. "The Human Side: A Brief History of Healing Gardens in Healthcare Settings." *Journal of Healthcare Design* 7 (September 1995).

Wilson, E. *Biophilia.* Cambridge: Harvard University Press, 1984.

WAYFINDING

16

Janet R. Carpman, Ph.D. and Myron A. Grant, MLA

P icture this: *You are an elderly man who has been healthy all his life and who has managed to avoid being hospitalized. But recently, it's been more difficult to do the normal tasks of life, like walking down the sidewalk to retrieve the newspaper, without becoming short of breath. Your doctor has ordered tests at the prestigious medical center downtown. You and your wife set out, anxious about the outcome of the tests; about negotiating the sprawling, unfamiliar buildings; about being on time for your appointment. How will you know where to park? Will you be able to tell which building is which? How will you find the Cardiology Department? Or was it Cardiopathy? Do they have colored lines on the floor to help you find your way, like you remember from the time your kids were born? How will you find your car again?*

There is no doubt that worries about the problems of finding their way and becoming lost in what seem like unfriendly, intimidating healthcare facilities adds to the stress felt by many unfamiliar patients and visitors. Although much of the stress associated with a visit to a healthcare facility is unavoidable (such as worries about one's health), wayfinding-related stress is avoidable. There are a number of ways wayfinding-related stress can be reduced, but, first, it is necessary to understand what wayfinding is and what it is not.

WHAT IS WAYFINDING?

Wayfinding is not the same as signage. *Wayfinding* refers to *behavior,* while signage refers to one of the many design-related elements that can affect that behavior. Wayfinding refers to what people see, what they think about, what they notice, and what they do to find their way from one place to another. It involves five deceptively simple ideas: knowing where you are, knowing your destination (including the correct terminology), knowing and following the best route to your destination, being able to recognize your destination once you arrive, and finding your way back.

275

Calling the issue "signage" is incorrect and simplistic. It assumes an automatic correlation between the posting of signs (regardless of their location, design, messages, accuracy, or lighting) and their viewing, comprehension, and adherence by healthcare facility users. It does not recognize the effects of other aspects of the physical and operational environments of wayfinding. This simplistic view leads to expensive and often ineffective attempts to solve complex wayfinding problems.

Many designers, facility managers, and others who deal with this issue have been trained to call it signage and to think about it in that way. Understanding wayfinding involves a paradigm shift of the type heard about in other areas of business and science (Kuhn 1970; Monteleone 1995). However, once that shift is made, and once wayfinding is understood as behavior affected by both environmental and operational factors, ease of wayfinding in healthcare facilities becomes an achievable goal.

HEALTHCARE FACILITIES ARE CONFUSING

Wayfinding confusion is certainly not limited to healthcare facilities. Most large-scale facilities including airports, museums, shopping malls, convention centers, major hotels, high schools, university campuses, and others end up being thought of as complex and confusing mazes.

However, healthcare facilities, particularly large hospitals, are among the most notoriously confusing buildings to negotiate in modern society. Numerous factors work together to make this so. Many hospitals started as small facilities that were easy to negotiate. They have been expanded incrementally, usually without a facility or campus masterplan to guide growth. Awkward corridor connections, floor misalignments, and poor functional adjacencies are all too frequent occurrences. As a result, destinations visited by a patient in a single visit may be nowhere near each other. Patients may need to walk long distances down winding corridors, they may need to travel from building to building and may end up feeling more like they've been in a labyrinth than in a hospital.

Furthermore, hospitals tend to use special terminology unfamiliar to the public. Thus, not only are buildings large and labyrinthine, signs may be unintelligible if they include messages like "Otorhinolaryngology." There is often a considerable difference in educational levels between medical personnel and the patients and visitors they serve, and many medical terms are typically not understood by those outside the medical world.

Large buildings, winding halls, and unfamiliar terminology in healthcare facilities need to be negotiated by the people under the most stress in our society. Elderly people, sick people, those worried about loved ones, people who physically can't walk long distances, and people who either temporarily or permanently don't have the mental faculties to solve the maze are the ones forced to negotiate complex and confusing healthcare environments.

WAYFINDING NEEDS

What do patients and visitors need in order to find their way to, through, and out of a complex healthcare facility? The following is a list of performance guidelines for how a successful wayfinding system should work and quotes from patients and visitors in several hospitals around the country reflecting how many existing wayfinding systems actually work.

Patients and visitors need to know how to find the facility from their home or office.

I lost my map before I came. The doctor's office said to follow the signs. The only problem is that, from where we were coming from to where we ended up, there weren't *any signs.*

We thought we could follow the "H" signs. There were several. When I saw the first "H," I thought it was intended for Children's Hospital, but it wasn't.

It's kind of confusing, the fact that the exit off the highway isn't well marked. It says "hospital," but if it said which *hospital, it would be better.*

Once I took the wrong turn and missed the way to the hospital. I had to turn later and then got confused about where to park. This construction makes it very difficult to get around.

Patients and visitors need to know the name of the building where their appointment is or where they will be visiting.

I didn't know there were different buildings. I thought they were all one place. I didn't know they had names.

The first time, I didn't know which building to go into. It took me 15 extra minutes, and I was late because I went all the way to Emergency. But I needed to come to Radiology.

We had a map, but it's not that easy to read. The buildings—there's nothing to let you know where you are—no signs on the outside of the buildings. You have to guess what building it is.

Patients and visitors need to know where to park.

This parking situation is ridiculous. I had to wait and I finally followed someone, and I feel like I am parked in the North Pole!

You need a bigger sign that says "Visitor Parking" with an arrow pointing. You have to quickly read all the 12 things on the sign out there. I ended up turning around in Emergency.

I wasn't sure where to park. I didn't even know which door to use. I found it very confusing.

Patients and visitors need to know how to find the correct entrance to the building once they have parked.

There are so many buildings and not enough signs leading to the different parts. I never know which doors to use. Now, with these expansions, I am always confused.

Patients and visitors need to know and understand the name of their destination.

(What do you think "Oncology" means?) I have no idea. That's kidney isn't it?

(What do you think "Concentrated Care" means?) I know what the two words mean, but I don't know what they mean in relation to the hospital though.

Patients and visitors need to know the floor and room number (if applicable) of the destination.

I didn't know where the room was because I didn't see a sign on the door or wall. To me, when the elevator door opens, you should see a sign telling you to go this way or that way. For two days, there is no name tag on my sister's door. The only thing that told me it was the right room was the sound of her voice.

I always have trouble getting from the first floor in the main lobby to wherever I end up.

I'm always getting off on the wrong floor or the wrong area.

They've been remodeling for two or three years! With all the detours, it's hard to find your way around.

Patients and visitors need to know what vertical circulation (elevators or stairs) to use.

I just jumped on the first elevator I saw. Someone told me "B" were the only ones working at night.

The lady in registration said take elevator C. We didn't know where it was. When we found it, it was marked "G."

Patients and visitors need legible directional and identification signs to help them find their way along hospital corridors.

When I was walking in the other building, I couldn't see anything, no signs with room numbers or names.

We had some trouble because we missed a sign. It was near the ceiling and we didn't see it. We ended up somewhere where we weren't supposed to be and had to be directed back to Outpatient Registration.

I just wasn't familiar with where things were, so I asked questions. One time when my daughter was admitted here, I had to go across the street to the hospital from the ambulatory services building, through the tunnel, and I got lost. I didn't know where I was and couldn't see any signs.

Patients and visitors need to be able to recognize the destination once they arrive.

I was in an office on the seventh floor of the Medical Office Building and my son was looking for me. He went up and down the hall before he found it. The first time around, you've just got to keep walking until you find the series of numbers you're looking for. There should be something here—right on the wall.

I was looking for the Lab and ended up at the Morgue.

I went the wrong way. You're in such a hurry to get where you are going, you don't look! After I got to where I thought I was going, I asked somebody with a name tag to see if I was really there.

Patients and visitors should be able to get accurate directions from staff about how to find their destination.

I stopped by to ask, but the volunteer was on the phone.

The information desk faces the wrong way. I walked right by it and didn't know it was there.

I was told by the doorman to follow the blue line. When I got to the end of the blue line I was confused because I wasn't where I was supposed to be. I couldn't find anyone to ask directions of. Then I asked a doctor I saw, but he didn't know the directions to the OP lab. He asked someone else who gave me directions.

Patients and visitors need to be able to find their way to other destinations such as departments, reception areas, restrooms, the cafeteria, the gift shop, telephones, cashier.

> *When I got up on the floor, I didn't know where to go. I saw this room but there was no sign. I just saw the family waiting here. You need blinking lights that say, "Restrooms."*
>
> *We were in the Emergency Room and wanted something to eat in the cafeteria. You can't go through the hallway to get there—you have to go outside and around and through the parking lot to get to the cafeteria!*
>
> *I couldn't find anything. I didn't know where the coffee shop or parking were. My daughter was very sick and everything was upsetting. It's not like you can think clearly! If you could think clearly you probably could read the signs and figure things out.*

Patients and visitors need to be able to find their way back out.

> *I went out the Emergency Room door trying to find my car. There's a nice parking garage across the street, but it happens to be the wrong one.*
>
> *It's confusing, the way it's laid out. Finding your way to the X-ray department, the cafeteria, Main Office, you name it. The markings aren't good either. You don't know when you exit where you're gonna wind up!*

WAYFINDING AND MARKETING

There is no doubt that wayfinding has a considerable effect on the overall image a health facility projects to its consumers in the surrounding community. When visiting a hospital means anxiety about the prospect of being confused or lost as well as the experience of disorientation during the visit, the view of the institution as caring about its patients dims considerably. As more and more facilities tout their "user friendliness" and individual attention, there is a telling contrast between the desired image and the reality of wayfinding-related stress and frustration.

With healthcare in its present and likely continuing state of flux, the overall attractiveness and appeal of healthcare facilities shouldn't be underemphasized. When consumers cannot tell one institution from another on the basis of (generally high) quality of care, characteristics of the facilities in general, and ease of wayfinding in particular, can help them choose one provider over another.

As one staff member explained, staff assistance with patient disorientation is received positively, yet if patients and visitors become too confused in a healthcare facility, they may not choose to return.

The strange thing about that is, when somebody gets lost, a lot of times they feel that it's their own fault, and some of the best PR we have probably is showing someone where they are supposed to go. Then you've rescued somebody. It sounds silly, yeah, you are not being productive at your job, but it's probably some of the best PR we have— "Oh here, let me show you where that is." Then the person says, "Thank you, I'd never have found it without you." But . . . long-term, it doesn't help us, because they don't want to come back to this hospital, because they will get lost again.

STAFF WAYFINDING

Patients and visitors are not the only people confused in large healthcare facilities. Staff often have a difficult time too. It is assumed they will learn their way around the whole facility and be able to direct others to various public destinations, but this frequently is not the case. Staff learn their way around eventually, but it is often difficult and takes considerable time. Some staff learn only the few routes they use every day and become lost if they have to get to a new area. They rarely have the advantage of receiving adequate orientation to the facility when they first start work. Teaching hospitals frequently have new personnel, as well as new groups of residents and other entering students all needing to learn their way.

Staff disorientation can have serious consequences. When ambulance drivers cannot find the emergency room, when code blue teams are delayed by taking a wrong turn, or when critical lab specimens don't arrive at the lab on time because a messenger was confused, patient care suffers.

When patients and fellow staff are confused, knowledgeable staff may need to take time away from their official duties to play the unofficial role of guide. They may frequently be called upon to give directions and/or may take the time to escort people to their destinations. This hospitable but otherwise unproductive time can result in considerable opportunity costs and lack of productivity (Zimring 1990). As one staff member put it:

It's a tremendous amount of time when you multiply how many times this is going on, times your staff. It adds up really quickly. It's probably a lot more than anybody has ever thought, if you take a minute times 3,000 employees every day. If every employee gets stopped for one minute to give somebody directions, it sounds stupid but when you multiply it up, it's a lot.

What do staff need in order to find their way to, through, and out of a healthcare facility and to give directions to others? The following is a list of performance guidelines for how a successful wayfinding system should work and quotes from staff in several hospitals around the country reflecting how their existing wayfinding systems actually work for them.

Staff need to have some orientation to the facility when they first begin work.

> *I've been here going on 11 years. I've been through a couple of these reconstructions that we've gone through, so I was thinking back on the orientation that I had when I first started. I think about one walk through the hospital and, by the way, "Here's your workload, and you find your way from there." We didn't have a hospital orientation, per se, when I first started, and in most of these things I've learned, I've learned just kind of by guess and by golly.*
>
> *When they go, they just stop in the middle of the hall and they point. "This is so-and-so." You have no idea what is in there when you get in. And I can understand part of the disruption with 30–40 people, because these orientation classes are big. But still, they say, "This is so-and-so," and they keep right on walking down the hall. It is very confusing.*

Staff need to understand the layout of the facility themselves and negotiate it efficiently.

> *To this day, after 11 years on the job, I find the basement and the second floor are the two most difficult to get to. I still get turned around in the basement going to Pharmacy or going to MIS. I start down the hallway and say, "That's the wrong way!" I have to turn around and go back the other way. They're not marked well.*
>
> *The hardest thing for me was, when I would get in, they'd say, "You work on 4-SW today." Get on the elevator and you get on the floor, and you say, "Okay, which way is 4-SW?" I don't even know where 4-Main is yet! And you are looking around and, well, I don't know which way is 4-SW. Ask the lady up there at that desk, and, half the time, she doesn't know!*

Staff need to be able to confidently direct patients, visitors, and fellow staff.

> *You know what I do when I get those people that look for Ultrasound? I give them the phone number and let them call it and ask them where they are located. That is how I*

handle it at the Information Desk when they come up. I don't know where Ultrasound is, so I give them the number for that department, and they call down there.

It's not a welcoming feeling sometimes, because you are out there like a stranger in your own company, and you feel ridiculous. And when a patient asks you where something is and you have to tell them to ask someone else because you don't know, that's sort of embarrassing as well.

Staff need to keep up with wayfinding changes: knowing where departments have moved, knowing what departments have changed names, and so on.

I work the Information Desk. And it is not very easy, because there is constant change. Although we have an escort man that helps us out, even he doesn't know where to go. And the quickest way is to call that department and find how to get there. Because, like I said, the changes are constant, and it makes it hard. And I try to offer a few suggestions, like maybe having a quick turnover on the information like a Rolodex system, where you could pull that out. And that we should be the first ones to be informed, after Administration, or that department. But a lot of times, we are far behind, and it makes it very inconvenient.

The department heads don't always notify the people. I've heard them call, "Code Blue—Cardiac Arrest," and I've seen residents running around, like, "Where is this?" First-year residents can't even find the ER. In the Professional Building, you have residents running around wondering where this person is now? That's bad, because seconds count.

Part of the problem is, too, there are people, and you can hear them giving instructions with great authority, and they're giving instructions for a location that has moved. So they sound like they really know what is going on, and their intentions are really good, but things are changing so rapidly.

Staff need to know how to access wayfinding information if they don't have it themselves.

People expect you to know, and when you don't that makes you feel bad. I usually have to ask, especially for certain areas, I usually ask to see their doctor's orders. But you can only get them so far. You have to be a very educated staff person in order to get them where they are going.

A WAYFINDING SYSTEM

As mentioned previously, signage (a product) is not the same as wayfinding (behavior). But signage (if well designed and appropriately located) can help people find their way. How should we think of signage in relation to wayfinding?

According to environmental psychologist Gerald Weisman, people find their way around confusing places as a result of:

- Designed aspects of the physical environment (*design elements*), only one of which is signage
- Policies and practices relating to how people find their way (*operational elements*)
- People's own wayfinding-related experiences, behavior, and attitude (*behavioral elements*) (Weisman 1982)

These three factor groups comprise a *wayfinding system.*

Design Elements

There is a long laundry list of design elements that can assist or detract from peoples' abilities to find their way around a complex hospital. For each of these design elements, there is an associated set of performance guidelines. There is insufficient space in this chapter to cover these in detail, but you may wish to consult other sources, such as our book, *Design that Cares: Planning Health Facilities for Patients and Visitors* (Carpman and Grant 1993).

Wayfinding-related design elements include:

- Off-site exterior signage
- Legibility of the institution
- Site layout, including exterior circulation
- Location of parking in relation to entrances
- On-site exterior signage
- Parking lot circulation and signage
- Parking structure circulation and signage
- Relation of parking areas to main entrances
- Building identification
- Legibility of main entrances
- Building layout, including horizontal circulation (corridors) and vertical circulation (elevators, escalators, and stairways)
- Interior identification, information, and directional signage
- Handheld maps
- "You-are-here" maps

- Emergency exit maps
- Color coding
- Special environmental features

Operational Elements

There is a shorter list of operational elements—the policies and practices that can help a wayfinding system work well or doom it to failure. However, the brevity of the list shouldn't mislead the reader into thinking that any of these elements are easy to accomplish.

Wayfinding-related operational elements include:

- Terminology selection and use
- Floor numbering
- Room numbering
- Wayfinding staff training programs
- Spoken directions
- Previsit information
- Wayfinding system maintenance

Behavioral Elements

No doubt there are as many approaches to finding one's way as there are individuals. However, wayfinding strategies usually fall into four main categories (Weisman 1982). The first strategy has to do with being able to see your destination and making your way steadily, if somewhat circuitously toward it. This tends to be more useful outside than inside, although views to and through buildings can be helpful.

The second strategy involves following a path that leads to a destination. Colored floor lines are the common environmental response to this strategy. Escorts also provide this type of service. This "blind navigation" approach has several disadvantages. Colored floor lines or other continuous cuing devices can work only when a very limited number of destinations is being called out. Otherwise, patients and visitors can be overloaded with too many colors, and those who are colorblind may not be able to distinguish some colors. This approach also means that people really have no idea where they are in relation to where they started. The only way they can make their way back is to reverse the route. Shortcuts are beyond their comprehension, and mistakes can't be corrected easily. In addition, many patients visit several destinations during one hospital visit, and, if they were to reverse their routes, following multiple continuous cuing devices would become overly complex and confusing.

The third strategy is to use signs and landmarks to provide information along the way. These can supply reassurance that one is on the right track and help clarify choices where decisions need to be made.

The fourth strategy involves forming and using a mental image, or *cognitive map,* of the environment. This means understanding how one place is spatially related to another place. It implies that people can use this understanding creatively, to find more efficient ways of moving from here to there.

In addition to these strategies, alone or in combination, recent experience with the facility or with a similar facility helps people find their way.

Wayfinding planners need to understand that different people may favor different wayfinding strategies and that the same individual may use different strategies in different situations. This is one reason why "redundant cues" (the same information given in different ways) are an important part of a wayfinding system.

WAYFINDING EXPECTATIONS

One of the principles of total quality management, a currently popular way of thinking about the delivery of health services, is that, in providing a service, an organization should not only *meet* the expectations of its consumers, it should *exceed* such expectations (Berwick, Godfrey, and Roessner 1990). This way of thinking is useful when considering wayfinding in health facilities.

When they come to a large hospital, patients and visitors have different expectations about what it will be like to find their way. To oversimplify for the purposes of argument, and as illustrated in Table 16.1, they either expect to have some difficulty ("lost"), don't think about it at all ("no expectation"), or expect to be able to find their way without much trouble ("not lost"). Sometimes, patients who expect to become lost take preventive measures, such as studying the facility map, allowing extra time to find their appointment, or even driving to the healthcare facility the day before and finding out the exact location of the department.

Expectations are always compared with realities, and again, to oversimplify, patients and visitors will either have difficulty finding their way during the visit ("lost") or find their way with relative ease ("not lost").

It is useful to look at all six combinations formed by these three expectations and two realities (Table 16.1). The best scenario is a patient or visitor who expects to be lost, but finds his or her way with relative ease. This is the situation in which the healthcare facility has exceeded the consumer's wayfinding expectations. Next best are the other two cases where the patients' or visitors' reality is "not lost," when they have "no expectation" and find their way easily, and when they do not expect to become lost and find their way easily.

TABLE 16.1   HOW REALITY LIVES UP TO EXPECTATIONS

| | EXPECTATION | | |
	Lost	*No Expectation*	*Not Lost*
Reality: Lost	Unhappy, but not surprised	Unhappy	Unhappy & angry
Not Lost	Happiest	OK	OK

If the patient expects to become lost and does, she or he may be unhappy about the outcome, but not surprised. When this expectation matches reality, the patient's negative opinion about the confusing nature of the facility may be confirmed. If the patient has no wayfinding expectations and becomes lost, he or she is likely to be unhappy, but probably not angry.

The worst-case scenario is when someone does not expect to become lost, but does. In this case, expectations for a smooth wayfinding experience do not match reality. This is probably why people find it much more difficult to cope with wayfinding-related changes in a facility they feel they know well than to try to negotiate an unfamiliar facility for the first time. Such wayfinding-related changes might include relocating departments, rerouting public circulation routes, or renaming services. Healthcare facilities need to recognize the difficulties such wayfinding changes can cause patients and visitors (as well as the damage to consumer satisfaction caused by unmet expectations) and work hard to communicate clearly about these changes.

WAYFINDING SYSTEM DECISION MAKING

Creating and maintaining design elements and operational elements that enable unfamiliar users to find their way around healthcare facilities with ease involves the collaboration of many disciplines: architects, interior designers, landscape architects and site planners, facility planners, facility managers, wayfinding consultants, graphic designers, lighting consultants, healthcare facility administrators, government regulators and inspectors, public relations and marketing staff, sign fabricators, artists, nursing staff, physicians, maintenance staff, and others. Just as it's a fallacy to believe wayfinding concerns only signs, it's another fallacy to think wayfinding system improvements can be made by any single department or profession. The political nature of wayfinding system decision making within a particular institution must be understood and respected or that system is likely to fail.

At the start of wayfinding system planning, careful thought needs to be given to the various constituencies within the organization (and possibly outside it too) who will be affected in one way or another. There are groups who will be asked to fund the system, those who will set its policies, those who will participate in its planning, those who will participate in its day-to-day operations, and those who will be affected by it. Strategies should be developed for keeping these various groups informed about the development of the wayfinding system at a minimum, and for involving some of them in that development, as appropriate.

For instance, top management needs to be involved in terms of philosophical support and financial backing. Its blessing will bring others along. The marketing department needs to see the connections between wayfinding and the hospital's image and the impact of the design or marketing materials such as maps and brochures on users' ease of wayfinding. The chief of staff needs to be consulted or at least apprised of changes being considered, as does the nursing director. The human resources department needs to be brought in to discuss initial and ongoing staff physical plant orientation programs.

It's one thing to involve professionals from inside and outside the organization and another to work though all the complex and difficult issues wayfinding touches upon, from terminology to site planning. Unfortunately, there is really no other way to end up with a wayfinding system that works initially and that will continue to work in the future. The more invested these various groups are in planning wayfinding system improvements, the more likely they will be to put in the effort needed to make the new system work.

THE NEED FOR WAYFINDING EXPERTISE

It is important to consider hiring outside wayfinding planning expertise. Common pitfalls of trying to do wayfinding planning in-house can be thought of as *benign neglect, camels,* and *shopping sprees.* Benign neglect occurs when no one is responsible for managing the wayfinding system. Signs are the only wayfinding element thought to be important. Old signs aren't removed when new ones are installed. New signs are commissioned at the whim of the powerful. Paper signs proliferate because no one has taken time to thoroughly understand the macro and micro circulation patterns within the facility or the decision points where wayfinding information is needed.

As the saying goes, a camel is a horse designed by committee. Although many points of view are needed in order for a wayfinding system to work effectively, when a committee is responsible for managing and designing a wayfinding system, the effectiveness of the system can be derailed by group dynamics and compromise solutions. Due to the difficulties involved in simply getting people together for meetings, critical wayfinding problems may not be solved in a timely fashion.

Shopping sprees can occur when all responsibility for a wayfinding system is left to a sign company. Busy managers, overwhelmed with decisions to make and thousands of details to consider, leave the decision making to a sign fabricator. They end up with a lot of expensive signs that may or may not be necessary, may or may not be appropriate, and may or may not solve the facility's wayfinding problems. Other design-related and operations-related components of the wayfinding system aren't even considered.

As healthcare organizations do for strategic planning, architectural master plans, total quality management programs, and other major management endeavors, they need to consider wayfinding important enough to get outside help. Having experts on board can help guide the necessary paradigm shift, offers an opportunity to seek information about existing wayfinding experiences, can produce a well-thought-out plan for change, and may help diffuse some of the political battles that occur within every organization.

GUIDELINES FOR ARCHITECTURAL DESIGN

Detailed information about design-related wayfinding elements and associated performance guidelines is available elsewhere. However, issues of exterior and interior architectural design and wayfinding need to be expanded upon. Architectural design is a critical component of a good wayfinding system. The irony is that architectural design that supports wayfinding is not enough to ensure a good wayfinding system. However, when poor architectural design leads to wayfinding confusion, it is difficult to dramatically improve wayfinding ease.

Exterior Architecture

To facilitate wayfinding when designing the facility's exterior, incorporate the following:

- Design healthcare facilities that are recognizable as such. Unfamiliar users need to be able to distinguish the healthcare facility from other buildings in the surrounding environment.
- Allow for illuminated building identification signage on each major building.
- If most people will be arriving by automobile, carefully consider the relationship of building entrances to parking structures and parking lots.
- Make the main entrance and other major entrances architecturally obvious.

- Allow for illuminated entrance identification signage at or near the main entrance and other major entrances.
- Design different buildings on a medical campus to look different from each other so that patients and visitors can easily distinguish them.

Interiors

When designing the interior, consider the following:

- Use interior architecture and interior design tools (including color, floor materials, lighting, and artwork) to create strategically located, unique-looking places within the health facility. These can be used both as landmarks and as destinations for direction giving.
- Design places to locate artwork of varying shapes and sizes. These works of art will act as landmarks people will notice as they move in one direction and will remember having seen as they make their way back.
- Consider special lighting to illuminate the artwork.
- Consider using lighting variations (in type or color) to indicate transition zones from one area to another.
- Think carefully about creating places, such as fascias or soffits, where directional and identification signage can be placed.
- Design lighting that will highlight directional signs, identification signs, and directories.
- Locate major information desks within direct lines of sight from main entrances.
- Make reception and waiting areas look obvious.
- Locate elevators along public circulation routes so they are visually obvious.
- Locate departments that patients use in sequence, like Outpatient Registration, Lab, and X-Ray, near one another in order to create good functional adjacencies.
- Regarding circulation planning, avoid circular circulation paths; avoid corridors that meet at odd angles (other than 90 degrees); provide exterior or interior views along interior circulation areas, if possible.

CONCLUSION: WAYFINDING MYTHS

Part of the reason wayfinding is such a problem in many large healthcare facilities is that much of so-called "conventional wisdom" is simply untrue. More appropriately called *wayfinding myths,* these include the following:

- If people can't find their way around, it's their own fault.

- Making it possible for people to find their way in a healthcare facility is nice, but not very important.
- Once staff have worked in a healthcare facility for a while, they don't have any trouble finding their way around.
- Color coding can solve the wayfinding problem.
- Facilities can easily solve wayfinding problems in-house.
- Wayfinding doesn't need to be thought about until the end of a building project.
- Once the wayfinding system has been designed and implemented, the job is done.
- And of course, there is the most pervasive wayfinding myth: signs alone will solve the problem of people getting lost, as illustrated by this story:

A physician who practices in a large, urban hospital notices that many of his patients arrive late for their appointments. When he asks why, the patients tell him that they find the large building in which he works very confusing; they try to follow the signs, they say, but they still become lost.

As the physician talks about the problem with his colleagues, he realizes that they too share his frustration. So the physician makes an appointment to meet with the head of the hospital's facility management department to work out a solution.

The physician is ten minutes late for the meeting. Never having been in the hospital's basement, he himself becomes lost trying to find the facility manager's office. Once there, he explains the problem and complains that his practice, especially the overall quality of patient care, is suffering because he is often forced to spend less time with patients who are late because they were lost.

"This problem needs immediate attention," the physician says.

The facility manager nods in total agreement. "No problem," he replies. "We'll just put up more signs!"

Janet R. Carpman and Myron A. Grant are partners in Carpman Grant Associates, Wayfinding Consultants, in Ann Arbor, Michigan. They have worked on more than 70 different wayfinding projects for healthcare facilities and other clients in the United States, are authors of numerous publications, and have involved more than 6,000 patients, visitors, and staff in systematic research studies.

References

Berwick, D. M., Godfrey, A. B., and Roessner, J. *Curing Health Care: New Strategies for Quality Improvement.* San Francisco: Jossey-Bass Publishers, 1990.

Carpman, J. R. and Grant, M. A. *Design that Cares: Planning Health Facilities for Patients and Visitors.* 2nd ed. Chicago: American Hospital Publishing, Inc., 1993.

Kuhn, T. S. *The Structure of Scientific Revolutions.* Chicago: University of Chicago Press, 1970.

Monteleone, F. "Step Carefully, Then Go for the Gusto" *Computerworld* 29 (May 29, 1995): 35.

Weisman, G. D. "Wayfinding and Architectural Legibility: Design Considerations in Housing Environments for the Elderly." In *Housing for the Elderly: Satisfaction and Preferences,* edited by V. Regnier and J. Pynoos. New York City: Garland Publishing, 1982.

Zimring, C. "The Costs of Confusion: Non-Monetary and Monetary Costs of the Emory Hospital Wayfinding System." Prepared for Innerface, Inc., 1990.

IV
APPENDIXES

HEALTHCARE FURNITURE MANUFACTURERS

ADD Specialized Seating Technology
6500 South Avalon Boulevard
Los Angeles, CA 90003-1934
213/752-0101

The Children's Furniture Company
3800 Buena Vista Avenue
Baltimore, MD 21211
410/243-7488

Haworth, Inc.
One Haworth Center
Holland, MI 49423
616/393-3000

Health Design
A Division of Brayton International, a Steelcase
Design Partnership Company
P.O. Box 7288
255 Swarthmore Avenue
High Point, NC 27264
910/434-4151

Hill-Rom
1069 State Route 46E
Batesville, IN 47006-9167
812/934-7777

Kimball International
1180 E. 16th Street
Jasper, IN 47549
800/451-8090

Krug Furniture Inc.
421 Manitou Drive
Kitchener, Ontario CANADA
N2C IL5
800/851-8174

Kusch & Co.
175A East Second Street
Huntington Station, NY 11746
516/271-6100

LA-Z-Boy
1284 N. Telegraph Road
Monroe, MI 48161
313/241-4700

LUI Corporation
5500 E. Lombard Street
Baltimore, MD 21224
410/522-4135

Midmark Corporation
60 Vista Drive
Versailles, OH 45380
513/526-3662

Milcare Inc., A Herman Miller Company
P.O. Box 302
Zeeland, MI 49464-0302
616/654-8062

Nemschoff
2218 Julson Court
P.O. Box 129
Sheboygan, WI 53082-0129
414/457-7726

Sauder Manufacturing Company
600 Middle Street
Archbold, OH 43502
419/446-3331

SMED International
4315-54th Avenue S.E.
Calgary, Alberta T2C 2A2
403/279-1400

Steelcase, Inc.
P.O. Box 2608
Grand Rapids, MI 49512
616/698-1554

Tuohy
42 St. Albans Place
Chatfield, MN 55923
507/867-4280

R. M. Wieland Co.
13737 N. Main Street
Grabill, IN 46741
219/627-3686

Wilkahn
150 East 58th Street
New York, NY 10155
212/486-4333

ASSOCIATION OF CONTRACT TEXTILES (ACT) TEXTILE PERFORMANCE GUIDELINES

B

FIRE RETARDANCY

Application	Minimum Standard
Upholstery	Class I (Pass) California Technical Bulletin 117 Section E
Direct Glue Wallcoverings	Class A ASTM E-84 (adhered method)
Panel and Upholstered Walls	Class A ASTM E-84 (unadhered method)
Drapery	NFPA 701 Small Scale

COLORFASTNESS TO WET AND DRY CROCKING

Application	Minimum Standard
Upholstery	Dry Crocking—Class 4 minimum Wet Crocking—Class 3 minimum AATCC-8-1974
Direct Glue Wallcoverings	Dry and Wet Crocking—Class 3 minimum AATCC-8-1974
Panels and Upholstered Walls	Dry and Wet Crocking—Class 3 minimum AATCC-8-1974
Drapery	Dry and Wet Crocking—Class 3 minimum Solids—AATCC-8-1974 Prints—AATCC-116-1974

COLORFASTNESS TO LIGHT	
Application	*Minimum Standard*
Upholstery	Class 4 minimum at 40 hours AATCC 16A-1974 or AATCC 16E-1976
Direct Glue Wallcoverings	Class 4 minimum at 40 hours AATCC 16A-1974 or AATCC 16E-1976
Panels and Upholstered Walls	Class 4 minimum at 40 hours AATCC 16A-1974 or AATCC 16E-1976
Drapery	Class 4 minimum at 60 hours ASTM D3691 16A-1974 or ASTM D3691 16E-1976

PHYSICAL PROPERTIES	
Application	*Minimum Standard*
Physical Properties Upholstery	Brush Pill 3–4 minimum—ASTM D3511 Breaking Strength 50 lbs. minimum in warp and weft— ASTM D3597-D1682-64 (1975) Seam Slippage 25 lbs. minimum in warp and weft—ASTM D3597-D434-75
Panels and Upholstered Walls	Breaking Strength 35 lbs. minimum in warp and filling— ASTM 1682-64 Grab Method Seam slippage 25 lbs. minimum in warp and weft—ASTM D3597-434-75
Drapery	Seam Slippage—Fabrics over 6 oz./sq. yd. in warp and weft—ASTM D3597-434-75 Seam Slippage—Fabrics under 6 oz./sq. yd.—15 lbs. minimum in warp and weft—ASTM D3597-434-75

ABRASION	
Application	*Minimum Standard*
Heavy-Duty Upholstery	30,000 double rubs* Wyzenbeek Method ASTM 3597 modified (#10 cotton duck) or 40,000 cycles Martindale Method ASTM D4966 (with 21-oz. weight)
General Contract Upholstery	15,000 double rubs Wyzenbeek (#10 cotton duck) ASTM 3597 Modified

Author's Note: These ACT standards represent a minimum. Although it is generally agreed by technical authorities that abrasion test performance and abrasion performance in the field (wear) is a complex subject to correlate because of the variables that may differ for each use. While the subject does not deserve simplistic formulas to predict wear, it is generally observed that, where very heavy-duty use and wear and intensive scrubbing may be involved, fabrics that exceed 50,000 double rubs (#10 cotton duck) and preferably those exceeding 100,000 double rubs are probably desirable. However, there is no evidence to suggest that, in the most demanding healthcare applications, fabrics that exceed 200,000 double rubs provide any further meaningful durability to the practical life cycle of a fabric than fabrics that achieve 200,000 double rubs. It should be a combination of durabilityy, cleanability, and resultant satisfactory appearance retention that is a determinant of appropriate wear life and acceptable appearance.

ENVIRONMENTALLY RESPONSIBLE PRODUCT MANUFACTURERS

AFM Enterprises
1960 Chicago Avenue, Suite E7
Riverside, CA 92507
909/781-6860
909/781-6892 fax

Angeles Metal Systems
4817 E. Sheila Street
Los Angeles, CA 90040
213/268-1777
213/268-8996 fax

Auro Sinan Company
P.O. Box 857
Davis, CA 95617
916/753-3104

BASF Fibers
1675 Broadway, 35th floor
New York, NY 10708
212/408-9703
212/408-9740 fax

Benjamin Moore Paints
51 Chestnut Ridge Road
Montvale, NJ 07645-1862
800/826-2623; 201/573-9600
201/573-9046 fax

Big City Forest
Bronx 2000
1809 Carter Avenue
Bronx, NY 10457
718/731-3931
718/583-2047 fax

Blumenthal Wallcoverings
979 Third Avenue
New York, NY 10022

212/752-2535
212/838-5668 fax

Buchner Panel Manufacturing
1030 Quesada Avenue
San Francisco, CA 94124
415/822-7300
415/822-8540 fax

Coyuchi Inc.
P.O. Box 845
Pt Reyes Station, CA 94956
415/663-8077

Crown Corp.
1801 Wynkoop Street
Denver, CO 80202
800/422-2099; 303/292-1313
303/292-1933 fax

DLW/Gerber Ltd.
P.O. Box 4944
Lancaster, PA 17604
717/299-5035
717/394-1937 fax

DesignTex
200 Varick Street, 8th floor
New York, NY 10014
212/886-8212
212/886-8219 fax

Dodge-Regupol
P.O. Box 989
Lancaster, PA 17603
717/295-3400
717/295-3413 fax

EcoTimber International
350 Treat Avenue
San Francisco, CA 94110
415/864-4900
415/864-1011 fax

Flexiwall Systems
208 Carolina Drive
P.O. Box 89
Liberty, SC 29657
800/843-5394

Forbo
P.O. Box 667
Hazelton, PA 18201
800/842-7839

The Gage Corp
803 South Black River Street
Sparta, WI 54656
800/786-4243
608/269-7622 fax

Glidden Paints
925 Euclid Avenue
Cleveland, OH 44115
216/344-8216

Guilford of Maine
5300 Corporate Grove Drive, SE
Suite 200
Grand Rapids, MI 49512-5512
616/554-2250
616/554-2255 fax

Gridcore Systems International
1400 Canal Avenue
Long Beach, CA 90813
310/901-1492
310/901-1499 fax

Homasote Co.
P.O. Box 7240
West Trenton, NJ 08628-0240
800/257-9491; 609/883-3300
609/530-1584 fax

Images Carpet
Hwy 140, Box 5555
Armuchee, GA 30105

800/722-2504
404/234-3464 tax

Ipocork
586 Bogert Road
Riveredge, NJ 07661
800/828-2675
201/265-1407 fax

Livos Plant Chemistry
1365 Rufina Circle
Santa Fe, NM 87501
505/438-3448
505/438-0199 fax

Louisiana Pacific Corporation
111 SW 5th Avenue, Suite 400
Portland, OR 97204-3604
800/299-0028, ext. 604
503/241-2387 fax

Medite Corporation
P.O. Box 4040
Medford, OR 97501
800/676-3339

Milliken Carpets
201 Lukken Industrial Drive West
LaGrange, GA 30240
800/231-8453

Pace Chem Industries
779 La Grange Avenue
Newbury Park, CA 91320
805/499-2911

PallasWalls
1330 Bellevue Street
Green Bay, WI 54308
414/468-2600
414/468-2661 fax

Phenix BioComposites
P.O. Box 609
Mankato, MN 56002-0609
800/324-8187
507/387-5900 fax

SCS
One Kaiser Plaza, Suite 901
Oakland, CA 94612
800/829-1416; 510/832-1415
510/832-0359 fax

Syndesis Studio
2908 Colorado Avenue
Santa Monica, CA 90404
310/829-9932
310/829-5641 fax

Smart Wood
Rainforest Alliance
65 Bleeker Street
New York, NY 10012
212/677-1900
212/677-2187 fax

Terra-Green Technologies
1650 Progress Drive
Richmond, IN 47374
317/935-4760
317/935-3971 fax

3M Center
Takfast Carpet System
Building 301-1E-03
St. Paul, MN 55144
800/440-2965

United Recycling
3119 Lynn Avenue South
St. Louis Park, MN
612/929-7175
612/929-7923 fax

WF Taylor
11545 Pacific Avenue
Fontana, CA 92337
800/397-4583

AUTHOR'S NOTE: *All of these sources are listed in* The Green Pages: The Contract Interior Designer's Guide to Environmentally Responsible Products and Materials *by Andrew Fuston and Kim Plaskon Nadel. For information on obtaining the guide and its annual updates, call 212/779-3365 or 718/369-2578; 212/481-1697 fax.*

accent lighting: directional lighting to emphasize a particular object or to draw attention to a part of the field of view. See **directional lighting.**

accommodation: the process by which the eye changes focus from one distance to another.

adaptation: the process by which the visual system becomes adjusted to more or less light, or to light of a different color, than it was exposed to during an immediately preceding period. It results in a change in the sensitivity of the eye to light intensity or light quality.

ambient lighting: lighting throughout an area that produces general illumination.

average luminance (of a luminaire): the luminous intensity at a given angle divided by the projected area of the luminaire at that angle.

average luminance (of a surface): the average luminance (average photometric brightness) of a surface may be expressed in terms of the total luminous flux (lumens) actually leaving the surface per unit area. Average luminance specified in this way is identical in magnitude with luminous existence, which is the preferred term.

baffle: a single opaque or translucent element to shield a source from the direct view at certain angles or to absorb unwanted light.

ballast: a device used with an electric-discharge lamp to obtain the necessary circuit conditions (voltage, current, and waveform) for starting and operating the lamp.

brightness: see **luminance,** and **veiling luminance.**

bulb: the glass enclosure of an incandescent filament lamp.

candela (cd): (formerly candle) the unit of luminous intensity.

candlepower, $I=d(/d)$ (cp): luminous intensity expressed in candelas.

candlepower distribution curve: a curve, generally polar, representing the variation of luminous intensity of a lamp or luminaire in a plane through the light center.

ceiling area lighting: a general lighting system in which the entire ceiling is, in effect, one large luminaire. Note: Ceiling area lighting includes **luminous ceilings.**

central (foveal) vision: the seeing of objects in the center or foveal part of the visual field, approximately two degrees in diameter. It permits seeing finer detail than does peripheral vision.

coefficient of utilization (CU): the ratio of the luminous flux (lumens) from a luminaire calculated as received on the work plane to the luminous flux emitted by the luminaire's lamp alone.

color rendering: general expression for the effect of a light source on the color appearance of objects in conscious or subconscious comparison with their color appearance under a reference light source.

contrast: see **luminance contrast.**

contrast sensitivity: the ability to detect the presence of luminance differences. Quantitatively, it is equal to the reciprocal of the contrast threshold.

cut-off angle (of a luminaire): the angle, measured up from nadir, between the vertical axis and the first line of sight at which the bare source is not visible.

diffused lighting: light that is not predominantly incident from any particular direction.

direct glare: glare resulting from high luminances or insufficiently shielded light sources in the field of view or from reflecting areas of high luminance. It usually is associated with bright areas, such as luminaires, ceilings, and windows that are outside the visual task or region being viewed.

direct lighting: lighting by luminaires distributing 90 to 100 percent of emitted light in the general direction of the surface to be illuminated. This usually refers to light emitted in a downward direction.

directional lighting: illumination on the work plane (or on an object) that is predominantly from a single direction. See **accent lighting.**

disability glare: the effect of stray light in the eye whereby visibility and visual performance are reduced. See **veiling luminance.**

discomfort glare: glare producing discomfort. It does not necessarily interfere with visual performance or visibility.

downlight: a small direct-lighting unit that directs light downward. It can be recessed, surface mounted, or suspended.

efficiency: see **luminaire efficiency.**

fenestration: any opening or arrangement of openings (normally filled with media for control) for admission of daylight.

fixture: see **luminaire.**

fluorescent lamp: a low-pressure mercury electric-discharge lamp in which a fluorescing coating (phosphor) transforms some of the ultraviolet energy by discharge into energy within the visible spectrum.

flux: see **luminous flux.**

footcandle (fc): the unit of illuminance, in older texts, where the foot is taken as the unit of length rather than the meter. It is the illuminance on a surface one square foot in area on which there is a uniformly distributed flux of one lumen.

general lighting: lighting designed to provide a substantially uniform illuminance throughout an area, exclusive of any provision for special local lighting requirements.

glare: luminance within the visual field that is sufficiently greater than luminance to which the eyes are adapted that causes annoyance, discomfort, or loss in visual performance and visibility. See **direct glare, disability glare, discomfort glare,** and **reflected glare.**

high-intensity discharge lamps (HID): a general group of lamps consisting of mercury, metal halide, and high-pressure sodium sources.

illuminance, E = d(/dA):   the density of luminous flux incident on a surface or a point. The average luminous flux on an area is the quotient of the total flux incident on the surface to the area of the surface.

illuminance (lux or footcandle) meter: an instrument for measuring illuminance on a plane. Instruments that accurately respond to more than one spectral distribution are color corrected. Instruments that accurately respond to more than one spatial distribution of incident flux are cosine-corrected, i.e., the response to a source of unit luminous intensity, illuminating the detector from a fixed distance and from different directions, decreases as the cosine of the angle between the incident direction and the normal to the detector surface. The instrument is a form of photodetector, with or without filters, driving a digital or analog readout through appropriate circuitry.

illumination: the act of illuminating or state of being illuminated. The term has been used for density of luminous flux on a surface (illuminance) and such use is to be deprecated.

incandescent filament lamp: a lamp in which light is produced by a filament heated to incandescence by an electric current.

indirect lighting: lighting by luminaires distributing 90 to 100 percent of emitted light upward, rather than toward a horizontal task plane below the luminaire.

intensity: a shortening of the terms luminous intensity and radiant intensity. Often misused for **illuminance.**

lamp: a generic term for a man-made source of light. By extension, the term is also used to denote sources that radiate in regions of the spectrum adjacent to the visible. Note: a lighting unit consisting of a lamp with a shade, reflector, enclosing globe, housing, or other accessories, is also called a "lamp." In such cases, in order to distinguish between the assembled unit and light source within it, the latter is often called a "bulb" or "tube," if it is electrically powered. See also **luminaire.**

lamp lumen depreciation factor (LLD):   the multiplier to be used in illumination calculations to relate the initial rated output of light source to the anticipated minimum rated output based on the relamping program to be used.

level of illumination: see **illuminance.**

light: radiant energy that is capable of exciting the retina and producing a visual sensation. The visible portion of the electromagnetic spectrum extends from about 380 to 770 nanometers.

light loss factor (LLF):   a factor used in calculating illuminance after a given period of time and under given conditions. It takes into account temperature and voltage variations, dirt accumulation on luminaire and room surfaces, lamp depreciation, maintenance procedures, and atmospheric conditions. Formerly called **maintenance factor.**

local lighting: lighting designed to provide illumination over a relatively small area or confined space without providing any significant general surrounding lighting.

localized general lighting: lighting that utilizes luminaires above the task and also contributes to the illumination on the surround.

louvered ceiling: a ceiling area lighting system comprising a wall-to-wall installation of multicell louvers shielding the light sources mounted above it. See **luminous ceiling.**

lumen (lm): the unit of luminous flux.

luminaire: a complete lighting unit consisting of a lamp or lamps together with the parts designed to distribute the light, to position and protect the lamps, and to connect the lamps to the power supply.

luminaire dirt depreciation factor (LDD): the multiplier to be used in illuminance calculations to relate the initial illuminance provided by clean, new luminaires to the reduced illumination resulting from dirt collection on the luminaires just prior to the time when cleaning procedures will be instituted. This is one component of the **light loss factor.**

luminaire efficiency: the ratio of luminous flux (lumens) emitted by a luminaire to that emitted by the lamp or lamps used therein.

luminance (photometric brightness): the luminous intensity of any surface in a given direction per unit area of that surface as viewed from that direction. All things visible have some luminance. Units are candelas per square meter (SI), candelas per square foot in older texts.

luminance contrast: the relationship between the luminances of an object and its immediate background.

luminance ratio: the ratio between the luminances of any two areas in the visual field.

luminance threshold: the minimum perceptible difference in luminance for a given state of visual adaptation.

luminous ceiling: a ceiling area lighting system comprising a contiguous surface of transmitting material of a diffusing or light-controlling character with light sources mounted above it. See **louvered ceiling.**

luminous efficacy of a source of light: the quotient of the total luminous flux by the total lamp power input. It is expressed in lumens per watt.

luminous flux ((): the time rate of flow of light.

lux (lx): the International System (SI) unit of illuminance. It is the illumination on a surface one square meter in area on which there is a uniformly distributed flux of one lumen, or the illumination produced at a surface of which all points are at a distance of one meter from a uniform point source of one candela.

maintenance factor (MF): a factor formerly used to denote the ratio of illumination on a given area after a period of time to the initial illumination on the same area. See **light loss factor.**

matte surface: a surface from which the reflection is predominantly diffused, with or without a negligible specular component.

peripheral vision: the seeing of objects displaced from the primary line of sight and outside the central visual field.

portable lighting: lighting by means of equipment designed for manual portability.

portable luminaire: a lighting unit that is not permanently fixed in place.

reflectance of a surface or medium, (= (r/(i: the ratio of the reflected flux to the incident flux.

reflected glare: glare usually from specular reflections of high luminance in polished or glossy surfaces in the field of view. It usually is associated with reflections from within a visual task or areas in close proximity to the region being viewed. See **veiling reflection.**

reflection: a general term for the process by which the incident flux leaves a surface or medium from the incident side.

reflector: a device used to redirect the luminous flux from a source by the process of reflection.

refraction: the process by which the direction of a light ray changes as it passes obliquely from one medium to another in which its speed is different.

shielding angle (of a luminaire): the angle between a horizontal line through the light center and the line of sight at which the bare source first becomes visible. See **cut-off angle (of a luminaire).**

specular surface: a surface from which the reflection is predominantly regular.

stray light: light from a source that is scattered onto parts of the retina lying outside the retinal image of the source.

supplementary lighting: lighting used to provide an additional quantity and quality of illumination that cannot readily be obtained by a general lighting system and that supplements the general lighting level, usually for specific work.

task lighting: lighting that is directed at a specific surface or area for providing illumination for specific visual tasks. See **general lighting** for comparison.

transmission: a general term for the process by which incident flux leaves a surface or medium on the side other than the incident side.

transmittance, $T = (t/(i$: the ratio of the transmitted flux to the incident flux.

tungsten-halogen lamp: a gas-filled tungsten incandescent lamp containing a certain proportion of halogens. Note: The tungsten-iodine lamp and the quartz-iodine lamp belong in this category.

veiling luminance: a luminance superimposed on the retinal image that reduces its contrast perception. It is this veiling effect produced by bright sources or areas in the visual field that results in decreased visual performance and visibility.

veiling reflection: regular reflections superimposed upon diffuse reflections from an object that partially or totally obscure the details to be seen by reducing the contrast. This is sometimes called **reflected glare.**

visibility: the quality or state of being perceivable by the eye. In many outdoor applications, visibility is defined in terms of the distance at which an object can just be perceived by the eye. In indoor applications, it usually is defined in terms of the contrast or size of a standard test object, observed under standardized viewing conditions, having the same threshold as the given object.

visual acuity: a measure of the ability to distinguish fine details. Quantitatively, it is the reciprocal of the angular size in minutes of the critical detail that is just large enough to be seen.

visual angle: the angle subtended by an object or detail at the point of observation. It usually is measured in minutes of arc.

visual field: the locus of objects or points in space that can be perceived when the head and eyes are kept fixed. The field may be monocular or binocular.

visual perception: the interpretation of impressions transmitted from the retina to the brain in terms of information about a physical world displayed before the eye.

visual performance: the quantitative assessment of the performance of a task, taking into consideration speed and accuracy.

visual surround: includes all portions of the visual field except the visual task.

visual task: conventionally, this designates those details and objects that must be seen for the performance of a given activity, and includes the immediate background of the details or objects.

Source: Illuminating Engineering Society of North America, "Lighting for Hospitals and Healthcare Facilities," Recommended Practice RP-29-95, New York, New York, 1995.

ADDITIONAL SOURCES

American Institute of Architects (AIA)
Academy on Architecture for Health
1735 New York Avenue, N.W.
Washington, DC 20006
800/242-3837
202/626-7518 fax

Speciality group within AIA membership that holds regular meetings, disseminates information, and sponsors special projects on healthcare architecture.

American Society of Interior Designers (ASID)
Healthcare Design Specialty Network
608 Massachusetts Avenue, N.E.
Washington, DC 20002-6006
202/546-3480
800/654-2732 fax-on-demand
e-mail: rosalyn.cama@asid.noli.com

Specialty group within ASID membership that provides an on-line network, fax-on-demand services, conferences, publications, and speaking networks.

Association for the Care of Children's Health
7910 Woodmont Avenue, Suite 300
Bethesda, MD 20814
301/654-6549
301/986-4553 fax
e-mail: acch@clark.net

Membership organization of healthcare institutions that provides care for children. Publishes resource materials on design and sponsors annual conference.

The Carpet and Rug Institute
P.O. Box 2048
Dalton, GA 30722-2048
706/278-3176
706/278-8835 fax

National trade association whose members represent 95 percent of all carpet produced in the United States. Offers over 30

informational and technical publications for design professionals, facility managers, builders, building owners and managers, and consumers.

The Center for Health Design
4550 Alhambra Way
Martinez, CA 94553
510/370-0345
510/228-4018 fax
e-mail: CTR4HD@aol.com

A nonprofit, nonmembership organization whose mission is to facilitate, integrate, and accelerate the creation of health and life-enhancing environments. Provides free technical support for design professionals and healthcare executives, publishes a variety of healthcare design resources (covering research, case studies, news, and trends), and produces the Symposium on Healthcare Design (held each year in November). Individuals are encouraged to join its free network by having their names added to the Center's mailing list.

Design for Aging Network
1735 New York Avenue, N.W.
Washington, DC 20006-5292
202/879-7750
202/626-7425 fax

A constituent program of the American Institute for Architectural Research (a division of the AIA) in cooperation with the Association of Collegiate Schools of Architecture, this membership organization links design professionals, product manufacturers, educators, facility owners, building developers and managers, healthcare executives, and others concerned with improving the quality of facilities for the elderly. Directory of members, design-for-aging bibliography, and other publications are available.

Good Wood Alliance
289 College Street
Burlington, VT 05401
802/862-4448 tel./fax
e-mail: warp@together.net

Nonprofit membership alliance of individuals, businesses, and organizations concerned about the impact of wood consumption on the world's forests. Promotes the conservation of temperate, tropical, and boreal forest resources through education, research, and fieldwork.

Illuminating Engineering Society of North America
120 Wall Street
New York, NY 10005-4001
212/248-5000
212/248-5017 fax

Membership organization of lighting designers and engineers, whose mission is to disseminate information on the art and science of illumination. Healthcare committees include: Lighting for Health Care Facilities and Lighting for the Aged and Partially Sighted.

Institute on Aging and Environment
School of Architecture and Urban Planning
University of Wisconsin—Milwaukee
P.O. Box 413
Milwaukee, WI 53201
414/229-6481
414/229-6976 fax

The mission of this university-based organization is the enhancement of the quality of life of older persons through the improvement of and innovation in housing, institutional, and service settings. Facilitates research, university and community education, and innovative environmental planning, programming, and design practice. Produces conferences, a monograph series, and a newsletter.

Institute for Family-Centered Care
7900 Wisconsin Avenue, Suite 405
Bethesda, MD 20814
301/652-0281
301/652-0186 fax

A nonprofit, nonmembership organization that serves as a resource for policy makers, design professionals, healthcare providers, and others on the implementation of family-centered

care in communities. Develops educational materials, conducts policy and research initiatives, disseminates information on the best practices, and helps institutions translate the concept of family-centered care into practice.

International Society of Interior Designers (IIDA)
Healthcare Forum
370 Merchandise Mart
Chicago, IL 60654
312/467-1950
312/467-0779 fax

Speciality group within IIDA membership that provides information and resources on healthcare design, including a newsletter and annual conference held at the Merchandise Mart in Chicago.

New York University School of Continuing Education
Health Care Environments Program
11 West 42nd Street
New York, NY 10036
212/790-1345
212/790-1656 fax

Offers courses for architects, interior designers, and facility managers on healthcare design, including a unique Healthcare Design Certificate program.

Society for the Arts in Healthcare
45 Lyme Road
Suite 304
Hanover, NH 03755
603/643-2325
603/643-1444 fax

A nonprofit membership organization of arts consultants, design professionals, and healthcare arts administrators whose mission is to promote the use of art in healthcare facilities. Offers an annual conference and has a database of over 200 articles on art and healing on file.

ON-LINE WEB SITES

AIA Home page
http://www.aia.org

Association for the Care of Children's Health
http://www.wsd.com/acch.org

The Center for Health Design
http://www.healthdesign.org

Envirosense Consortium
http://www.envirosense.org

Home page of a strategic group of companies dedicated to educating building owners and facility managers on the environmental, legal, and productivity issues of indoor air quality.

Health*Online*
http://www.healthonline.com

Home page of a subscriber service for healthcare executives and others interested in improving health and quality of life. Features an Architectural and Design Gallery.

Hospital Audiences, Inc.
http://www.hospaud.org

Home page of an organization that makes the arts accessible and available to people with physical and mental disabilities.

INDEX